Difference at the Origin

Derrida's Critique of Heidegger's Philosophy of the Work of Art

Inaugural-Dissertation
zur Erlangung des Doktorgrades der Philosophischen Fakultät
der Westfälischen Wilhelms-Universität zu Münster (Westfalen)

Vorgelegt von

Paul Manithottil
aus Manjoor, 1963

ATLANTIC
PUBLISHERS & DISTRIBUTORS (P) LTD

Published by
ATLANTIC
PUBLISHERS & DISTRIBUTORS (P) LTD
B-2, Vishal Enclave, Opp. Rajouri Garden,
New Delhi-110027
Phones : +91-11-25413460, 25429987, 25466842

Sales Office
7/22, Ansari Road, Darya Ganj,
New Delhi-110002
Phones : +91-11-23273880, 23275880, 23280451
Fax : +91-11-23285873
web : www.atlanticbooks.com
e-mail : info@atlanticbooks.com

Branch Office
5, Nallathambi Street, Wallajah Road,
Chennai-600002
Phones : +91-44-64611085, 32413319
e-mail : chennai@atlanticbooks.com

D 6
Tage der mündlichen Prüfungen: 26.und 27.04.2007
Dekan: Prof. Dr. Dr. h.c. Wichard Woyke
Referent: Prof. Dr. Josef Früchtl
Koreferent: Prof. Dr. Dr. Klaus Müller

ISBN 978-81-269-0919-3

Printed in India
at Nice Printing Press, Delhi

Preface

Philosophy is the way of thinking, the activity of philosophizing. There is a saying that 'to philosophise is to create concepts' and traditional philosophy is considered as the play of concepts. Heidegger's way of thinking has left an immense legacy for post-modern philosophers, particularly for Jacques Derrida, who has greatly influenced philosophy and literature in our time. The writings of Derrida have enhanced my interest in Heidegger, whose question of Being and the retrieval of the meaning of Being play a vital role throughout his writings. The present book is an attempt to explore the meaning of origin in Heidegger and Derrida by explaining how Derrida's difference depends upon and differs from Heidegger's notion of ontological difference. This has helped me to see the solid foundation of classical philosophy.

I am deeply indebted to Prof. Dr. Josef Früchtl, who has provided me with the necessary guidance and valuable suggestions throughout my writing of this book. I would also like to express my gratitude to the Bishop of Münster for his inspiration and advice here. Also I need to thank all the professors in the Department of Philosophy from whose scholarly classes I have benefited a lot. Finally, I want to express my gratitude to Manfred Schneider, whose linguistic support has helped me heighten my language awareness.

Paul Manithottil

Contents

Introduction

Metaphysics that considers beings as Being is the objectifying thinking. Aristotle, the father of Western metaphysics, asks 'what is being (i.e. entity) as being.' Everything that is, by which Aristotle means, that is a being.[1] Standing in a long tradition of metaphysics Heidegger too asks the question of the meaning of Being. But he reformulates Aristotle's basic question, 'what is being as being,' as to what is the Being of beings? For him philosophy is not a science of beings but of Being,[2] because we can understand something as a being if we understand it as Being. The meaning of beings is thought along with the universal concepts. We conceptualize beings under the category of beingness (*Seiendheit*) or objectivity. It suggests the precedence of the understanding of Being before the discoverability of the concrete beings. A being can be discovered only if the Being of the beings is already disclosed. Then what is the ground of Being? The search for the origin of truth by Heidegger[3] and Derrida[4] builds the gist of this work.

Heidegger as an existentialist exposes the origin in terms of the truth of *Dasein,* the human subject whose existence precedes his essence.[5] In order to destruct the subject-centred traditional metaphysics, he begins the analysis of Being not with the meaning of entity, but with the existential structure of human *Dasein*, which is the only thing-which-is (only *Seiendes*) that can ask question of Being. Human *Dasein,* which exists as the *Being-in-the-world*, is devoid of Self. Later, in the essay on *The Origin of the Work of Art*, he explains the relationship between truth (philosophy) and art in order to explain the structure of Being itself, which, according to Pattison, is 'the earliest manifestations of the later Heidegger.'[6] His question of Being, being influenced largely by Nietzsche's concept of overcoming or going beyond the metaphysical values, is the critic of the origin, which breaks the long reign of subject-centred philosophy and inaugurates the new era of the understanding the meaning of things.[7] Heidegger's basic question, 'what is Being,' is based on Nietzsche's philosophy of two mutually irreconcilable principles: The Will to Power and The Eternal Recurrence of the Same.[8] In *Nietzsche* Vol. III, Heidegger admits that he finds in Nietzsche sum and substance of the Western thought. Calling him as 'the *last metaphysician* of the West,'[9] Heidegger tries to break with the long metaphysical tradition of the West. By asking the meaning of entities, traditional philosophy exerts an assault upon material reality (upon what is present), such as trees, Socrates, etc., because it determines the meaning of entities in terms of categories of Being, which are already given as self-evident and as something that exist. It is Heidegger's contention that Western philosophy, as onto-theology, has always determined Being in terms of what is (beings), which results in the forgetfulness the ontic-ontological difference. Heidegerian destruction is of the view that meaning and concepts in the traditional philosophy are fundamentally muddled with metaphysics of presence. It has forgotten the Being for beings. As he evaluates, the whole of Western philosophy takes its origin in the elaboration of Platonic-Aristotelian thinking, accordingly the entire systems of thought and their manifoldness are rooted on the underlying determinations of Being.[10] The underlying principle, which is present in everything, is called truth or unconcealedness (*alētheia*). Heideggerian destruction of metaphysics is a de-structuring of philosophy in order to arrive at the meaning behind the structure of Being. For Heidegger origin of truth is neither the *a priori* categories nor the truth of proposition, but non-originary origin, which is explained in terms of the disclosedness or truth of *Dasein* and that of work of art.

As Heidegger does, Derrida too understands that in the Western philosophy the meaning of beings has been determined by metaphysics of presence. Derrida's philosophy can be called post-Heideggerian. However, unlike Heidegger, Derrida does neither begin his philosophical career with a question on Being nor take up philosophical positions, traditional or otherwise. Those who ask the question of the meaning of Being come back to its shelter; Derrida, therefore, does not ask any meaning of Being. He does not engage in any rational inquiry of the meaning, which is always directed to the centre, reason. His philosophy falls short of being identical, or falls short of circular, which postpones the return of the identical to itself. Derrida argues that the metaphysical thought that Heidegger fails to destruct the metaphysical tradition of the Western philosophy, for its spirit is re-visited in Heideggerian thought and listed him among the subjectivists of the West. The purpose of the present study is the critical evaluation of Derrida's claim that he deconstructed one of Heidegger's most important essays, *The Origin of the Work of Art*, by which he tries to overcome the metaphysics of presence.

Rockmore holds the view that in post-modern philosophical circles, especially those who committed to Heideggerian exegesis in France, among them Derrida emerged with his own original thinking.[11] David Wood maintains that along with the whole range of thinkers, such as Saussure, Freud, Nietzsche, Heidegger, Levinas, etc., Derrida too finds difference at the origin of truth.[12] Hills Miller argues that Derridean thought is essentially built up on Heidegger's destruction of metaphysics, and Husserl's subjective form of transcendental experience.[13] His work is a continuation of ideas developed by the above mentioned predecessors, particularly by Nietzsche, Husserl and Heidegger. His method of deconstruction is phenomenological. Like Heidegger he too argues that philosophers at all time have gone wrong in trying to make sense of meaning by looking for essential truth lying with the 'essence of things.'[14] For Heidegger the aim of philosophizing is 'to go the thing itself,' which he inherited from Husserl. However, the phenomenological reduction carried out by Derrida prevents any attempt to reach to the 'thing itself.'[15] There is a difference between Heidegger's destruction and Derrida's deconstruction. Heideggerian destruction is something positive, it is not aimed to do away with metaphysics; rather its phenomenological reduction is oriented towards the reconstruction of meaning of beings which is found mixed within the hard layers of Being.[16] Heidegger's concept of ontological difference, as Derrida remarks, is insufficiently radical since his critique of Western metaphysics is motivated by a longing for the origin and a desire for its restoration.[17] Carrying forward the task initiated by his above said predecessors Derrida tries to dismantle the objective pretensions of truth and such like concepts.[18] Derridean deconstruction radicalizes the task of destruction inaugurated by Heidegger. His writing is a radical critique of Western metaphysics and of its basic notions of absolute truth.

Theme

The thought of Derrida and Heidegger questioning the possibility of totalization is critical of the epistemic and systematic exigencies of philosophy. They observe that the metaphysical tradition of the West is grounded in a philosophy of presence—that is the desire to make present the presence of a Being in beings.[19] Traditional philosophy supports the determination of Being or truth of entity as presence. Thus all the categories of beings fall under metaphysics of presence. They together hold the view that the entire history of philosophy is the forgetfulness of the meaning of Being since it is controlled and determined by the metaphysics of presence. Both of them try to purify philosophy from its false structure and work out philosophy devoid of metaphysical spell.

Philosophers are destined to tie their concepts to the unitive position of Being so that they are to be accepted as philosophers. There is no philosophy devoid of this intuitive *telos*. Both Heidegger and Derrida advocate the philosophy of difference that resists the philosophy of Being and its manifold versions, which institute a power-structure of presence in the history of philosophy. They react against the dominant tendency of logocentrism and liberate philosophers from a particular pattern of thinking by advocating the unrestrained thought. It becomes the hallmark of present day philosophy, the end of the reign of Being. As Heidegger's thought revolves around the undecidability of the common matrix, a unit of oppositions and contradictions, which is similar to Heraclitus' thought, Derrida inaugurates the beginning of non-philosophy by removing the centre off thought from the field of philosophy. However, his concept of infrastructure, which generates and holds together oppositions and contradictions, is in effect similar to the concept of Heidegger's destruction of metaphysics.[20] Both of them destroy the basis of traditional metaphysical system of thought, and do not re-constitute any alternative system of thought in the sense of the truth of correctness.

For Heidegger difference is at the very origin of truth. At the moment we speak of the truth in relation to Being and being, we encounter originary, irreducible difference. Derrida accepts this basic notion of Heideggerian truth, and argues that since difference is at the origin, any inquiry into the truth of Being does not favour to catch at the origin; it is infinitely elusive. Instead of trying to travel to the end, he wishes to accept the disseminative character of truth. Philosophy cannot comprehend meaning because there is no reality with intrinsic meaning. He reduces philosophy to literature to mean that there is no truth, no origin, but only signifiers. Therefore, his dictum: "There is nothing outside of the text."[21] This dictum simply denotes his important argument that every referent in a text, all reality has the structure of a differential trace.[22] In other words, the proclamation, 'there is no outside-text,' breaks the borderlines or margins between oppositional elements of truth since the inside, presence being infected by the outside, the non-presence. Meaning is essentially related to an irreducible alterity. He says that every metaphysical text carries within itself the resources for its own criticism.[23] He deconstructs various texts of philosophy from Plato to Heidegger, calling into question all basic ideas and belief, that legitimise current institutional forms of knowledge. Derrida's reading attempts to draw out the deconstructive activity already implicit in various philosophical and literary texts. His deconstructive reading exposes the unsettling forces in a text he wants to deconstruct.[24] This work deals with the encounter between Heidegger and Derrida and evaluates critically Derrida's deconstructive reading of Heidegger's aesthetic philosophy given in *The Origin of the Work of Art*.

Relevance

Philosophy is born with the question 'what is...?' and it at all times deals with the fundamental principles of truth which defines and determines what a thing is. After Nietzsche come Heidegger and Derrida who challenges this central issue of philosophical inquiry. For them nothing is real in itself, and therefore, their philosophy is basically the denial of the metaphysics of presence which defines and determines the truth. Heidegger's relentless critique of the so-called metaphysics of presence is known as the overcoming of metaphysics or destruction and Derrida's deconstruction. They are undoubtedly the most influential, controversial and complex thinkers of our time.

Both destruction and deconstruction of metaphysics rest in their declared task to purify philosophy from its false concepts. Heidegger's concept of *Dasein* and aesthetic philosophy open the structure of Being and show the irreducible difference between Being and beings. For him difference is philosophy. Derrida on the other hand reads different philosophical texts in order to bring out the contradictions and paradoxes of metaphysical concepts to light; he calls into question the notions of Being as presence and applies his deconstructive terms to different texts from Plato to Heidegger. His greatest contribution to philosophy is his concept of *différance*, which is, according to him, older than the truth of ontological difference. He reduces philosophy to text as he says philosophy is literary or non-philosophy.[25] The quarry, 'how to get out of the logocentrism,' undoubtedly led both Heidegger and Derrida to the field of meaninglessness. However, the possibility of absence in the edifice of metaphysics still remains before us a problem unsettling.

Methodology of procedure

This dissertation is the exposition of Heidegger's overcoming of metaphysics and Derrida's criticism of the same. It is the encounter between two important modern thinkers: Heidegger-Derrida under two important terminologies: difference and *différance*. The primary sources of this study are the reliable English translations of their important books. The secondary sources include books and articles on their major works.

I have developed this dissertation into four chapters, with an introduction and conclusion with a critical appraisal. The introduction sets the context and the position of Heidegger and Derrida in the history of philosophy and explains the purpose and the general view of the work in nutshell. The first chapter entitled *In pursuit of Being: Heidegger and Derrida* sets up the position of Heidegger and Derrida with the question of the meaning of Being. Taking note of (mentioning) how Nietzsche's reversal of Platonism reconstitutes the 'other' of metaphysics, Heidegger is well aware of the pervasive nature of metaphysics of presence in all systems of thought. He calls the metaphysics of presence Platonism. His search of the truth of Being overtakes Platonic and Aristotlean concept of truth and reaches up to the mytho-poetic thinkers who meditated the concept of Being as Being (*Physis*), not as being. Heidegger wants to uphold the difference between Being and being as the truth of Being. Along the pattern of thought of Heidegger, Derrida too argues that what is at issue is the metaphysics of presence that reigns the history of Western philosophy from Greek till today. According to him it is an intellectual slavery of reason to which all philosophers till today succumbed. His criticism is the thirst to burst out this suppressive system of metaphysics and calls for an absolute free-thinking in the limitless, groundless world of thought. He reads many different texts of philosophy with this particular aim. At the very outset, it should be noted that only his purpose justifies the methodology of deconstruction.

In order to evaluate correctly Derrida's criticism of Heidegger's essay on the work of art, it is necessary to describe Heidegger's basic positions and arguments particularly in the direction of the overcoming of metaphysics. It is the thrust of the second Chapter, *The origin of the truth of the work of art: Heidegger*. He disagrees with the traditional concept of truth as *aletheīa*, revealment. The truth of *Dasein* and that of work of art describe how the structure of the truth Being as revealment consists in concealment. The 'other' constitutes the truth of Being; the revealment of this 'hidden other' in the centre of presence is the task of overcoming metaphysics in Heidegger. The truth of Being is caught up in the tension between Being and non-Being. The irreducibility of the truth of Being is given by the interpretation of the meaning of *Dasein* and that of work of art. The retrieval of metaphysics inaugurates a new thinking entirely different from the metaphysical thought.[26]

In his book *The Truth in Painting*, Derrida claims that he deconstructs Heidegger's thought on work of art. The third chapter, *Derrida's critique of Heidegger's philosophy of the work of art* concentrates Derrida's treatise on Heidegger's one of the most famous works, *The Origin of the Work of Art*. Derrida isolates one of the paragraphs from Heidegger's essay on work of art, in order to carry out his particular objective namely, to show how Heidegger's essay remains in the traditional philosophy. Through the description of product-being of a product Heidegger became an *effective* tool in the hands of Derrida. In his critique, Derrida deals with the concept of truth of a product and claims that Heidegger is not free form Platonic-Aristotelian way of thinking, which he (Heidegger) himself wants to overcome. Derrida's claim that he discovers the metaphysics of presence in Heideggerian essay and deconstructs it is challenged in this Dissertation.

Having replaced the transcendental truth of traditional philosophy with the notion of difference, the thought of Heidegger and Derrida gets outside of the orbit of metaphysics. The fourth chapter, *The non-originary origin of truth: Heidegger and Derrida*, discusses how the principle of differentiation precedes identity. For Heidegger and Derrida, there is no reality outside of the structure of difference: difference is the meaning of Being. For both the difference is prior to all determination, meaning and concepts. In search of the truth of Being, Heidegger with his question of the meaning of Being, casts a look back, whereas Derrida does not. Heidegger opens the grand discussion of difference and Derrida carries forward it to the *finishing* point of difference, truth as disseminative. Without Heideggerian concept of difference Derrida's thought remains beyond the human understanding. In his search for the meaning of Being he looks for an infrastructure which underlies all metaphysical concepts. This infrastructure is coined by a neologism *différance*. In this respect their vision of origin of truth as difference is also different. Derrida's endeavour is dangerous for the importance of philosophy and it is much less to apply to different philosophers like Plato, Rousseau, Kant, Husserl, Heidegger, etc. Here the question remains unanswered that how can one dissolve transcendental truth into simple signifiers of literature? How can one throw away the metaphysical truth even if he could destroy its structure? Is not his philosophy of *différance* residing within the milieu of a structure? Is not the truth transcending all structures of determinations as well as undecidability?

References

1. Aristotle, *Metaphysics: Books Z and H*, Z 1, 1028b 4, trans. David Bosteock, Oxford, Oxford University Press, 1994, 1-2.
2. Martin Heidegger, *The Basic Problems of Phenomenology*, trans. Albert Hofstadter, Bloomington and Indianapolis, Indiana University Press, 1982, 11.
3. Martin Heidegger was born in 1889 in Messkirch, in Germany. He studied catholic theology, mathematic and philosophy in Freiburg. He was awarded Ph.D. for the dissertation *The Doctrine of Judgment in Psychologism*. In 1915 he attained Habilitation in *The Doctrine of Categories and Signification in Duns Scotes*. Afterwards he became lecturer at the University of Freiburg. In 1917 he married to Elfriede Petri. From 1923 to 1928 he was professor in philosophy in University of Marburg. In 1927 his famous work *Being and Time* was published. In 1928 he became Husserl's successor, Professor of philosophy, at the University of Freiburg. He has written a number of outstanding books in philosophy. In 1976 he died in Freiburg.
4. Jacques Derrida was born in 1930 in El Bair in Algeria, of Jewish parents. In 1950 he studied philosophy at the *École Normale Supérure*, in France. There he taught philosophy (1964-84) and since 1984, he is been Director of Studies at the *École des Husstes Études en*

Sciences Sociales, in Paris. His writing is a radical critique of Western metaphysics. In 1967 he moved quickly to the French philosophical scene with the publication of three books: *Of Grammatology, Writing and Difference and Speech and Phenomena and Other Essays on Husserl's Theory of Signs*. In these books he deconstructs metaphysical thoughts of some eminent thinkers like Husserl, Saussure, Rousseau, etc. Again in 1972 he published three important works: *Dissemination, Margins of Philosophy and Positions*. He has written a number of famous books like *Limited Inc* (1977), *The Truth in Painting* (1978), in which he criticised Immanuel Kant and Martin Heidegger. Since 1972 he has taught philosophy at Yale and Johns Hopkins Universities in the USA. In 1980, he defended his thesis based on his works. On 16 May 1992, Cambridge University conferred on him its honorary award for distinguished people. He was also involved with GREPH (*Groupe de Recherches sur l'Enseignement Philosophique*), set up to examine institutional aspects of teaching of philosophy. He died in the USA on 9.10.2004. Ref. Christopher Norris, *Derrida*, Cambridge and Manchester, Harward University Press, 1987, 11, 239-45. Jeff Collins and Bill Mayblin, *Derrida for Beginners*, ed., Richard Appignanesi, Cambridge, Icon Books Ltd., 1996, 10.

5. George Pattison, *Later Heidegger*, London and New York, Routledge, 2000, 8.
6. *Ibid.*, 21.
7. *Ibid.*, 107-08.
8. Ernst Behler, *Confrontations: Derrida, Heidegger, Nietzsche*, trans. Steven Taubeneck, Stanford and California, Stanford University Press, 1991, 21, 23.
9. Martin Heidegger, *Nietzsche*, Vol. III and IV, ed. David Farrell Krell, San Francisco, Harper & Row, 1979-1987, 8.
10. Martin Heidegger, *The End of Philosophy*, trans. Joan Stambaugh, New York, The University of Chicago Press, 2003, 10-11.
11. Tom Rockmore, *Heidegger and French Philosophy: Humanism, Antihumanism and Being*, New York, Routledge, 1995, 127.
12. David Wood, *Following Derrida*, in *Deconstruction and Philosophy*, ed. John Sallis, Chicago and London, The University of Chicago Press, 1987, 146.
13. J. Hillis Miller, *Derrida's Others*, in *Applying to Derrida*, eds. John Brannigan, Ruth Robbins and Julian Wolfreys, London, Macmillan Press LTD., 1996, 158.
14. Alan Bullock and R.B. Woodings, eds., *The Fontana Dictionary of Modern Thinkers*, London, Fontana Press, 1992, 178.

15. Husserl's return to the thing itself is mainly a subjectivist method of reduction. It is a method of leading the mind back to a juncture where interpretations no longer intervene, so that the mind can come into direct intuitive contact with what things essentially are. Whereas Heidegger's 'return to the thing itself' is indirect, exposing the structure of the truth of the work. In both Heidegger and Derrida, thing itself is unknown; in their effort to return to the thing, they find the irreducible alterity, the non-originary originary.
16. Martin Heidegger, *Being and Time*, trans. John Macquarrie and Edward Robinson, Oxford and Cambridge, Blackwell, 2004, 44.
17. Steven W. Laycok, *Mind as Mirror and the Mirroring of Mind: Biddhist Reflections on Western Phenomenology*, New York, State University of New York, 1994, 44.
18. Jenny Teichman, ed., *An Introduction to Modern European Philosophy*, London, Macmillan Press Ltd., 1995, 157.
19. The 'presence of Being in beings' is typically the problem of question of Being in the Heideggerian philosophy. In Derridean thought this question reveals the logocentric bias of Western metaphysics — a desire to be involved in the presence of the logos.
20. Infrastructure is the minimal unity of self and 'other' before presence. It means that self can take place only in relation to the 'other'. The meaning of infrastructure in Heidegger denotes the meaning of Being as equi-primordial. It implies the infinite withdrawal of the Being without constituting a centre. Derrida dissolves different philosophical texts to the truth of infrastructure. In this work the term infrastructure is substituted by different terms like, the general structure of referral or general structure of reference or synthesis of referential structures or differential structures or the truth of structural moment.
21. Jacques Derrida, *Of Grammatology*, trans, Gayatri Chakravorty Spivak, Bltimore and London, The Johns Hopkins University Press, 1974, 158.
22. Jacques Derrida, *Afterword: Toward an Ethic of Discussion*, in *Limited Inc*, Evanston, Illinois, North Western University Press, 1977, 148.
23. Jacques Derrida, *Différance*, in *Margins of Philosophy*, trans. Alan Bass, Chicago, University of Chicago Press, 1982, 60.
24. Christopher Norris, *Derrida*, 19.
25. Jacques Derrida, *Qual Quelle: Valéry's Sources*, in *Margins of Philosophy*, trans. Alan Bass, Chicago, The University of Chicago Press, 1982, 293.
26. Martin Heidegger, *Letter on Humanism*, in *Basic Writings*, ed. David Farrell Krell, London and New York, Routledge, 1993, 265.

1

In Pursuit of Being: Heidegger and Derrida

Philosophy as a science of truth deals at all times with the question what are entities or what is the Being of entities. This very question of the pre-Socratic thinkers, who marked the beginning of Western philosophy and civilization, denotes the ontological difference, the difference between beings and Being, to which their answer was '*physis*,' i.e. self-disclosing of beings. They understood entities as 'emerging' and 'abiding.' Being, according to the earliest Greek experience, is appearance as a definite mode of emerging self-manifestation, in which things emerge from concealment into truth in the sense of un-concealment. Heidegger's most famous argument is that the origin (emergence) is the ambivalence of both truth and untruth in the sense that concealment involves in every unconcealment. Asking about and defining the beingness of entities, i.e. what beings show up *as*, the history of philosophy overlooked the truth itself, the emergence, what makes the presence of entities possible, i.e. the presencing of what is present. From the very beginning, Greek philosophy thought of the Being of entities, the truth that underlies all our understanding of reality, but it did not ask what is Being or what is the truth of Being. Heidegger's the basic question is not concerned with the beingness of entities, but it deals with Being in respect to its ground, what Being itself is.[1]

It is the human attitude towards entities that makes the meaning of Being. Entities are uncovered by human concern. The human understanding of things, particularly in and through the languages of historical people, preserves and controls what originally holds sway—*physis*—the difference between Being and beings. The humanization of truth began with the meaningful articulation of the earliest Greek experience of truth of entities. By subjugating entities *as* tree, *as* animal, etc., human intelligibility undertakes to govern the power of the overpowering of Being. Our understanding of beings is subjected to the culture and practices, and the belief and the knowledge of the historical people, rather than the original meaning of Being itself.[2] Both Heidegger and Derrida criticize the humanization of truth, the subject-centred metaphysics, such as, for example, concept of *logos,* our understanding of the essence of beings or Being of entities, which underlies particular things.

The earliest Greek experience of Being, has been transformed through the history of metaphysics; Heraclitus' concept of aboriginal strife is the first step towards the science of ontology, which explained the *how* of things. It has reached its fulfilment in the metaphysics of Plato and Aristotle, who veiled what is revealed by the pre-Socratic Greek thinkers. In asking about the meaning of entities and experiencing entities as what comes to presence, the Greek thinkers overlooked what makes this presencing possible, i.e. the presencing of what is present. Thus, according to Heidegger, Being itself remains forgotten. Instead thinking of Being, the Greeks focused on beingness as the essential property of actually existent entities. Philosophy from its very inception defines truth as the 'correspondence between intellect and thing.' It is Heidegger's contention that the truth lies unsaid at the very base of what is said by the Greeks.[3] He exposes 'Platonism' as the forgetfulness of the meaning of Being in the entire history of philosophy, and takes a more originary way to the question of the meaning of Being in order to deal with what remains unsaid, i.e. truth, in the history of philosophy. Since Platonism has predefined all subsequent ways of experiencing things till today, in other words, since things are predefined by the humanization of truth from the very beginning of Greek philosophy till today, Heidegger initiates an originary way to the question of the meaning of Being in order to retrieve the original meaning of Being of the earliest Greeks. Even though he does compare neither the meaning of *physis* nor

Heraclitian Being, the truth of aboriginal strife, to the origin of the truth of aestheticism, he regards them as the right path to reach the origin of truth. The background of this thesis is Heidegger's critique of metaphysics, i.e. from the very inception of philosophy the distinction between presencing and what is present is ignored, which is the starting point of his philosophy of origin of truth that Derrida shares too.

Heidegger's aesthetic philosophy in the essay *The Origin of the Work of Art*[4] is the retrieval of the meaning of Being in an originary or the Heideggerian way, and by reducing the origin of truth to the discord of concealment and unconcealment he claims that the essay overcomes the 'metaphysics of presence,' the claim that Derrida challenges. Even though Derrida shares the same standpoint of Heidegger's critique of metaphysics, he criticizes Heidegger's philosophy of the work of art and remarks that it is not free from the grip of metaphysics of presence.[5] Derrida does not search for the origin of truth; his critique of metaphysics is known as the 'philosophy of deconstruction,' which is no way a search for the origin or the meaning of Being in the traditional sense. Since the truth of metaphysics is fabricated out of the necessity of asking about and finding the meaning of Being, he argues that the history of philosophy from the beginning to Heidegger remains 'logocentric,' which he wants to demolish without reconstituting further a centre or coming back to an another origin.[6] For him any search for the root of truth is in vain, since it is elusive in nature.

In the post-modern era metaphysics becomes the battlefield, where Heidegger and Derrida come up with the same goal. However, Derrida's claim that he deconstructs one of Heidegger's outstanding texts, *The Origin of the Work of Art*, and thereby calls into question Heidegger's effort to overcome the metaphysics of presence is thought-provoking. This thesis is concerned with the encounter between Heidegger and Derrida and its centre is the question of the 'origin of truth' in terms of Heidegger's question of the meaning of Being, to which the Derridean deconstruction is added.[7] In order to describe the philosophical positions of Heidegger and Derrida, the first part of this chapter expounds Heidegger's search for the meaning of

Being, the critique of traditional metaphysics, and his reading of archaic Greek philosophy. Derrida's critique of logocentrism, his aim and method of deconstruction are dealt in the second part.

Heidegger's question of the meaning of Being

Thing is given in truth or Being. Heidegger's fundamental question of metaphysics is: "Why are there beings at all instead of nothing?"[8] We are always questioning and thinking beyond the usual regions of beings. Our day to day experience is concerned with things that are ordered beyond their usual, ordinary state. "Philosophizing, we can now say, is extra-ordinary questioning about the extraordinary."[9] His destruction of metaphysics is the removal of cover of Being, the *extra*, that prevents our attempt to reach to thing itself. The destruction of metaphysics is carried out to reach to the origin of truth.

For Heidegger forgetting of the difference between Being and beings forgets the essence of Being. In the history of philosophy, the relationship between presencing and what is present remains unthought. In metaphysics even the *early trace* of the difference is erased or obliterated when presencing appears as something present and thereby Being finds itself the highest being present.[10] He holds the view that the essence of truth as unhiddenness, the appearance of what is present in its appearance, cannot be grounded in reason, thinking, or subjectivity;[11] because the presence or disclosure of entities has the structure of withdrawal. In other words, entities become apparent in appearing (Being) which withdraws itself, or effaces itself. Since Being that is taken as presence or disclosure cannot appear as such in entities that are disclosed, in other words, the presence or disclosure of entities has basically the structure of withdrawal. In *The Anaximander Fragment* he describes the trait or 'withdrawal' as the basic characteristic of Being.[12] Being that opens the first relation withdraws itself simultaneously without constituting a pure moment. Gasché says that concealment is the basic structure of the Heideggerian truth. Revealing and concealing, or coming forth and folding back constitute the basic characteristic of the truth of Being. Gasché describes Heidegger's truth as Being-as-retreat, which does not give rise to any truth as subjective consciousness of an object, but it refuses to reify any permanent relation by thinking it in terms of pre-given principles. Heidegger's concept of the trait of Being (Being *as* Being-trait) can be better understood in terms of the disclosure of thing in and through 'poetry and language'; thing revealed in poetry does not have any objective *nature* as such, which later becomes the underlying thought in Derrida.[13] Being *as* Being-trait, i.e. opening and concealing, makes our understanding of the meaning of beings limited. What remains hidden in the history of philosophy is not this or that being, but rather the Being of these beings that sheds shadows to our effort to know the origin of truth. Being is covered up so extensively that it becomes forgotten and there no longer is any question which arises about it and its ultimate meaning. Therefore, Heidegger undertakes this very important task in his philosophizing, namely the very question of the meaning of Being.[14] It is his critique of traditional metaphysics, which is to blame for the oblivion of the meaning of Being initiated by Plato and Aristotle.

Heidegger's critique of metaphysics

Metaphysics is the science of Being, ontology, which deals with the unity of Being: beings and Being.[15] Etymologically the term 'metaphysics' derives from the Greek *meta ta physika*.[16] *Meta* means trans or extending out or going beyond. *Physika* means physical beings. Metaphysics is the philosophical questioning about beings as such.[17] The term *meta*-physics literally means the things beyond the physical things, or the things coming after the material or physical things. It implies ontic-ontological difference.

The term *Being* denotes meaning in terms of which something becomes intellible to us as something. Heidegger's question of the meaning of Being is essentially the critique of Western metaphysics. In Aristotelian definition of metaphysics, Heidegger finds the meaning of Being as the fundamental relationship between Being and beings. Aristotle identifies phenomena (i.e. that which show themselves in themselves) with entities. Truth is understood as phenomena 'things themselves,' 'things that are,' or 'what shows itself,' which mean that entities in the *how* of their uncoveredness.[18] According to Aristotle the fundamental function of metaphysics is to ask 'what are beings as beings?' The answer to this question is that Being gives beings their *is*.[19] The traditional concept of Being, Heidegger formulates accordingly, is that which determines a being as a being or that by which a being is what it is.[20] Being is the meaning of beings as being. In traditional metaphysics he finds the problem of the meaning of Being, which determines beings, i.e. what they are. He argues that the Aristotelian doctrine of metaphysics as a manifold of meaning of beings, which dominates the history of Western metaphysics, ignores the fundamental distinction between Being and beings.[21] Heidegger holds the view that "aesthetics as a philosophical discipline arose as a consequence of the forgottenness of the ontological difference between Being (*Sein*) and beings (*Seiendes*), and therefore of the emphasis being placed on the particular being."[22] In Aristotle the primordial meaning of Being is ignored by asking what entities are. Even though Being is considered as the 'most general of generalities, which transcends all categories and has no real content, Western philosophy ignores the meaning of Being by reducing it to the level of reality or to the centrality of substance, thinghood of thing. Instead of thinking Being, Western philosophy asks the beingness (*Seiendheit*) of entities, which it considers their essential, self-evident and underlying property. It results in the forgetfulness of the meaning of Being because it is regarded as the sum total of independently existing entities that exist for the observer.[23] Plato explains the world of Ideas as something that independently exists is the root cause of the meaning of entities. Together with Heidegger, Gadamer too thinks that in Plato and Aristotle the question of Being and that of being as such are inseparable.[24]

In *Nietzsche* Vol. III, Heidegger holds the view that the entire history of metaphysics is a distortion of the meaning of Being because it is thought as *what* and *how* every being is to be. For him, Being, which is the root cause and the fundamental meaning of beings, is to be questioned.[25] In *Metaphysics*, Aristotle thinks metaphysics, the totality of beings, from the standpoint of being as beings and thereby material beings (physics) determine the essence of Being. From this point of view, truth of Being is defined as the presence of beings. In traditional philosophy Being is the meaning of beings. Our knowledge is true if there is a correspondence between Being and beings and to 'know means to be able to stand in the truth.'[26] A thing is defined and determined in terms of its truth and thus, particularly from Plato onwards, the distinction between Being and beings has disappeared from the field of metaphysics, something that Heidegger calls 'Platonism.'

According to Heidegger, the primordial disclosure of the beings as such and taken as a whole, the question concerning Being of beings, and the beginning of Western history are one and the same. In *Nietzsche* Vol. III, he calls for thinkers to challenge the metaphysical definition of truth as being as a whole and to begin to think 'the *questionableness* of beings as a whole.'[27] Metaphysics as the science of Being as beings is perversion of truth, which originated mainly with Plato and Aristotle. An attempt to think metaphysics as the being of beings rather than Being, originates first in Plato's turn from truth as uncoveredness to the truth about that which is uncovered.

Heidegger accepts truth as disclosure, which he explains it in terms of the disclosure of *Dasein* and that of the work of art.[28] He finds a relationship between truth and art (*technē*), the mode of knowing.[29] The Greek term *technē* denotes the way of bringing entities out of their concealdness into the unconcealdness, the way of revealing of beings. In his search for the meaning of Being he returns to Heraclitus' concept of truth as '*unhiddenness*,' which, according to him, is reformed by Plato and Aristotle as correctness.[30] Western Philosophy takes its origin in this transition from "*alētheia qua* unhiddenness to truth *qua* correctness."[31] In Aristotle there is an adequation between beings and Being; his concept of truth eliminated the subject-object distinctions. In *Metaphysics* he asks: "'What is being?' - is the question 'What is substance?'"[32] He equalizes the being with Being. Substance is the what-being of a thing that underlies.[33] It is what permanent, self-evident and always remains there through all changes. According to Aristotle, philosophy studies entities as such and this study is the study of substance itself, because he applies the primary sense of Being to substance that which is (particular things).[34] Western philosophy defines truth as "the bringing of the thought or proposition into alignment with the thing,..."[35] Truth is an agreement between a proposition and that which is represented. Propositional truth is equal to the represented reality itself. The correspondence theory, establishing truth through the alignment of thought and thing, marked the end of metaphysics by bringing down the trans-temporal or supra-dimensional aspect of truth to the temporal or physical level. How can there be truth in *correspondence* between our thought (the content of our consciousness) and the outside world?

Heidegger does not consider the origin of truth as the agreement. Setting aside the truth as revealment, he understands that truth that happens has some other source, a more originary source, to which concealdness and unconcealedness belong, which he explains in terms of the disclosedness of *Dasein* and that of work of art.[36] Wolin argues that Heidegger's truth as uncoveredness is an empty generality without having been any objective truth. Disclosure of beings in *their immediacy* provides us the sufficient knowledge of the topology of truth, i.e. the disclosure is the condition for the appearance of truth as untruth.[37] Heidegger criticizes the objectivity of our subjective impression because he finds an irremediable distinction between two separate entities: the thinking subject and the independently existing object. Metaphysics, by defining the truth of entities as something what it is, reduces the irremediable distinction between thought and entities.[38] He finds the hallmark of Western metaphysics in Plato and Aristotle, in which metaphysics lost its meta-dimension of truth since it is confined to the truth of physical things.

a. *Platonism: the oblivion of the meaning of Being*

In *Plato's Doctrine of Truth* Heidegger says that it is Plato who is taken to task for forsaking the original Greek concept of truth and initiating, with his theory of Idea, the content of knowledge and understanding, which Heidegger deplores as the humanization of truth.[39] In Platonism, revealment denotes our understanding of beings as what they are. Metaphysics is the Being of beings as being. In *Introduction to Metaphysics*, Heidegger criticizes the whole of Western metaphysics, from Plato to Nietzsche, for persisting in oblivion of the truth of Being. The entire history of European philosophy from Plato to Nietzsche is the history of metaphysics, which Heidegger calls Platonism, in which Being as such remains in oblivion.[40]

i. Platonic Idea: truth as revealment

The entire history of metaphysics considers truth as non-concealment, which for Heidegger is the forgetfulness of the meaning of Being compared to the archaic Greek understanding of *physis*. According to him, Plato shifts his attention from the pre-Socratic Greek understanding of the truth of Being as emergence, *physis*, the process by which things of a certain look *emerge* into view, to the shining forth of the look itself, to what the view offers for observation, namely the enduring presence, the Idea, with its nature as a look. The Idea is that which provides a thing with existence and essence and it makes it possible for anything to show up as existent. The truth of entities is the Idea and therefore, the entire history of philosophy from Plato is forgetfulness in which entities obtrude as actually existing and possessing essential properties while Being remains concealed. The concealment or withdrawal occurred in Plato through rational contemplation and thinking. In order to explain the shift of the locus of truth from a thing that emerges to the rational Idea, the content of the thing that emerges, Heidegger interprets the allegory of the cave in Plato's *Republic*.[41] In the allegory, what is called unhidden is the beings and is taken as such. In each stage there is a passage and progress from hiddenness towards unhiddenness.[42] "The more the unhidden is unhidden, the closer do we come to beings."[43]

For Plato the Ideas are the most unhidden, self-evident and the truth of things; when we perceive a thing correctly, we perceive the reality that of Idea. Though the truth is explained as the revealment of beings in four distinctive stages, the truth in the final stage as correctness is related to the Ideas. In the final stage things show themselves as what they are. The Greeks call the look of a thing *eidos*, or Idea, through and by which a thing is accessible to us as *what* it is.[44] In the allegory of the cave Plato has neglected the process, the transition (i.e. the transition from one stage to another, in which a change happens in the mind), by which a thing comes into the light in its look; and he concentrates upon the look as the foreground. Heidegger says that Greek philosophy has never returned to its roots, instead it continues to hold that the essence of truth is presence, what is revealed.[45]

Plato's interpretation of the allegory of the cave reveals the Ideas as the beingness of beings, the most unhiddenness that is permanent and endures in beings. Beings that are unhidden in the first stage as the shadow-like beings become more-being or more unhidden in the second stage in the light of the fire, the image for the sun. Again, beings that are more unhidden in the second stage become most beingful in the light of the sun in the third stage. Here our knowledge of a thing unites with the beingful beings, Ideas. It is the level of seeing a thing with the faculty of the soul. Beings attain their truth through the participation in Ideas. In one of the most celebrated passages Plato identifies Ideas with entity that is most unhidden. He calls Ideas the being which has being.[46] A thing is what it *is* only in Idea; thing that is revealed is true. In order to indicate that which is pure, unhidden being, Plato uses the term true. Truth for Plato is the revealment or beingness of beings, which for Heidegger is the error of metaphysics, since it concentrates only on one aspect of truth i.e. *what* things are, and forgets to ask *how* things are, the truth of emergence, in which confluence of subjective-objective dimensions takes place.

In Plato, truth is disclosure of a thing as what it is. Disclosure is important because it lays open to sight the appearance of what appears and the *form* of what is seen. What matters to Plato is the appearance of the forms in disclosure, the essence or continuous presence of a substance, which remains unchanging. Plato's concept of the eternal form of things as well as Aristotle's substance is known as the Being of an entity, the ground that provides foundation for it.[47] Things that are visible outside the cave denote what the proper being of beings consists in. Particular things are what they are only in their visible forms or Ideas, in which things present themselves.[48] Form constitutes the substance or the beingness of being. Individual forms or Ideas are the Being of particular things insofar as they (particular things) participate in the individual forms.[49] In Plato unhiddenness can be understood as the visible form of things in which they can be accessible *as* something.[50] The visible forms of Plato enable beings to appear; the Idea is the visible form, the essence of beings, which offers a view of what things are. A thing is what it is only because of the visible form, Idea, which is the truth and look of a thing. An entity can appear to us as what it is in its visible form, Idea.[51] Platonic truth as the revealment of an entity *as* something ignores the truth of emergence, the truth of what is present in presencing.

ii. The Idea as the original source of the knowledge and of the meaning of beings

Plato calls Idea the most beingful of beings, what-being of beings, the essence of beings, image, look and *eidos*, which as essence is antecedent to the appearance of a particular thing.[52] Our recognition of a thing *as* something is an antecedent view. The Idea as the most beingful of beings makes all other beings visible and intelligible. The continuous presence of a substance is called *ousia*. We can perceive thing *as* something in and through the presence, the appearance of thing.[53] For example, when we recognize a house *as* a house, we are seeing this particular thing in its truth, seeing it with the faculty of the soul.[54] The self-showing of the *whatness* of a being is its Idea, which is the most unhidden and in which thing is accessible to us as what it is.

Thus Idea is the underlying factor of the meaning of beings and the foundation of our knowledge. In the allegory of the cave there is a relationship between the sun as the source of light and the things visible. The fire in Plato's cave is the image for the sun; any form of unveiling is possible only in the light.[55] Our true knowledge of things refers to the antecedent illumination, the Idea of all Ideas.[56] In the analogy of the cave, the sun that shines outside the cave symbolizes the highest Idea, the form of the Good, which supplies the forms to particular things and illuminates their forms with truth and being. It is the Idea of all Ideas which makes all Ideas visible. The Idea of Ideas or the Idea of the Good is that which makes all sight, appearance, and disclosure possible. It is the reason (ultimate ground) for the possibility of all that is, it is what enables everything else to be.[57] Our knowledge is the recollection of the eternal truth or Idea, to which the truth of a thing belongs through participation. The Idea of the Good shines by itself; it has the power of visibility which accomplishes all shining.[58] The essence of the Idea is called good because it constantly stands in view wherever beings show themselves. The Idea is the original source of all that is right and also all that is fine or beautiful. In *Republic* Plato says that the Goodness makes things knowable; it enables the philosophers to know things.[59] Idea is the source of truth and knowledge. In Plato, Heidegger finds the humanistic aspect of the truth of beings, which is directed by or subordinated to the Idea. "With this transformation of the essence of truth there takes place at the same time a change of the locus of truth. As unhiddenness, truth is still a fundamental trait of beings themselves. But as correctness of the 'gaze,' it becomes a characteristic of human comportment toward beings."[60] Plato's doctrine of truth as it is revealed in the allegory of the cave indicates the dominance of Idea over truth. The revealment of beings as something, *what* they are, is primarily a humanization of truth, since beings become present in its whatness.

In Plato, truth in its original sense as 'uncoveredness' is subordinated to the dominance of the Idea, and so too the notion of truth changes from uncoveredness to that of the correctness or correspondence. This humanistic aspect of truth can be detected from the very beginning to the present day of philosophy. Plato and Aristotle received the concepts of thought and being from Parmenidean concept of the meaning of Being, according to which truth is the thought of beings. Parmenides (Fragment 3) held the view that thought and beings are one and the same. "For the same thing is for thinking and for being."[61] A thing and the thought of it are identical because we can think of something that which *is*, and that which *is not*, is unknowable or unthinkable. Plato's ontological concept of the forms of particular things is based on Parmenidean requirement for knowledge. In Plato too the essence of truth is correctness, i.e. the identity between Idea and being. Real is accessible to knowledge, unreal is not.[62] "In the idea we see *what* every being is and *how* it is, in short the *being* of beings (*das Sein des Seienden*)."[63] Idea is the ground or origin of particular things. It is to be noted that in Plato's thought the essence of truth is the unhiddenness of beings, which ultimately means our understanding of beings as *what* they are: the essence of truth as correctness, knowing of thing in truth or in terms of its whatness. "Truth is no longer, as it was qua unhiddenness, the fundamental trait of being itself. Instead, as a consequence of getting yoked under the idea, truth has become correctness, and henceforth it will be a characteristic of the knowing of beings."[64] Truth as unhiddenness in Plato means the unhiddenness of beings *as* this or *as* that, in other words, our understanding of the essence of beings.

Truth as correctness is impossible without truth as the unhiddenness of being; it is the act of seeing or knowing what is revealed.[65] Truth in Plato and in Aristotle consists in the unhiddenness of things, which is the foundation of truth as correctness or untruth in the sense of incorrect. Truth as correctness becomes the characteristic of the entire Western thought.[66]

iii. *The Idea and the truth of production*

There is a relation between Platonic Idea and the truth of a work produced. The production of a work is the presencing of its anticipated look.[67] Even though Plato considers the truth of production of works of art is a mere imitation, it is a mode in which the original or Idea itself appears or shows itself. The Greek term for production of work as well as for art is called *technē,* which does not mean the art or production of work, but the *mode of knowing*.[68] Clark explains the three levels of Platonic understanding of reality: first, the universal non-sensuous intellectual forms, second, the imitation of the ideas in objects of the world, such as table, trees, and third, the artistic imitation, which is considered as the shadows of the shadows.[69] Production manifests the mode of the Idea's self-manifestation. Heidegger illustrates it with the example of a potter. A potter shapes a vase out of clay after its pre-image (Idea). That which is formed or stamped is a creation of the imagination. The Idea (the anticipated look of a thing) and the figure of a thing are intertwined; in production the pre-image of the work directs the activity of the producer to provide the work with a particular shape.[70] Heidegger explains, for example, how the relation between *morphe* and *eidos* (look) constitute the truth of a being. The word *morphe* refers not only to the spatial figure but to the total stamp of a thing, from which we perceive it.[71] The stamping or shaping of an entity means the conferring meaning to it. In ordinary Greek usage, the model for the understanding of perceived entities is the productive activity of the craftsman, e.g., the activity of a potter to form a vase. His activity of stamping lends to the produced entity its characteristic look, the *eidos,* by which we see what has been produced. "...the *eidos*, the look of a thing is founded, grounded in the *morphe*, stamp."[72] In perception we apprehend the look via the *morphe* or shape. It shows the relationship between thing produced and its meaning. Heidegger says that in Greek ontology, sense perception means the perception of the unchangeable essence of things, the Being, Idea.[73] Therefore, concealment accompanies every emerging-into-presence. In Platonist ontology, the configuration or stamp of the particular entity is explained by, and thus grounded in, the look, which is understood as prior to and independent of the particular entity, in the way that the pre-image is prior to and independent of the artefact to be constructed in its light. In Platonism, we move from the *eidetic* look (pre-image) to the production of the perceived being.[74] The concept of production ultimately deals with Being-in-itself, the prototype of Platonic Idea, which exists in the craftsman's mind, by which he anticipates what he intends to produce.[75] In Platonic sense, argues Heidegger, a work produced has the truth of *mimesis*, imitation, which is not a mere copy, but a mode of Idea's self-manifestation. The meaning of a work or product is Being; Being is the presenting of the anticipated look (production, bringing forth, *her-vor-bringen*), which stems from the *event* (*Ereignis*) of presence that does not maintain itself since it withdraws.[76] In order to describe truth Heidegger explores the nuances of the Platonic concept of art as *mimesis*, uncoveredness, the appearing of what is present in its appearance.[77]

What Plato considers as the look of the being is in fact how the being looks to human cognition, which is already predetermined. Here Idea is more related to imagination and therefore Idea is conceived as possibility rather than actuality.[78] The Idea is called an anticipatory look, which Heidegger assimilates to the Aristotelian essence, to "that which a being already was."[79] The Idea or look is common to all of its existing instances, through which a thing is the very thing that it is. Heidegger understands the Idea as the analogical unity underlying substance and the other categories; it is the universal or general concept of Being that is initiated by Plato and Aristotle, and remains the defining mark of Platonism throughout its history.

b. *Truth as correctness: the turn in Plato and Aristotle*

The Greek word for truth is *alētheia*, which originally means unhiddenness in the sense of *physis*. The original meaning of the early Greek concept of truth as *physis* changes time and again;[80] particularly it takes an unexpected turn in Plato and Aristotle, who reformed or transformed the fundamental Greek experience of truth as unhiddenness into the essence of truth as correctness.[81] "In Greek, unhiddenness is called ἀλήθεία, a word that we translate as 'truth.' And for a long time now in Western thinking, truth has meant the agreement of the representation in thought with the thing itself: *adaequatio intellectus et rei*."[82] The adequation theory is the humanistic determination of truth. Correspondence is a relation, a relation between intellect and thing. In Aristotle's correspondence theory, Heidegger finds three implications of truth: (a) the locus of truth is the proposition or assertion (judgement); (b) the essence of truth lies in the correspondence or agreement between a judgement and its object; and (c) truth is relegated to judgement.[83] Judgement is also a kind of relation between a real or physical fact to which judgement refers and the ideal content of the judgement itself. In this definition of judgement one can grasp truth as the alignment, truth as the relation between ideal being and physical entity. The ontological dimension of a judgement is characterised as demonstration of what a thing *is*.[84]

Western philosophy with its definition of truth as correspondence and as revealment takes its origin from the very beginning of Greek philosophy. Heidegger criticizes the concept of Platonism and calls into question the content of truth as revealment, "'true means what something no longer has."[85] He also criticizes that truth as unhiddenness has nothing to do with assertion and the measurement of truth in terms of correctness and correspondence.[86] The transition from truth as unhiddenness to truth as correctness marks the beginning of Western philosophy, which, according to Heidegger, is an erroneous and fateful course.[87] He holds the view that the very Greek interpretation of truth in the sense of correspondence or alignment is a fatal error.[88]

Physis as nature: the degradation of the archaic Greek meaning of Being

Physis is the first Greek name for beings themselves and for the beings taken as a whole. It implies the meaning of entities as emergence-abiding sway. *Physis* as beings' emergence implies that which rises and comes forward, and goes back again into itself. Nature (*physis)* is the self-contained in the sense that entities' coming-into-presence involves the meaning of withdrawal. Heidegger argues that one cannot ascribe the presence to the notion of emergence of beings and to the presencing, because concealment accompanies every emerging-into-presence. With the human concern and the question of the meaning of beings began the degradation of the earliest meaning of Being as *physis*. The humanization of truth determines the truth of things in a rational way. If man tries to gain a foothold among beings and proceeds to master them in one way or another, then his advance against them is guided by a knowledge of them which is called *technē*. Originally *technē* does not have the meaning of producing something; rather it designates that kind of knowledge which supports every human concern in the midst of things, the meaning of beings.[89] *Technē* denotes the mode of knowing things in the sense of truth as revealing out of concealing. The terms Being and art imply the meaning of emergence which denote the ontological difference. The etymological implications of the term *physis* and its corresponding Latin translation *natura*, nature, indicate how the original meaning of Being as *physis* is degraded into physics, what a thing is, the meaning of beings as being in Western philosophy.[90]

Etymologically, the term *physis* derives from the Indo-Germanic root *bhū*, *bheu* (corresponding Greek word is *phuō*), which means self-emergence, "to emerge, to hold sway, to come to stand from out of itself and to remain standing."[91] Accordingly the root meaning of Being denotes the implications of self-subsistence and self-emergence of entities. *Physis* is Being itself, which is by nature in-itself-abiding and self-unfolding. It means growing or emerging. *Physis* is accordingly explained as that which emerges from itself, or self-opening unfolding.[92] It is the coming forth and unfolding, the self-opening, which at the same time returns to its source: withdrawal. *Physis* as a ground word means the emergence into the open, the emergent return into itself.[93] Heidegger's etymological analysis of the meaning of *physis* as Being indicates the meaning of self-emergence, not the whatness of beings that emerge. In presencing and emergence of beings and all that is present, difference is more originary than the pure presence of the origin. This more originary nature of beings is covered up by the presence of the origin.

Heidegger translates *physis* as Being.[94] The term Being, which is translated as to be, to emerge, to dwell, and to abide, attains the etymological implications of *physis*.[95] He interprets *physis* as Being to denote that which originally holds sway.[96] Heidegger ascribes difference to the very origin (the source) or to the emergence of what is present from presencing. As the root word *bhū* indicates, the term *physis* denotes truth in the sense of a self-manifestation of being; that which emerges in itself (*phū*) shows itself in the process of growth (*pha* or *phyein*). The Greek terms *phū* (to emerge) and *pha* (it is translated to *phos*, light. It is the root meaning of phenomenon) constitute different moments of the meaning of *physis*. They mean the unfolding that rests in itself which is also called showing itself, shining forth, self-manifesting, or appearance. Phenomenon means 'that wherein something can become manifest, visible in itself.'[97] For Clark, the terms such as Being, *physis,* and *alētheia* denote the Greek meaning of Being, i.e. Being as self-unfolding that rests in itself and self-manifesting.[98] The word *physis* means "what emerges from itself (for example, the emergence, the blossoming of a rose), the unfolding that opens itself up, the coming-into-appearance in such unfolding, and holding itself and persisting in appearance-in short, the emerging-abiding sway."[99] *Physis* means the emerging—abiding sway. The verb *sway* is the translation of German verb *walten,* which means to prevail, to reign or to dominate. In relation to the emergence of beings, the verbal noun of the German word *das Walten* means the powerful upsurge of the presence of beings. Heidegger interprets the Greek word *physis* as the Greek word for Being, which denotes the ontological difference, the emergent-abiding presence of beings as such.[100] *Physis* brings beings to the 'world,' to be as they are. The meaning of *physis* implies in its original meaning physics;[101] i.e. the meaningful appearance of entities. "*Phusis* is Being itself, thanks to which the thing first becomes and remains observable."[102] *Physis* as emergence implies revealment of beings as something in a given culture in which concealment subsists. *Physis* has the same meaning of poesy, bringing-forth, or arising of something from out of itself (e.g. the bursting of a blossom). Work of art has the meaning of *physis* in the sense that it brings to the fore the prior value of beings.[103] Heraclitus described the character of this concealed truth (*physis*) as the strife that holds sway before every actuality, divine or human. For Heidegger the origin of truth is the aboriginal strife.[104]

The distortion of the concept of *physis* took place with the translation of *physis* into Latin as *natura* (*nasci*), which means 'to be born,' 'to originate.' By this translation the fundamental meaning of *physis* is already ignored. Here we understand *physis* not in the originary sense of the emerging and abiding sway, but rather as the *nature* of things, as being prior to all beings.[105] Thus, in the course of time, the fundamental Greek experience of *physis* is turned into the philosophy of nature, "a representation of all things according to which they are really of material nature."[106] Heidegger explains the meaning of representation in his book *Nietzsche* Vol. IV, where he interprets Descartes' *cogitare* as taking possession of something with the certitude in grasping.[107] Clark explains the Heideggerian meaning of representation as something *presenting to oneself* by *presenting before oneself*. Consciousness of an object is possible only in and through the ego, self-consciousness of it, which is the *ground* of representation, in which things are standing against (opposing) us. Thus Western philosophy speaks of the *nature* of spirit, the *nature* of history to mean not only the material determination of beings but also their whole essence.[108] The *nature* of things means "*what* things are in their 'possibility' and *how* they are, regardless of whether and to what degree they 'actually' are."[109] In Plato, the essence of truth as the correctness of the representation, and thereby, philosophy becomes the inquiry into the truth of beings in terms of Ideas.[110] His thinking causes the change in the essence of truth; *physis* is turned into the *look* of beings as being, the real is interpreted and determined by Ideas. And this change in the essence of truth dominates the entire history of philosophy till today.[111] Western philosophy was born with thinking of beings as such and as a whole; metaphysics is the articulation of the truth of beings as a whole.[112]

In Aristotelian metaphysics, the narrowing down of the meaning of *physis* takes place in the direction of a physical or materialistic interpretation of this term (*physis*). He describes the *nature* as "the grounds of beings as such," 'what is, as such and as a whole.'[113] In short, beings—as such and as a whole—is *physis*, to mean the emerging-abiding sway as their essence and character; but the narrowing down of *physis* takes place to mean *what* naturally or physically is. *Meta*-physics is concerned with the question 'beyond beings:' Being of beings; but from the very beginning of philosophy to Nietzsche *physics* determines the essence and the history of metaphysics.[114] In all systems of thought, the concept of Being is thought of in terms of the truth of beings. Thus the question of the meaning of Being turned into the question of the meaning of beings. In this context, the definition "metaphysics is the fundamental knowledge of beings as such and as a whole,"[115] announces the essence of Being. It deals with the truth of the entities; truth means truth of something. "Metaphysics is inquiry beyond or over beings, which aims to recover them as such and as a whole for our grasp."[116] Metaphysics is the conceptualization or the objectification of entities. It is an expression that may be translated as the existent altogether or the being of beings altogether. Metaphysics thinks Being as the being of beings.[117] The Greek word *physis* as disclosure of closure becomes narrowed down in the history of metaphysics with its meaning as revealment, the absolute foundation of truth. Heidegger's question of Being deals with the history of philosophy as oblivion of Being. He holds the view that the concept of Being as such remains in oblivion.[118]

The conceptualization of the meaning of beings, the humanization of truth, leads to the distortion of the original Greek experience of the meaning of *physis*. Metaphysics is the distortion of the archaic meaning of *physis*. "The systematic articulation of the truth at any given time 'about' beings as a whole is called metaphysics."[119] In metaphysical knowledge historical humanity preserves and hands down the truth of its relation to beings as a whole and the truth about those beings themselves. In order to explain the truth, Heidegger uses the term *technē*, a form of knowledge that brings to the fore the truth (Platonic *eidos*, the antecedent appearance of things) in production. Indicating Aristotelian categories and the four causes that define the thingness of a thing *as* something, Heidegger says that *physis* in Aristotle is a kind of *technē*.[120] Aristotle's *Metaphysics* presents physics as metaphysics. However, Heidegger observes that the essence of *physis* as *nature* originated with Anaximander, Heraclitus and Parmenides.[121] The definition of Being in terms of identity (Anaximander) and *polemos* (Heraclitus) conceals the originary experience of Being and reveals what beings are. Concealing and revealing (or rest and movement) are the two irreducible aspects of Being as emergence.[122] *Physis* as the originarily emergent self-upraising of the originary forces of what holds sway, does not let beings be reduced to presence. The pre-Socratic concept of world and also the Christian concept of world or cosmos designate, however, the mode of Being of things or the how (*wie*) of the Being of the beings rather than these being themselves. This *how* defines beings in the totality of the meaning, and at the same time it is the possibility for the *how* of every being. This *how* of the beings taken as a totality is *a priori* (*vorgängig*),[123] which is *prior* to and determines all beings. *Physis* can be defined as the prevailing of beings as a whole. The concept of Being given by Parmenides and Heraclitus is the first step towards the ontology, which tries to define the *nature* of beings. In addition, Heidegger mentions the fulfilment of Greek ontology in Aristotle, the four Aristotelian causes as the *origin* in terms of the originary, *a priori* meaning of beings.[124] Aristotle's interpretation of *physis* as material thing, as what it is as such and as a whole, has already inaugurated, according to Heidegger, the end of Greek philosophy.[125]

In poetry and thought the Greeks experienced Being, in that way *physis* is disclosed to them as Being, which is *prior* to all beings and gods. *Physis* is an *event* of standing forth, which implies that everything comes into presence as what it is from the concealment.[126] The coming-forth of beings from concealment and their abiding presence in themselves signify the meaning of *physis*. For the Greeks *physis* means the poetic meditations of Being, which comprises all material, living things and also immaterial. *Nature* is the underlying, universal truth which is prior to all determination of beings. Heidegger refers to one of Hölderlin's hymns (*As when on feast day...*), which describes the *nature* as the Being, which is beyond all beings and gods of Occident and Orient and upon which (*nature)* rest history and subjectivity.[127] In *Elucidations of Hölderlin's Poetry*, Heidegger describes the meaning of *physis* as self-opening in the sense that that which is rising is at the same time going back to itself. In other words beings are entering or presenting themselves or showing themselves in their outline, in Being: *physis*.[128] *Physis* means concealed truth, prior to all actuality, even to gods and to all determinative concepts. Things come to the presence as what they are in their truth. Heidegger's ontological difference implies the truth of *physis*: the concealed-truth or the concealment in the revealment of entities.

From Platonism to Heideggerianism

For Heidegger, the fundamental question of metaphysics, the meaning of Being is a historical question through and through. What is the meaning of Being as historical? It does not take the objective of historical science which deals with the truth of beings, but rather it deals with the metaphysical dimension of truth, which implies the meaning of difference at the origin.[129] In him the meaning of Being remains undiscoverable. He makes it explicit in terms of the truth of the work of art, e.g. van Gogh's painting and Greek temple that open up the world of historical people, their values and practices. For example, what is the meaning of Being in relation to van Gogh's painting as a pair of peasant's shoes? The peasant's shoes are the truth of painting, what *is* there, the *Da* of *Sein*. When we say the painting is a pair of peasant's shoes, we make no distinction between Being and being; it is the oblivion of Being. Even though Heidegger determines to avoid the reign of metaphysics in the history of work of art, there are thinkers like Gethmann-Siefert, Pattison who argue that his works reflect the German culture and politics of that time, between the two world wars, and particularly *Being and Time* and *The Origin of the Work of Art* represent his political views.[130]

Having criticized the entire history of Western philosophy as Platonism Heidegger feels the need to take another starting point to mark a new origin in the search of the meaning of Being. Gethmann argues that even though Heidegger denies the truth of adequation, he does not answer to the question of the meaning of Being in a satisfactory way to those who search the origin of truth.[131] However, for Heidegger the kernel of truth is the emergence of beings, in which both concealment and unconcealment play a vital role. The entire history of metaphysics is concerned with what is originated, or emerged, and thus having said what truth is, it remains indeed unsaid. By directing our attention to the visible thing, and so to visibility or presence as the property that is common to and thus defines anything whatsoever, Plato is criticised for concealing from our view, the real character of truth, process of emergence or of rendering visible. From Plato onward, philosophers conceive of Being as a general term that expresses what is common to all things.[132] For the Greeks the fundamental experience of *alētheia*, the unhiddenness of beings, was something self-evident.[133] By 'thing' is meant any definite or identifiable entity whatsoever. What has already emerged, the thing, then acquires the character of presence as showing. The underlying notion is that natural beings are those things that emerge from a process of manifestation that is complete in itself.[134] In order to bring to light what remains unsaid in Platonism, Heidegger tries to overcome Platonism via the mytho-poetic meditations of the pre-Socratic era. Plato ignored the basic pre-Socratic thought of the meaning of Being, especially that of Heraclitus' (Fragment 123) that "The holding sway of beings, i.e. beings in their Being, loves to conceal itself."[135] Heidegger accepts this argument and considers the self-concealment of Being in revealment as the destiny of Being. Forgetfulness of the question of Being is originated at the very beginning of Western metaphysics because of the very nature of Being itself. One shall not ignore the archaic Greek experience which suggests that the nature of *physis* is self-concealing: "The real constitution is accustomed to hide itself."[136] Heidegger's work shows how being loves to conceal itself in revealment. Heideggerianism indicates the concealment of Being in revealment. He argues that the truth of being is to be understood as ontological difference, which cannot be reduced to the presence. Prof. Dr. Josef Früchtl has provided me with deep insight into the irreducibility of the Heideggerian truth: "Truth-I depends upon truth-II."[137] Truth as self-disclosing opens up another context, from which it comes into the fore: the truth of *Dasein* and that of the work of art manifest the infrastructural character of truth, its referentiality.[138]

Derrida's critique of Western logocentrism and his philosophy of deconstruction

Derrida is generally regarded as the father of the contemporary philosophy of deconstruction. The Derridean deconstruction can be considered as sustained critique of Western metaphysics. Taking up the Heideggerian criticism, Derrida too attacks the metaphysics of presence.[139] He argues that the history of philosophy has always and everywhere been controlled by logocentrism.[140] He questions its basic notions of absolute truth and observes that philosophy at all times is the relentless search for ground, fundamentals, principles; he branded it logocentrism. At the beginning of *Of Grammatology*, he substitutes the word logocentrism for metaphysics in order to show that metaphysics has always been determined by *logos*.[141] In his writings he identifies metaphysics with logo-philosophy. Metaphysics is the presence of *logos*, which determines the entire Western tradition. There is nothing beyond the grip of it. Philosophy from its beginning to Heidegger is under the control of the determination of the truth of Being. To deconstruct the pervasive nature of metaphysics means to demolish the entire edifice of Western philosophy as a whole.

The Derridean deconstruction radicalizes the task of destruction inaugurated by Heidegger. Behler concludes that the both terms, destruction and deconstruction, denote the demolition or dismemberment in the sense that they stand for the removal of the sedimented layers and covers that hide the original meaning of Being.[142] Even though Heidegger's critique of metaphysics is very important for Derrida, he needs to overcome Heidegger in order to mark his own distinctive way of thinking.[143] Derrida calls Western metaphysics the philosophy of presence extending from the beginning to Heidegger. Derrida writes, "the history of (the only) metaphysics, which has, in spite of all differences, not only from Plato to Hegel (even including Leibniz) but also, beyond these apparent limits, from the pre-Socratics to Heidegger, always assigned the origin of truth in general to the logos..."[144] He criticises that Heidegger remains faithful to the traditional metaphysics with his two important works, *Being and Time* and *The Origin of the Work of Art*.[145] The aim of his deconstruction is to undo the transcendental absolute[146] of Western metaphysics. Therefore, he reduces every concept to the 'play' of 'text.'[147] The fundamental theme in Derrida's thought is the textuality of philosophy, which does not reconstitute any centre. By deconstructing the metaphysics of presence in several philosophical texts he tries to put an end to the reign of metaphysics, the possibility for the centrality of meaning for reference. Some of the important deconstructive terms of Derrida such as *writing* (*grammatological writing or arche-writing*), *trace, différance,* etc.,[148] are synonymous terms, which he uses to point to a movement or a realm anterior to the presence. He lays bare the pervasive nature of presence in various philosophical texts and applies his deconstructive terms to them, in order to indicate difference prior to presence. He favours neither the concept of presence nor that of difference. His philosophy of deconstruction has the logic of *neither...nor*. Therefore, the fundamental theme in his philosophy is the concept of textuality.[149] It is the negation of presence and the impossibility of the centrality of meaning. Like Heidegger, he too opposes the absoluteness of meaning and stands for relativity of meaning.

Logocentrism: Derrida's critique of Western metaphysics

Derrida observes a long and complex Western heritage of the reign of *logos*, from which he wants to disengage. It is his contention that the entire Western philosophy is logocentric as it is founded on the undivided origin, *logos*. This system of metaphysics is violent and suppressive because it suppresses its *other*. He perceives that metaphysics is functioning from Plato to today by the institution of the hierarchical opposition. Thus, metaphysics asserts its meaning on the exclusion of its opposite, which according to him is a violation.[150] He says that there is no presence in its real sense because it can be shown as a product of an unjust system. Deconstruction exposes the impossibility of presence of one genre, by excluding the *other*.

What is logocentrism? It is the determination of the meaning of Being of beings as presence. The metaphysics of presence, which constitutes the basic trait of Western philosophy, has been termed logocentric philosophy. Derrida observes that the history of Western philosophy always centres its understanding on notions of presence. What does he mean by metaphysics of presence? The meaning of Being in general is known as the philosophy of presence. All the terms, which refer to the fundamentals, the principles, or to the centre, have the content of presence.[151] Being, essence, existence, substance, subjectivity, consciousness, God, transcendentality, self-presence of cogito, etc., are some of the examples of fundamental terms, which contain the notion of *logos* as presence.[152] The logocentric tradition of Western philosophy, the meaning of Being is defined as the presence of Being. He has termed this belief in the self-presentation of meaning 'logocentrism,' coined from the Greek word *logos,* meaning, speech, logic, reason, the Word of God.[153] Different systems of thought in the history of philosophy belong to this philosophy of *centrism*, which determines the meaning of Being.

a. *The history of metaphysics as the determination of Being as presence*

The meaning of being is determined by the presence of Being. In *Writing and Difference* Derrida explains that all the determinations of beings take the notion of presence in all sense of the word.[154] Whitehead's famous description of the European philosophical tradition as a series of footnotes to Plato[155] indicates the impact of Plato's thought in Western philosophy. With the question of Being, the metaphysical thinking of Plato and Aristotle acquired a clear onto-theological significance.[156] The transcendental signified[157] (all that has content of presence, e.g. Plato's Form, Aristotle's universals, St. Thomas' *esse*, Husserl's Transcendental Ego, Heidegger's Being, etc.) is the source of universality and univocality that controls the entire history of Western philosophy till today.[158] Metaphysics is philosophy's main mode of existence. All thoughts are different versions of presence or meaning of Being. He says that the aim of both Western Scholastic and Modern philosophy is to characterise the capital *T*, the *T*ruth of things. The failure of that undertaking is considered as the failure of the philosophy of presence—and the failure of the system itself.[159] In his essay on *Ousia and Grammē* Derrida ascribes metaphysics of presence to the Heideggerian concept of *Dasein:* "How could one think Being and time *otherwise* than on the basis of the present, in the form of the present, to wit a certain *now in general* from which no experience, by definition, can ever depart?"[160] Heidegger's thought on what is unthought by the history of philosophy, argues Derrida, has not displaced any *centre*; the displacement of one centre by the other does not imply any *absence*, rather it signifies another presence. "An other centre would be an other now."[161] In *Being and Time*, Heidegger replaces one centre (presence) with the other (*Dasein*) and his essay on the work of art too reconstitutes another centre by way of substitution. However, Derrida argues that his deconstructive decentring prevents the possibility for constituting another centre.

b. *Different gestures of logocentrism*

In the history of philosophy, the question of the meaning of Being assumes different forms and notions that depend on the value of presence. The influence and control of logocentrism is found everywhere at all times. The authority of presence, its power of valorisation, controls and structures all our thinking. The notions of making clear, grasping, demonstrating, revealing, etc. invoke presence. All these indicate that in the history of philosophy, the metaphysics of presence is pervasive, familiar, and powerful.[162] Derrida comes to the conclusion that this logocentric tradition has influenced every aspect of human understanding attributing priority to the transcendental terms. In *Of Grammatology*, he denotes the long tradition of the privilege of voice (truth or meaning) over writing extending from Aristotle to Hegel, and this tradition extends further onto Heidegger by determining Being of entity as presence.[163] In traditional philosophy, the reality of an entity is regarded as presence. The meaning of being or the presence is seen in the immediate relationship with voice or mind. Our mind is intimately related to the universal truth. This immediacy between speech and idea is called phonocentrism. Derrida identifies phonocentrism to the general principles of different systems of thought throughout the entire history of philosophy.

Western systems of thoughts belong to the powerful traditional chain stretching back to Plato and Aristotle, and this "motif of homogeneity, the theological motif *par excellence*, is decidedly the one to be destroyed"[164] It is argued that the origin of truth is a direct insight into the meaning of beings and this divine eye provides the valid ground for truth. As traditionally interpreted, the ontological question presupposes an ordered ground. It is this transcendental reality which defines the logocentric motive of Western philosophy—the desire to illuminate and to articulate the order and structure in things.[165] George Steiner observes: "Western theology and the metaphysics, epistemology and aesthetics which have been its major footnotes, are 'logocentric.' This is to say that they axiomatize as fundamental and pre-eminent the concept of presence. It can be that of God (ultimately it must be); of Platonic 'Ideas;' of Aristotelian and Thomistic essence... It is to these pivots that spokes of meaning finally lead. They insure its plenitude. That presence, theological, ontological or metaphysical, makes credible the assertion that 'there is something in what we say.'"[166] Entities derive their meaning from the onto-theological signified. For example, in St. Thomas, thing (*ens,* being) means thing-in-Being (*ens*-in-*esse)*; thing derives its meaning from Being (*ipsum esse* = God). In Thomistic philosophy the science of thing (*ens*) becomes the science of Being (*esse)*; thing means that which has Being. It is because of this reason that the proper name of God, the thing whose essence is Being, is Being itself.[167] Derrida wants to clear or throw away the centrality of Being from the field of philosophy since it controls philosophical discourse from the beginning to this time. He declares that there is no concept or sign before *writing* or difference. He reverses the traditional relationship of the voice to writing in order to deconstruct the hierarchy of voice over writing.[168]

The concept of deconstruction

The word deconstruction is closely related to the term *analysis*, which etymologically means to *undo*, a synonym for to deconstruct. It analyses the warring forces of signification within a text itself.[169] Deconstruction uncovers the so-called irreducible *other* from the metaphysical texts. It is a positive response to an alterity, the irreconcilable force within a text. It reveals that the meaning of Being or our understanding of reality functions like a 'text' and this textual phenomenon within a metaphysical text suggests the necessity with which what an author does see is systematically related to what he does not see.[170] Deconstruction consists in the ambivalent force of disparities and inconsistencies in a concept due to the functions of heterogeneous elements, which constitute it.

Derrida develops deconstructive theories of meaning based on the idea of difference and seeks to nullify the fundamental ground for certainty, an organizing centre within which all truth inquiries can find protection. His deconstructive terms, i.e. *writing, différance, trace, textuality, supplement, re-mark, hymen, pharmakon*, etc. stand for relativity of meaning and they do not carry any fixed meaning, they have no essence.[171] They function within a text, deconstruct it into an undecidable one and at the same time they prevent any kind of re-inscription. Deconstruction infects the text from within itself; it is an internal critique of the text. Every text carries within itself the tool for its own deconstruction. Culler argues that deconstruction is "rigorous argument within philosophy and displacement of philosophical categories and philosophical attempt at mastery."[172] With the terms 'rigorous argument' and 'displacement' Culler criticizes Derrida's philosophical reading something that does not have a vital role in philosophy.

a. *Deconstruction as an internal critique*

The Cambridge Dictionary of Philosophy defines deconstruction as a demonstration of the incompleteness or incoherence of a philosophical position using concepts and principles of argument whose meaning and use is legitimated only by that philosophical position. Therefore, it is a kind of internal conceptual critique in which the critic implicitly and provisionally adheres to the position criticised.[173] With the introduction of his concept of *différance*, Derrida argues in favour of the impossibility of final reference for meaning. He places difference prior to the transcendental content of a text. There is no ultimate ground that is found devoid of the play of difference. His deconstructive thought is *infolding* into the bottomless abyss of a text that does not have a centre. In Derrida's philosophy, there is no place for Being, there are only texts—traces or elements—in differential relationships.

b. *The aim of deconstruction*

The purpose of deconstruction is to uncover the reality of the irreducible *other* in traditional philosophy. With his own way of thinking, Derrida is relentlessly engaged in the war against the logocentric prejudices and traditional unitive notions of thinking. Through his works he claims that he deconstructs the logocentric spell of metaphysics in many eminent Western thinkers such as Plato, Rousseau and Saussure, Hegel, Freud, Kant and Heidegger. Exposing the univocity of meaning in all these thinkers, he introduces the free play of endless difference, in order to destroy their self-validity.

Deconstruction has two important functions within a text: the first phase consists in showing that any origin or teleological end is inseparable from the play of difference,[174] and that it is therefore not the origin or end it proclaims itself to be. The second phase of deconstruction marks the application of the new concept, which displaces the centre in question. Derrida's new concept does not constitute another centre; it remains on both sides: presence-absence. His anti-epistemological deconstructive thought has the meaning of undecidability, a science of *neither...nor.*[175] Chapter 3 is a typical example how Derrida infects a text with his own aim and applies his deconstructive meaning of undecidability by decentralizing it into the position of *neither...nor*. In *The Truth in Painting*, he describes how van Gogh's painting opens many worlds, the world of a peasant woman, of a city man, of Heidegger and that of Schapiro. Derrida claims that he deconstructs the traditional philosophy in Heidegger's essay on the work of art by undoing the centre of the text, i.e. by attributing van Gogh's shoes to none of them.

c. *The method of deconstruction*

The purpose of deconstruction determines its methodology too. In a practical sense, Derrida says, it is a way of reading. Deconstructive reading is a certain way of re-reading philosophers. It is a philosophical strategy applied within philosophical texts. Deconstruction does not destroy structures of a text from outside. Instead, it must work from within the structures it chooses to work on, inhabiting those structures in a certain way, so that it can show its failures and contradictions.[176] Chapter 3 shows how Derrida's critique infects Heidegger's essay on the work of art from within. It is a certain way of reading a text (essay on the work of art) to carry out Derrida's intentions. His deconstructive reading is a practice of a question of strategy, through which the contradictions and dissimilarities of a text brought forward. He finds in each philosophical text the necessary resources which are necessary for the deconstruction of that heritage itself. Thus his famous dictum, "language bears within itself the necessity of its own critique,"[177] indicates the transcendental signified of a text, which he wants to deconstruct. It is the strategy of using the only available language, while not subscribing to its premises, or operating according to the vocabulary of the very thing that one delimits. Derrida's essay on *Restitutions*, in *The Truth in Painting* shows how he uses the same internal matter in Heidegger and Schapiro to attack the logocentric spell of their positions, without re-constituting further a new realm of meaning.[178]

The destruction and the deconstruction: Heidegger and Derrida

Heidegger applies the method of phenomenology to the truth of *Dasein* and that of the work of art in order to expose the structure of truth of Being. His concept of truth does not give any sense of pure presence, since concealing is also the essence of Being. In Heidegger and in Derrida the origin or the meaning of beings is given in structural, in withdrawal, in disappearing. The infrastructure[179] of the truth implies the origin as a withdrawal, which does not impart a meaning. Derrida's deconstruction is based on Heidegger's critique of the truth as revealment. The so-called presence can be thought only within infrastructure, which does not yield the purity of presence. "The first step or this deconstruction of philosophy, which attempts to locate that which is *present* nowhere in philosophy i.e. that which philosophy must hide in order to remain philosophy, is precisely the examination of the notion of *presence* as undertaken by Heidegger. Heidegger, says Derrida, recognized in the notion of presence the destiny of philosophy, and the reference to the Heideggerian deconstruction of presence is a constant throughout Derrida's works."[180] There is no Derrida without Heidegger. The simultaneous existence of the opposites in the infrastructure of truth makes the pure presence impossible. Truth, in both of them, opens up the truth of *other* contexts, and the irreducibility of difference leads to the erasure of the question of Being: *what is*. This question is possible only in ontology, which Heidegger and Derrida want to destroy. If one could speak of anything originary, only *différance* could be originary. But, "To say that *différance* as originary is simultaneously to erase the myth of present origin. Which is why 'originary' must be understood as having been *crossed out*, without which *différance* would be derived from original plenitude. It is non-origin which is originary."[181] Deconstruction is the critique of the classical concept of origin as presence and simplicity, to which everything else can be deduced. It advocates the pluralization of origin. The origin is not simple or single, but a certain heterogeneity; at the beginning there are sources or origins.[182]

Even though Heidegger and Derrida are inseparable, there are some differences between them, since Derrida has fulfilled what Heidegger has undertaken. Heidegger confesses in *Being and Time* that his aim of the destruction of metaphysics, the negative sense of shaking its ground, is to be regarded as something positive or productive to the question of Being.[183] He investigates the structure and meaning of beings in order to overcome all predeterminations, which construct the meaning of Being. "Construction in philosophy is necessarily destruction, that is to say, a deconstructing of traditional concepts carried out in a historical recursion to the tradition. And this is not a negation of the tradition or a condemnation of it as worthless; quite the reverse, it signifies precisely a positive appropriation of tradition. Because destruction belongs to construction, philosophical cognition is necessarily at the same time, in a certain sense, historical cognition."[184] The positive aspect of destruction of metaphysics is the removal of concealment of the truth of Being. Truth as revealment is in fact concealment; its removal is the positive effect of deconstruction, i.e. truth is both: unconcealment and concealment.

Derrida's reading of Heidegger is more prejudiced with his intension to go beyond the Heideggerian difference: "There may be a difference still more unthought than the difference between Being and beings. We certainly can go further toward naming it in our language. Beyond Being and beings, this difference, ceaselessly differing from and deferring (itself), would trace (itself) — this *différance* would be the first or last trace if one still could speak, here, of origin and end."[185] Derrida's claim that *différance* is *older* than the ontological difference is to be critically examined because both ontological difference and deconstructive *différance* basically stand for the irreducibility of the alterity or the *other*. *Différance* does not yield any meaning; having no meaning in itself, it is the process of anteriority to the epoch of meaning and the loss of meaning.[186] However there is no *as such* to their philosophy, since they remove the transcendental signified from the meaning of Being.

Heidegger's inquiry into the meaning of Being asks about the exact meaning of the term correspondence or conformity. How is such conformity possible? What are the conditions which must be fulfilled in order to make this conformity possible? In every true statement there is a correspondence between the judgement and the thing judged. The correspondence is determined by the kind of relation that exists between statement and thing. Heidegger's destruction of metaphysics takes place with the substitution of the theory of correspondence with the theory of infrastructural references. The truth of *Dasein* as Being-in-the-world and the truth of the work of art as the strife between the world and the earth provide the truth of contextual reference, instead of conformity.[187]

In his essay *On the Question of Being* Heidegger expresses his aim of the destruction of metaphysics, which he has already undertaken in *Being and Time*, that it "has no other intent than to retain the originary experiences of Being belonging to metaphysics by deconstructing (*Abbau*) representations that have become commonplace and empty."[188] Heidegger's destruction of metaphysics removes the sedimented layers of the metaphysical thinking that have hidden the original nature of Being. In this respect, the Heideggerian destruction of metaphysics is related to Derrida's deconstruction of logocentrism. Even though both Heidegger and Derrida speak of the need for liberating metaphysics from false conceptions of suppressive systems, they are different with regard to their way of philosophizing. Heidegger deletes Being in order to denote the inarticulable nature of presence; Derrida's deconstructive terms stand for the erasure of Being marking the absence of presence.[189]

Derrida holds the view that the Heideggerian destruction is not enough to undo Western logocentrism; therefore, he goes a step further by removing the centre of metaphysics from the field of philosophical thinking. Since Derrida claims that he deconstructs one of Heidegger's important texts *The Origin of the Work of Art*, and challenges Heidegger's overcoming of metaphysics in it, the following two chapters deal with the Heideggerian truth of Being and Derrida's deconstruction of the same. Dealing with the question of the meaning of Being, Heidegger and Derrida stand for the same task, the overcoming of metaphysics of presence. However, Derrida's deliberate efforts to isolate a particular paragraph from Heidegger's essay on the work of art, in order to apply his deconstructive thought to it, ignores the context and content of the whole essay. Heidegger's essay on the work of art provides no fixed centre for the origin of the truth, and hence, Derrida's claim that Heidegger's essay fails to overcome Platonism is unfounded and unjustifiable.[190]

References

1. Martin Heidegger, *Introduction to Metaphysics*, trans. Gregory Fried and Richard Polt, New Haven & London, Yale University Press, 2000, 32, 107, 110.
2. *Ibid.*, 182-83.
3. Martin Heidegger and Eugen Fink, *Heraclitus Seminar*, trans. Charles H. Seibert, Evanston and Illinois, Northwestern University Press, 1979, 161.
4. Martin Heidegger, *The Origin of the Work of Art*, in *Basic Writings*, ed. David Farrell Krell, London and New York, Routledge, 1993.
5. Chapters 2 and 3 deal with Heidegger's aesthetic theory and Derrida's critique of Heidegger's philosophy of the work of art respectively. Chapter 4 deals with Derridean deconstructive thought with critical appraisal.
6. Jacques Derrida, *Of Grammatology*, in *A Derrida Reader*, ed. Peggy Kamuf, New York, Columbia University Press, 1991, 39-40.
7. The origin of truth according to Heidegger and Derrida is given in Chapters 2 and 4 respectively.
8. Martin Heidegger, *Introduction to Metaphysics*, 13.
9. *Ibid.*, 14.
10. Martin Heidegger, *The Anaximander Fragment*, in *Early Greek Thinking*, trans. David Farrell and Frank Capuzzi, New York, Harper and Row, 1975, 50-51.
11. Martin Heidegger, *Plato's Doctrine of Truth*, in *Pathmarks*, ed. William McNeill, New York, Cambridge University Press, 1998, 182.
12. Martin Heidegger, *The Anaximander Fragment*, 26.
13. Rodolphe Gasché, *Joining the Text: From Heidegger to Derrida*, in *The Yale Critics: Deconstruction in America*, eds. Jonathan Arac, Wlad Godzich, Wallace Martin, Minneapolis, University of Minnesota Press, 1983, 159-60.
14. Martin Heidegger, *Being and Time*, 21, 59.
15. *Seiende* and *Sein* are the two important terms in Heidegger's philosophy. *Seiende* is translated as "being or beings" means "what is" or "that which is," and *Sein* is translated as Being means "that by which it is." Being is not anything; it is not a being. Being, which is the abstract noun of 'to be,' is always a Being of some entities or Being of things-that-are; it is not something which is (*ein Seiendes*). Being, by its very nature, can offer itself only in a concealed manner, namely in and through beings. Being (*Sein*) as such remains hidden. Martin Heidegger, *Introduction to Metaphysics*, x-xi; Martin

Heidegger *Being and Time*, 22 Footnote 1, 25-26, 29, 61. Martin Heidegger, *Basic Problems of Phenemenology*, trans. Albert Hofstadter, Bloomington & Indianapolis, Indiana University Press, 1982, 19.

16. Martin Heidegger, *What Is Metaphysics?*, in *Basic Writings*, ed. David Farrell Krell, London and New York, Routledge, 1993, 106. Martin Heidegger, *The Fundamental Concepts of Metaphysics*, trans. William McNeill and Nicholas Walker, Bloomington and Indianapolis, Indiana University Press, 1995, 25.
17. Martin Heidegger, *Introduction to Metaphysics*, 18.
18. Martin Heidegger, *Being and Time*, 192-93, 261. George Pattison, *The later Heidegger*, 50.
19. Alan Code, *Aristotle's Logic and Metaphysics*, in *Routledge History of Philosophy*, Vol. 2, ed. David Furley, London and New York, Routledge, 1997, 57-66.
20. Martin Heidegger, *Being and Time*, 25-26
21. According to Aristotle there are as many meanings of Being as there are categories of entities. The primary category of substance is natural things that exist in their own rights and all other entities are attributes of substance either inhering in them or standing in relation them (quality, quantity, relation, place, time, action, affection, possession, position). Accordingly, we can predicate a naturally existing independent object, e.g., a stone, which is heavy, red, etc., that belong to the nature of that thing. Substances are the only entities that can exist in their own right; all other entities are attributes that need substances as the substrate for their existence. According to Aristotelian doctrine of metaphysics, 'to be' then means either to be a substance or to be attributes of a substance. Since Being can be predicated in different ways of its attributes, there is no unity of expression or univocal meaning of being, but 'analogy of Being.' Aristotelian definition of substance, or things, natural entities with attributes remains the central them in the entire history of ontology. Aristotle, *Metaphysics*, trans. Hugh Lawson-Tancred, New York, Penguin Books, 1998, Zeta 1-2, 102 8b ff, 168-71. Ref. Alan Code, *Aristotle's Logic and Metaphysics*, 62-66.
22. Keith Hoeller, *Introduction* to *Elucidations of Hölderlin's Poetry*, Martin Heidegger, trans. Keith Hoeller, New York, Humanity Books, 2000, 9.
23. Dorothea Frede, *The Question of Being: Heidegger's Project*, in *The Cambridge Companion to Heidegger*, ed. Charles B. Guignon, Cambridge, Cambridge University Press, 1993, 60. Martin Heidegger, *Being and Time*, 28, 96.

24. Hans-Georg Gadamer, *Hermeneutics and Logocentrism*, in *Jacques Derrida: Critical Assesments of Leading Philosophers*, Vol. I, eds. Zeynep Direk and Leonard Lawlor, London and New York, Routledge, 2002, 51.
25. Martin Heidegger, *Nietzsche*, Vol. III and IV, 6-7.
26. Aristotle, *Metaphysics*, Gamma, I, 1003a, 79. Martin Heidegger, *Introduction to Metaphysics*, 23.
27. Martin Heidegger, *Nietzsche*, Vol. III and IV, 6.
28. See Chapter 2.
29. Martin Heidegger, *The Origin of the Work of Art*, 184. The Greek word *technē* derives from the root word *tec*, which means "to make something appear, within what is present, as this or that, in this way or that way." The verb *tikto* means to bring forth or to produce, in terms of letting appear. Martin Heidegger, *Building Dwelling Thinking*, in *Poetry, Language, and Thought*, trans. Albert Hofstadter, New York, Harper & Row, 1971, 157.
30. Martin Heidegger, *On the Essence of Truth*, in *Pathmarks*, ed. William McNeill, New York, Cambridge University Press, 1988, 10-12. Martin Heidegger, *Plato's Doctrine of Truth*, 177-78.
31. Martin Heidegger, *The Essence of Truth*, trans. Ted Sadler, London and New York, Continuum, 2002, 12
32. Aristotle, *Metaphysics: Books Z and H*, Z 1, 1028b 4, 2.
33. *Ibid.*, Z 4, 1029b1, Z 6, 1031a 15, 4.
34. *Ibid.*, Z 1, 1028a 10-15, 1.
35. Martin Heidegger, *The Essence of Truth*, 6. "*Veritas est adaequatio rei et intellectus sive enuntiationis.*"
36. See Chapter 2. The origin of the truth as play is described in Chapter 4.
37. Richard Wolin, *Politics of Being: The Political Thought of Martin Heidegger*, New York, Columbia University Press, 1990, 121. Ref. Timothy Clark, *Derrida, Heidegger, Blanchot*, Cambridge, Cambridge University Press, 1992, 42.
38. Dorothea Frede, *The Question of Being: Heidegger's Project*, 61.
39. Martin Heidegger, *Plato's Doctrine of Truth*, 177. Ref. Plato, *Republic*, trans. Robin Waterfield, Oxford, Oxford University Press, 1993, 508e, 236.
40. Martin Heidegger *Introduction to Metaphysics*, 20.
41. Martin Heidegger, *Plato's Doctrine of Truth*, 168. The occurrence of *alētheia* (unhiddenness) is the content of the allegory of the cave, which provides the education of truth, which unfolds in the

conversation between Socrates and Glaucon. Plato presents the allegory of the cave in four different stages and the process consists of a series of transitions from one stage to another. In the first stage he explains a cave, an underground chamber, in which people from their childhood have their hands, feet, and heads fettered, with their eyes turned to the cave's wall. Their shackles do not allow them to turn their heads and to look around them. Behind them there is a small exit from the cave, through which light falls to the cave in the back of its inhabitants, so that heir own shadows necessarily fall on the wall lying opposite them. Fettered and bound firmly so that they can only look ahead of them, they see only their own shadows on the wall. Behind them, between them and the light, there is a path with a partition. On this path other humans, behind the prisoners, carry past all sorts of implements such as figures of men and animals made of stone and wood, and all sorts of other man-made artefacts. These objects throw their own shadows and are visible as moving objects on the opposite wall. The prisoners discuss among themselves what they see on the wall. What they see there is their world, actual beings. In so far as they have no direct experience with light, they see only shadows and experience these shadows as unhiddenness. In the second stage, one of the prisoners is released, so that he can turn around and look into the light. In the third stage, he can even move out of the cave and walk toward the light itself; he will first be dazzled and will only slowly become accustomed to the light and see the things that stand outside the cave in the light. The essence of truth as unhiddenness is given in the third stage. In the fourth stage, dazzled in the sunlight, he returns to the cave and converses once again with those who are sitting in the cave. What is common to each transition is that in each case his eyes are confused and he has to go through a process of adjustment so that he can discern whatever is given in the light. Each transition requires a profound transformation of the soul. Plato wants to show by this the condition for the possibility of recognizing something as a shadow in distinction from the real. If the cave dwellers were to see only what they see on the wall, they would never gain the insight that it is only shadows. The basic condition for the possibility of understanding the actual as actual is to look things in the light of the sun. Truth as unhiddenness means to understand things in their truth or to perceive the essence of a thing in advance. Plato, *Republic*, 514a-517a, 240-243. Martin Heidegger, *The Essence of Truth*, 18-24, 30-60; Martin Heidegger, *Plato's Doctrine of Truth*, 155-82.

42. Martin Heidegger, *Plato's Doctrine of Truth*, 172.
43. Martin Heidegger, *The Essence of Truth*, 26.

44. Martin Heidegger, *Plato's Doctrine of Truth*, 169-70.
45. Martin Heidegger, *Introduction to Metaphysics*, 63-64.
46. Martin Heidegger, *The Essence of Truth*, 49-50.
47. Michael E. Zimmerman, *Heidegger, Buddhism, and deep ecology*, in *The Cambridge Companion to Heidegger*, ed. Chharles B. Guignon, Cambridge, Cambridge University Press, 1993, 243.
48. Martin Heidegger, *Plato's Doctrine of Truth*, 164.
49. Plato, *Republic*, 507b, 235.
50. Martin Heidegger, *Plato's Doctrine of Truth*, 172-73.
51. *Ibid.*, 173-75.
52. Martin Heidegger, *Plato's Doctrine of Truth*, 170. Martin Heidegger, *The Essence of Truth*, 50.
53. Martin Heidegger, *The Essence of Truth*, 38. Martin Heidegger, *Plato's Doctrine of Truth*, 164.
54. Plato's recollection theory teaches that souls have latent knowledge of things. Ref. Robert Heinaman, *Plato: Metaphysics and Epistemology*, in *Routledge History of Philosophy*, Vol. I, ed. C.C.W. Taylor, London and New York, Routledge, 1997, 373-74.
55. Martin Heidegger, *Plato's Doctrine of Truth*, 173, 175. In Plato, the sun (the fire) is a visible analogue of the One. By providing an illuminating clearing, the Sun brings the many things of the earth together for a unified perception.
56. *Ibid.*, 164-65, 174-75. Martin Heidegger, *The Essence of Truth*, 33, 43. Ref. A.W. Price, *Plato: Ethics and Politics*, in *Routledge History of Philosophy*, Vol. I, ed. C.C.W. Taylor, London and New York, Routledge, 1997, 417.
57. Martin Heidegger, *The Essence of Truth*, 70-71. Martin Heidegger, *Plato's Doctrine of Truth*, 164, 175, 179.
58. Martin Heidegger, *Plato's Doctrine of Truth*, 173-74. Plato, *Republic*, 517c, 244.
59. *Ibid.*, 176. Ref. Plato, *Republic*, 517 c4.
60. Martin Heidegger, *Plato's Doctrine of Truth*, 177.
61. Edward Hussey, *Pythagoreans and Eleatics*, in *Routledge History of Philosophy*, Vol. I, ed. C.C.W. Taylor, London and New York, Routledge, 1997, 136. Ref. Martin Heidegger, *The Essence of Truth*, 39, See Footnote 9.
62. Plato, *Republic*, 476b-478a, 197.
63. Martin Heidegger, *The Essence of Truth*, 39.
64. Martin Heidegger, *Plato's Doctrine of Truth*, 179.

65. Martin Heidegger, *The Essence of Truth*, 26.
66. Martin Heidegger, *Plato's Doctrine of Truth*, 178.
67. See also *Self-disclosure and the origin of the work*, in Chapter 2.
68. George Pattison, *The later Heidegger*, 49. *Technē* means art and craft; *technitēs* means craftman and artist.
69. Ref. Timothy Clark, *Derrida, Heidegger, Blanchot*, 194-95, footnote nr. 4.
70. Martin Heidegger, *The Basic Problems of Phenomenology*, 106.
71. *Ibid*., 106. Martin Heidegger, *On the Question of Being*, in *Pathmarks*, ed. William mcNeill, New York, Cambridge University Press, 1998, 299.
72. Martin Heidegger, *The Basic Problems of Phenomenology*, 106.
73. Martin Heidegger, *On the Question of Being*, 298.
74. Martin Heidegger, *The Basic Problems of Phenomenology*, 106.
75. *Ibid*., 107.
76. Martin Heidegger, *On the Question of Being*, 302. The forgetfulness of the question of Being is inscribed in the original event (*Ereignis*) of Western metaphysics. This event indicates that Being is revealed itself only to instantly withdraw again. The instant or the now (*nun*) *is* never quite in the sense of being present. The so-called presence or 'now' is the singular occurrence of a *there is* (*es gibt*), which cannot be conceptualized because its withdrawal is inherent in it. A thing can, therefore, become manifest only in this concealment or withdrawal. The forgetting of Being is the very destiny of Being. Even though our thinking plays a vital role in the realization of the meaning of Being, it is to be noted that the history of metaphysics is not the creation of humans, instead it is something that happens from out of Being itself to humans. Different epochs in the history of philosophy are brought about by event (*Ereignis*), an event of coming-into-its-own. It suggests that if unconcealment happens from an event within Being, it follows that the concealment running through the history of metaphysics. Concealment accompanies every emerging-into-presence. Humans are innocent in the oblivion of the meaning of Being, because they think that nothing is hidden in what is revealed before them.
77. Heideggerian meaning of *mimesis* (imitation) as the appearance of Being.
78. Martin Heidegger, *The Basic Problems of Phenomenology*, 107.
79. *Ibid*., 107. According to Aristotle, the substance or essence is that in accordance with that which it already was and is. The substance is *per se*. Everything *that is* will be accounted for by reference to substance. Ref. Alan Code, *Aristotle's Logic and Metaphysics*, 62.

80. Plato and Aristotle could not conceive and enrich the pre-Socratic meaning of Being, *physis*. Aristotle considers *physis* to mean the ground of beings as such. The Greek term *physis* translated as *natura* means literally *originate*, *to be born*. This Latin translation does not carry the basic implications of the meaning of Being conceived by the mytho-poetic meditations of Greek thinkers. Martin Heidegger, *Introduction to Metaphysics*, 14, 17.
81. Martin Heidegger, *The Essence of Truth*, 11-12.
82. Martin Heidegger, *Plato's Doctrine of Truth*, 168.
83. Martin Heidegger, *Being and Time*, 257. Martin Heidegger, *Plato's Sophist*, trans. Richard Rojcewicz and André Schuwer, Bloomington & Indiana University Press, Indiana University Press, 2003, 10.
84. Martin Heidegger, *The Essence of Truth*, 6-9. The traditional understanding of the truth of a proposition consists in the discovering of something; propose means to bring into light. A proposition is true when it brings forward or brings into light what is as it is. The Greek understanding of truth also means to bring forth that which is, out of its hiddenness to light, to let it appear, shine forth in disclosure.
85. *Ibid.*, 8. The original Greek meaning of truth is different to the German word '*Wahrheit*' (truth), and also the Latin expression '*veritas*.' The original Greek expression for truth is *privative* which is to be translated as '*Un-schuld*' in its contrast to '*Schuld*' (guilt). Ref. *Ibid.*, 7.
86. *Ibid.*, 8.
87. *Ibid.*, 12.
88. *Ibid.*, 8.
89. Martin Heidegger, *Introduction to Metaphysics*, 110, 18.
90. Martin Heidegger, *On the Essence and Concept of Φύσις in Aristotle's Physics B,I*, in *Pathmarks*, trans. Thomas Sheehan, ed. William McNeill, New York, Cambridge University Press, 1998, 183.
91. Martin Heidegger *Introduction to Metaphysics*, 75. *Physis* is translated as nature (*natura- nasci)*, which means "to be born," "to arise," or "grow." The Greek root *γεν* means *natura*, which is understood as "that which lets something originate from itself." The meaning of this term indicates the meaning of *phyein*, the process of unfolding into the open, the process of coming forward into light, coming-into-presence. The Greek word *physis* or *phuō* derives from the Indo-Germanic root word *bhū* which means "to emerge, to hold sway, to come to stand from out of itself and to remain standing." That which emerges itself has the quality of showing itself. Thus, for the Greeks, the conception of *physis* (verbal form *phuein* as growing) is related to *pha*, or *phainesthai* (to show itself). The meaning of the

term *physis* is related to things that show themselves, (*phaos*) all designating light: illuminate, shine forth, visibility, or presence as a showing-forth. The meaning of the word *physis* is usually translated as nature, which has various nuances such as emerging, growing, showing, shining, etc. *Ibid.*, 14-15, 75. Martin Heidegger, *On the Essence and Concept of Φύσις in Aristotle's Physics B, I*, 183.

92. Martin Heidegger, *Introduction to Metaphysics*, 14-15.
93. *Ibid.*, 64.
94. *Ibid.*, 133. See Footnote 3. Heidegger investigates the Indo-Germanic root words to mention the different implications of the term 'Being.'
95. *Ibid.*, 75-76. Heidegger investigates the Indo-Germanic root words to mention three different implications of the term 'Being.' (1) The oldest term for Being is *es*, Sanskrit *asus*, which means "life, the living, that which from out of itself and in itself stands and goes and reposes." To the stem word *asus* belong the Sanskrit words *esmi, esi, esti, asmi* and the corresponding Greek terms are *eimi* and *einai*. The Latin words for this *asus* are *essum* and *esse*. The first implication of the term Being is "is" or to be (*ist, estin, est*); (2) The second implication of Being derives from the Indo-Germanic terms "*bhū, bbheu,* which mean "to emerge, to hold sway to come to stand from out of itself and to remain standing." The corresponding Greek word is *phuō*. Usually *bhū* is understood as *physis* (nature) and *phuein* (growing). These words are somehow identical implications; that which is growing or emerging is in turn coming to presence and appearing; and (3) 'Being' includes the meaning of the Sanskrit word *vasami* and the German verbs *sein* or *wesen, which* mean to dwell, to abide. The participle *wesend* is found in *an-wesend* (*ab-wesend*). *Wesen* originally does not mean what-ness (*Was-sein* or *quidditas*) but rather enduring as present (*Gegenwart*).
96. *Ibid.*, 66. In the earlier edition it is explained as "that which originally worlds," (*das ursprünglich Weltende*). *Ibid.*, see footnote 8.
97. Martin Heidegger, *Being and Time*, 50.
98. Martin Heidegger, *Introduction to Metaphysics*, 14-15, 75. Ref. Timothy Clark, *Derrida, Heidegger, Blanchot*, 24-25.
99. Martin Heidegger, *Introduction to Metaphysics*, 15, 132.
100. Gregory Fried and Richard Polt, *Introduction*, to *Introduction to Metaphysics*, Martin Heidegger, New Haven and London, Yale University Press, 2000, xiii.
101. Martin Heidegger, *The Fundamental concepts of Metaphysics*, 25.
102. Martin Heidegger, *Introduction to Metaphysics*, 15.

103. Martin Heidegger, *The Question Concerning Technology*, in *Basic Writings*, ed. David Farrell Krell, London and New York, Routledge, 1993, 317. See p. 80.
104. See Chapter II, *Truth as the strife.*
105. Martin Heidegger *Introduction to Metaphysics*, 14. The Latin word *Natura* means "that which lets something originate from itself." Martin Heidegger, *On the Essence and Concept of Φύσις in Aristotle's Physics B, I*, 183-84.
106. Martin Heidegger *Introduction to Metaphysics*, 16.
107. Martin Heidegger, *Nietzsche,* Vol. 3 and 4, 108.
108. Timothy Clark, *Derrida, Heidegger, Blanchot*, 21-22.
109. Martin Heidegger, *On the Essence and Concept of Φύσις in Aristotle's Physics B, I*, 183.
110. Martin Heidegger, *Plato's Doctrine of Truth*, 182.
111. *Ibid.*, 181.
112. Martin Heidegger, *On the Essence and Concept of Φύσις in Aristotle's Physics B, I*, 185.
113. Martin Heidegger *Introduction to Metaphysics*, 17. Aristotle, *Metaphysics*, Gamma, I, 1003a, 79.
114. Martin Heidegger *Introduction to Metaphysics*, 18-19.
115. Martin Heidegger, *Kant and the Problems of Metaphysics*, trans. Richard Taft, Bloomington and Indianapolis, Indiana University Press 1997, 5.
116. Martin Heidegger, *What is Metaphysics*, 106.
117. *Ibid.*, 5.
118. Martin Heidegger *Introduction to Metaphysics*, 20.
119. Martin Heidegger, *On the Essence and Concept of Φύσις in Aristotle's Physics B, I*, 185.
120. *Ibid.*, 192-97.
121. *Ibid.*, 186.
122. Martin Heidegger *Introduction to Metaphysics*, 64.
123. Martin Heidegger, *On the Essence of Ground*, in *Pathmarks,* ed. William McNeill, New York, Cambridge University Press 1998, 112-13.
124. Martin Heidegger *Introduction to Metaphysics,* 17.
125. *Ibid.*, 17-18.
126. *Ibid.*, 16. "*Phusis* ist das *Ent-stehen*, aus dem Verborgenen sich heraus- und dieses so erst in den Stand bringen." Heidegger shows the etymological connection between *Entstehen* (growth, genesis)

and *Stand* (state, situation). Generally the phrase *in den Stand bringen* means to "enable." The event of standing-forth from concealment enables an entity to take its stand, to appear as something.

127. Martin Heidegger, *Elucidations of Hölderlin's Poetry*, trans. Keith Hoeller, New York, Humanity Books, 2000, 79-81. Martin Heidegger, *On the Essence and Concept of Φύσις in Aristotle's Physics B, I*, 184
128. Martin Heidegger, *Elucidations of Hölderlin's Poetry*, 79.
129. Martin Heidegger, *Introduction to Metaphysics*, 46-47.
130. Annemarie Gethmann-Siefert, *Martin Heidegger und die Kunstwissenschaft*, in *Heidegger und die praktische Philosophie*, Hrsg. Annemarie Gethmann-Siefert und Otto Pöggeler, Frankfurt am Main, Suhrkamp, 1988, 251-56, 281. George Pattison, *The later Heidegger*, 26-27, 35, 40.
131. Carl Friedrich Gethmann, *Heideggers Wahrheitskonzeption in seinem Marburger Vorlesungen*, in *Martin Heidegger: Innen-und Außenansichten*, Forum für Philosophie Bad Homburg, Suhrkamp 1989, 125.
132. Martin Heidegger, *The Essence of Truth*, 10-12.
133. Martin Heidegger, *Plato's Doctrine of Truth*, 172.
134. Martin Heidegger, *Introduction to Metaphysics*, 75.
135. Martin Heidegger, *The Essence of Truth*, 9. Martin Heidegger and Eugen Fink, *Heraclitus Seminar*, 45.
136. Martin Heidegger, *The Essence of Truth*, 9. See footnote 5.
137. "Wahrheit-I setzt Wahrheit-II voraus." Ref. Prof. Dr. Josef Früchtl, Colloquium at the Faculty of the Philosophy of Westfälische Wilhelms-Universität, Münster, Winter Semester, 2005-2006.
138. See Chapter 2.
139. Metaphysics of presence means anything which is related to the fundamental principles such as Platonic Idea, transcendental truth, intuition, essence, existence, consciousness, etc. which have the characteristic of truth and in which all concepts are rooted. These fundamental principles of metaphysics can be called the concept of Being. Derrida observes that the entire Western philosophy, theology, epistemology, literature and all other disciplines have been in essence logocentric.
140. The Greek word *Logos* can mean logic, reason, the Word. Logocentrism means the system of thought based on the fundamental principles in which *presence* is characteristic of truth. Logocentrism denotes the philosophy of "centrism" by which the truth of Being is determined.

141. Jacques Derrida, *Of Grammatology*, 3.
142. Ernst Behler, *Confrontations: Derrida, Heidegger, Nietzsche*, 29.
143. Jacques Derrida, *Positions*, trans. Alan Bass, Chicago, The University of Chicago Press, 1972, 54.
144. Jacques Derrida, *Of Grammatology*, 3.
145. In his essay on *Ousia and Grammē* Derrida criticises Heidegger's *Being and Time* since he borrows uncritically the concept of time and terminological implications from traditional metaphysics. "At a certain point... the destruction of metaphysics remains within metaphysics, only making explicit its principles." Jacques Derrida, *Ousia and Grammē: Note on a Note from Being and Time*, in *Margins of Philosophy*, Alan Bass, Chicago, The University of Chicago Press, 1982, 48, 60.
146. The term *absolute* is most commonly used to mean without qualification, not relative, not comparative. In philosophy it is the term for the ultimate truth. The term 'transcendental' means the reality lying outside or beyond ordinary experience or knowledge.
147. Jacques Derrida, *Of Grammatology*, 158. In Derrida the concepts of play and text stand for the undecidability of the meaning of Being. He substitutes Heideggerian truth of Being for play of text. Derrida's concepts of play and text are given in the 4 Chapter.
148. See Chapter 4.
149. See Chapter 4.
150. Jacques Derrida, *Positions*, 41.
151. Jacques Derrida, *Structure, Sign snd Play*, in *Writing and Difference*, trans. Alan Bass, London and New York, Routledge & Kegan Paul Ltd., 1967, 353; Barbara Johnson, *Introduction* to *Dissemination*, Jacques Derrida, London and New York, Continuum, 1981, viii.
152. Jacques Derrida, *Of Grammatology*, 11-12.
153. Jacques Derrida, *White Mythology*, in *Margins of Philosophy*, trans. Alan Bass, Chicago, The University of Chicago Press 1982, 213. Ref. Jacques Derrida, *Dissemination*, London and New York, Continuum 1981, ix.
154. Jacques Derrida, *Structure, Sign snd Play*, 353.
155. Alfred North Whitehead, *Process and Reality: An Essay on Cosmology*, New York, Macmillan, 1929, 63.
156. Jacques Derrida, *Of Grammatology*, 14. The term 'onto-theology' is a combination of 'ontology' and 'theology,' which is the hallmark of ancient Greek philosophy and thereafter. It is the epoch of logos. In Derrida's works, onto-theology denotes the metaphysical determination of an entity as transcendental signified.

157. *Ibid.*, 18. Transcendental signified (or the transcendental ego or consciousness in general) guarantee the objectivity of experience and, thereby, the possibility of valid knowledge for all human beings. In Aristotelian-Thomistic philosophy, particulars are related to universals for their intelligibility and meaning. According to Derrida, the signified, such as truth or meaning, exists prior to inscription or writing. By reversing the traditional hierarchy, he tries to put an end to the reign to metaphysics.
158. Jacques Derrida, *Positions*, 49-50.
159. Eliot Beutsch, *Culture and Modernity: East-West Philosophic Perspectives*, Delhi, Motilal Banarsidas Publishers Pvt. Ltd., 1994, 57.
160. Jacques Derrida, *Ousia and Grammē: Note on a Note from Being and Time*, 38.
161. *Ibid.*, 38.
162. Jonathan Culler, *On Deconstruction: Theory and Criticism after Structuralism*, London, Melbourne and Henley, Routledge & Kegan Paul, 1983, 93-94.
163. Jacques Derrida, *Of Grammatology*, 11-12, 15, 18.
164. Jacques Derrida, *Positions*, 64.
165. Eliot Beutsch, *Culture and Modernity: East-West Philosophic Perspectives*, 57.
166. George Steiner, *Real Presences*, Chicago, The University of Chicago Press, 1989, 121.
167. St. Thomas Aquinas, *The Summa Theologica*, Vol. 1, 1.Q3.4, trans. Fathers of the English Dominican Province, London, Encyclopaedia Britannica, 1952, 16. Ref. Frederick Copleston, S.J., *A History of Philosophy*, Vol. I, Part 2, New York, Image Books, 1962, 51-52, 164-65.
168. Jacques Derrida, *Of Grammatology*, 14.
169. Barbara Johnson, *Introduction*, to *Dissemination*, Jacques Derrida, xv.
170. Jacques Derrida, *Of Grammatology*, 158-59.
171. Jacques Derrida, *Différance*, 25-26.
172. Jonathan Culler, *On Deconstruction: Theory and Criticism after Structuralism*, 85.
173. Robert Audi, ed., *The Cambridge Dictionary of Philosophy*, Cambridge, Cambridge University Press, 1985, 181.
174. See Chapter 4.
175. Jacques Derrida, *Dissemination*, 220-21.

176. Jacques Derrida, *Of Grammatology*, 24.
177. Jacques Derrida, *Structure, Sing and Play*, 358.
178. See Chapter 3.
179. The infrastructure denotes the referential structure, or structure of reference (*Verweisungsstrucktur*). Derrida's truth of infrastructure is known as *arche-trace*. See Chapter 4.
180. Alan Bass, *Introduction* to *Writing and Difference*, Jacques Derrida, trans. Alan Bass, London and New York, Routledge, 1989, xi.
181. Jacques Derrida, *Freud and the Scene of Writing*, in *Writing and Difference*, trans. Alan Bass, London and New York, Routledge, 1978, 255.
182. Jacques Derrida, *Qual Quelle: Valéry's Sources*, 277.
183. Martin Heidegger, *Being and Time*, 44.
184. Martin Heidegger, *The Basic Problems of Phenomenology*, 23.
185. Jacques Derrida, *Ousia and Grammē: Note on a Note from Being and Time*, 67.
186. Rodolphe Gasché, *Joining the Text: From Heidegger to Derrida*, 149.
187. See Chapter 2.
188. Martin Heidegger, *On the Question of Being*, 315.
189. Gayatri Chakravorty Spivak, *Preface* to *Of Grammatology*, Jacques Derrida, trans. Gayatri Chakravorty Spivak, Baltimore and London, The John Hopkins University Press, 1974, xvii.
190. See Chapter 4. *Derrida on Heidegger: a critical appraisal.*

The Origin of the Truth of the Work of Art: Heidegger

2

Heidegger upholds that the history of philosophy, which considers truth as unconcealment, conceals the essence of the truth, the emergence. For him the origin of truth[1] is the difference, the difference between Being and beings. Here the meaning of the genitive, the Being *of* beings, is the source or origin as the emergence of what is present from presencing.[2] For him the question of truth is essentially the question of art. Art is dis-closure in the sense of truth-happening. He considers that the disclosure of beings is, intrinsically, the concealment of beings.[3] In the essay on *The Origin of the Work of Art*[4] he reflects on the origin of truth, which he has already undertaken in *Being and Time* in terms of the 'truth of *Dasein*.'[5] He does not consider Being as the ground or the foundation of things, but it is nothing, an openness, in which things come *to be*. Since he refuses to accept the traditional concept of the truth as revealment, in the sense of correctness, he undertakes a new investigation into the meaning of Being as disclosedness. His concept of truth as revealment—the disclosure of *Dasein* as Being-in-the-world and of the work of art—opens up another context, upon which depends the meaning of what is present. The destruction or deconstruction of metaphysics positively suggests that a phenomenon[6] manifests itself not as what it is, but as what its essence is to be presented by the presencing of the world; and so the phenomenon shows itself in its otherness as what it genuinely is, namely by showing itself as what it *is* not. This is made clear by an example of one of the paintings of van Gogh,[7] which brings to light or discloses what this piece of equipment, a pair of shoes, in truth (in Being) *is*.

In the first part of the essay on the work of art Heidegger explores the traditional concept of the essence of things, the *a priori* non-concealment of a thing, the essence of entities. A thing *is* already there even before it appears to us. He also discusses the meaning of Being as presencing or *how* entities show up in their Being. For the disclosure or presencing of an entity there must be a nothingness or absencing: the 'withdrawal' of Being. Heidegger does not accept Being as the eternal foundation or ground of things. Being as presencing denotes *how* entities are revealed in Being: the 'clearing' that which makes presencing possible is withdrawal of Being. Thus the two important aspects discussed in the essay are: (1) the traditional concept of the truth of entities; and (2) the happening of truth, how things are coming to be in their Being: the clearing. Accordingly, the task is here twofold: The first part articulates the thingly aspect of the truth, which constitutes the traditional concept of the truth of Being and the second part explains the origin of the truth of the work as the strife.

The thingly character of the truth of the work of art

In his essay on the work of art Heidegger explains the traditional understanding of the truth of thing in terms of the essence of thing, the essence of equipment and the essence of work, which, according to him, is the assault upon the mere things itself.[8] He holds the view that concealment belongs to the truth of thing and criticises the presence character of metaphysics, the so-called origin of the truth. In the essay he criticizes the traditional philosophy's view that the reality is to be understood in terms of 'substance' or metaphysics of presence and tries to explore more original sense of things.

The essence of thing

What is a thing? This ontological question deals with the thingness of thing, the way of Being characteristic of the thing. Being is always a Being of some entities or Being of things-that-are; it is not something which-is. By its very nature, it can offer itself only in a concealed manner, namely in and through beings.[9] Even though Being as such remains hidden, beings are discoverable only in and through it. Thus there is a difference as well as interdependency between Being and beings or things-that-are.[10] Heidegger argues that traditional philosophy has forgotten the ontological difference between Being and beings because the Greeks, instead of thinking of Being, has focused on 'beingness,' which is understood as the essential property of entities.[11] In order to expose the forgetfulness (hiddenness or covering up) of the meaning of Being, the essay on the work of art analyses the structure of Being proceeding from beings. Metaphysics as a science investigates the truth of beings, the *reality* of a thing, which *is* before it appears to us.[12] Without this underlying *reality* nothing can appear to us; we cannot understand a thing as something without the prior knowledge of Being. In the first part of the essay Heidegger explores the truth of this *a priori* non-concealment of a thing, the *what-being* of entities. He gives three important aspects of the traditional understanding of the thingness of thing: (a) a thing is a composition of substance and accidence; (b) a thing is a unity of manifold of sensible properties; and (c) it is the unity of matter and form.[13]

a. *Thing as the composition of substance and accidence*

In the essay Heidegger deals with Greek ontology that makes a distinction between substance and accidence. The thing is understood as the bearer of properties. *Sub-stantia* literally means what *stands under* and is present throughout all change, the underlying reality or the substructure of a thing. The distinction between substance and accidence can be shown with the help of a piece of rock. It is a thing with different characteristics, for example it is hard, heavy, extended, of irregular shape, rough, grey, etc. These characteristics refer to something that is proper to the stone itself. They are its properties. The thing itself is not just the aggregate or the sum of these properties. The thing possesses these properties, accidence. One could also speak of the core of things; the Greek called the core of a thing substance (*hypokeinmenon*), which remains continuously present throughout the change. It is also known as the metaphysics of presence. The substance remains identical with the thing itself, whereas accidence means the attributes, for which the substance provides continuing support. For the Greeks the truth of a thing is something lying on the ground; it is already revealed and precedes properties of a thing. Western philosophy translates the Greek term *hypokeinmenon,* which originally refers to substratum, the underlying reality of a thing, as *subjectum* or subject (in opposition to object) marking the beginning of subjectivist philosophy which culminates in Hegel.[14] In *Nietzsche* Vol. IV, the section entitled *The Cartesian Cogito as Cogito Me Cogitare*, Heidegger describes the *underlying reality* as the self-consciousness, which is the essential ground for any representation.[15] Referring to the concept of perception of thing and intentionality, Pattison describes how a *mere* thing is perceived *as* something that it is from out of our lived out experiences. The meaning of a thing is attached to the dimension of intentionality.[16] Describing Heidegger's interpretation of Cartesian substance (*cogitare*), Clark points out that the truth of representation of a thing is essentially representing of one-self or self-representing.[17] Heidegger calls the subjectivist's position, the self or consciousness as *subjectum* or *hypokeinmenon* (what underlies, what already lies-before of itself), the rootlessness of Western philosophy because it took over the Greek words without the original experience of what the Greeks say.[18] In his view, thing shall not be determined on the basis of underlying, self-evident principle.[19] In the essay on the work of art and *Being and Time* Heidegger tries to put an end to the subject-centered philosophy.

In *The Thing,* Heidegger tries to think Being through things of common experience. He applies the term *thing* to any being which directs man back to an encounter with Being, to an antecedent knowledge with beings. There is a close relationship between thing and Being. In other words, things bring us into *nearness* or proximity,[20] which means that we can think of things only in terms of their pre-given relation. Here nearness means the open region, in and through which things are revealed in a given world: unconcealment, or to understand things as what they *are*, in the sense of Cartesian representation. For the understanding of any entity, we are always remaining in unconcealment. The phrase, thing *things*, world *worlds*, time *times*, space *spaces*, etc. denote the act of bringing-near, the presencing of presence. These verbal expressions designate the prior relation of an entity to its Being. These peculiar expressions denote our thinking of an entity in terms of its pre-given relations. Entities are revealed in their Being. In revealing, we are led to where we are already are; for Heidegger, nearness as such is Being itself.[21] Nearness as Being precedes our knowledge of a particular thing, by virtue of which we call a thing thing. The substance that underlies everything is characterized as *eidos,* the Idea, to mean the nearness of thing as something self-sustained, something that stands on its own. In this sense a thing is not merely an object opposite us, but it is to be grasped essentially as that what stands forth; thing is standing forth into the unconcealedness of what is already present.[22] A thing, for example a jug, comes to be a jug, because of the thinging of thing, i.e. in its *relation* to its Being. The thing *things* means that the thing lets itself be. For Heidegger, a thing that manifests itself *as* something in its relation to its Being does not have nature proper to it as such. A thing revealed is no-*thing*. It is not we who determine the Being of thing, but it is already there before us. When we see or understand a thing *as* something, we are be-thinged (*be-dingt*),[23] i.e. we think and understand a thing as what it is in accord with its pre-determinative meaning. Thus, the history of philosophy, according to Heidegger, is the forgetfulness of the difference between Being and beings since it accepts Being of entities as the underlying reality, the substance.

b. *Thing as the unity of the manifold of sensible properties*

The traditional metaphysical concept of thing suggests that the thingness of thing consists in the 'unity of the manifold of what is given in the senses.'[24] The sensible qualities of a thing are the necessary mediations by which we encounter it. For example, our perception of a tree consists of a certain unity of colours, shapes, smell; etc. In this sense, Western philosophy understands a thing in the same way as what the Greeks did by the senses.[25] For Heidegger, there is no simple thing in the sense that our sense experience is never *raw*, but always already interpreted, and therefore, we always understand thing *as* something. Our intuition involves some kinds of structuring of experience. According to Pattison, in relation to our intuition Heidegger accepts neither the Aristotle's table of categories nor that of Kant to explain the structure of our experience.[26] In Kant the essence of thing consists in the synthesis of recognition, "the unity of a manifold of what is given in the senses."[27] Kant places a special emphasis on *a priori*, unconditional concepts, which is known as the category of substance. For example, there is a tree as substance, which is responsible for the unity of tree-perceptions. We suppose that there is the tree that which lies behind (*hypokeimenon*) all sense experiences and ties them together. The reality of a tree *is* already there, even before it appears to us, our experience of a thing constitutes the important aspect of our understanding of the concept *tree*. Heidegger observes the metaphysical distinction between *a priori* and *a posteriori* aspect of truth in Kant, and considers the superiority of the spiritual, subjective aspect of the origin of truth as an assault upon material reality. He tries to overcome the metaphysical determination of particular things by the analysis of the truth of 'human *Dasein* as Being-in-the-world' and that of work of art.

c. *Thing as the unity of matter and form*

A thing is traditionally understood a formed matter. The thingly element in work of art is the matter of which it consists. It can be observed that in a thing matter stands together with its form.[28] The very moment we think things in terms of matter (*hyle*) we posit form (*morphē*) at the same time. Heidegger explains the *hylemorphic* structure of a thing in order to explain the modes of Being characteristic of pieces of equipment, where the form always determines the kind of matter that will be used, the form itself is, in turn, determined by the purpose which the piece of equipment is to serve.[29] The material is subordinated to the form, which in turn is determined by utility. The determination of a thing on the basis of its utility is primarily metaphysical. The essence of a thing is not the thing itself, but it is something prior to the thing. In his reflection on the essence of the work of art, Heidegger begins with the consideration of the thingness of thing, but he leaves this theme and turns to the essence of equipment which provides better insight into the origin of the work of art.

The essence of equipment

Equipment,[30] being man-made thing, has an intermediate position between mere thing and works of art, and the investigation of its way of truth gives us more insight into the essence of the work of art. A piece of equipment has the affinity with the work of art insofar as it is made and formed by humans. It is not a work of art, since it lacks self-sufficiency. Heidegger calls it half thing.[31] The essence of equipment consists in its serviceability and reliability.

a. *Serviceability and the essence of equipment*

Usefulness or serviceability[32] is the fundamental feature through which every piece of equipment faces us and presents itself to us as thing. A piece of equipment is made for some particular purpose. As it is already discussed, the interfusion of form and matter is in each case prescribed or determined by the purpose, which the equipment is to serve.[33] Heidegger opposes determination of thing on the basis of its instrumental values. By exposing the pre-historical understanding of equipment—both in *Being and Time* and in the essay on the work of art—he tries to save entities from the objectivity and representation.[34]

In *Being and Time* Heidegger explains the essence of equipment in order to prepare the ontological-existential conception of the world, which is the precondition of the 'truth of *Dasein*.' The essence of equipment like the essence of any other entities is essentially related to its standing out in-the-world.[35] It means the interrelatedness of entities among themselves; there is no such thing as an isolated piece of equipment.[36] What makes the essence of any piece of equipment there always corresponds to an equipmental totality in which a particular piece of equipment can be what it *is*. For a piece of equipment is basically something that is to be characterized by its 'something in-order-to' or the purpose to which it is made. At the same time a piece of equipment is what it is because of its belonging to other pieces of equipments with which it constitutes a totality. The Being of equipment is its involvement, which provides us with the intelligibility of it. In the totality of equipments everything is internally related. Thus, before a piece of equipment can be shown itself as that which it is, a totality of equipment has already been discovered in advance. Disclosedness makes discoveredness possible; intra-worldly entities can be discovered in its prior disclosedness.[37] He calls the *a priori* disclosedness of entities *transcendental generalization*,[38] which is the condition for the interpretation of any entity and by virtue of which (*woraufhin*) everything hangs together. Interpretation of a thing is related to the fore-structure of understanding, in which a thing is prior disclosed in particular culture and tradition of people. It is also called the *as*-structure or the pre-predication of the understanding of a thing, which has the implication of the withdrawal of the meaning of Being.[39] *To be* means, therefore, to be *already* revealed or understood as something, which results in the forgetfulness of the meaning of Being.

Entities are discovered in their functional relationship in which they are determined as something. An entity that is what it is in its equipmental relation shows the meaning of world. For Heidegger the worldhood is the essence of equipment that consists in its functional relationship such as, *in order to, for which, and for the sake of*.[40] It is the referential totality, which is also the possibility for the significance of a thing. For example, hammer, nails, wood, etc. in carpentry signify the purpose to build up a roof of a house. The act of hammering has the significance of *in order to* nail the wood together to make a roof. This kind of invisible purpose it enjoys is called *for-the-sake-of*. Different items subordinate themselves to the assignments (i.e. the equipmental relationships, or the determination of equipment on the basis of its relation to other equipment) of the in-order-to and accommodate themselves within the referential totality of *Dasein*'s world, called circumspection.[41] Equipment is discovered *in* something, in the equipmental totality. Davidson and Haugeland maintain that the totality of equipmental involvement and its assignment constitute the normative relationships among the equipments, e.g. what a hammer is *for* is driving in nails.[42] The totality of involvement as prior to any equipment has the structure of the world, which is the necessary condition for the revealment of entities.

There are three basic ways of Being such as, availableness or readiness-to-hand, occurrence or presence-at-hand, and '*Dasein*,' which provide modes of intelligibility or understanding of beings. All these three ways of truth of entities suggest that, instead of conformity, it is the referential relationships that provide the conditions for the possibility of the meaning of a thing.[43] The manual implications of equipment—or things made and used by man—as readiness-to-hand is a kind of being, which denotes our practical understanding of dealing with equipment.[44] Another significant mode of Being that underlies an entity is the theoretical understanding of it, the presence-at-hand; it is the ontological interpretation of an entity, which dominates the history of ontology.[45] Gadamer finds it difficult to express the peculiar implications of Heidegger's presence-at-hand, since it comprehends both the Greek concept of Being as presence, which is the theoretical and conceptual meaning of beings, and the modern concept of objectivity, which is the methodological understanding of the meaning of things.[46] An entity is discovered only when it has been referred or assigned to something, and referred as that entity which it is.[47] The meaning of equipment depends upon its totality of references sighted beforehand in circumspection.[48] Equipment is then *there*, as already been disclosed. The meaning and interpretation of entities always presuppose the world; the world is something *wherein* an entity already *was*.[49] Ready-to-hand has the character of *with-in*, which shows entity's involvement, which is described by the term assignment or reference.[50] Like the truth of equipment, *Dasein* as Being-in-the-world gives itself beforehand as something to be understood.[51] The way of Being of *Dasein* finds itself in the whole, in its relation to the world. *Dasein* as Being-in-the-world denotes the meaning of 'clearing,' in which things can show up what they *are*, is the fundamental thought in Heidegger's question of Being. Our understanding of an entity is possible only in and through the very understanding of its Being. This theoretical knowledge of things is more important than our practical involvement with them. World-disclosure implies that there can be no being without a prior understanding of Being, which is explained in terms of readiness-to-hand, presence-at-hand and that of *Dasein*. The truth of an entity consists in its prior-structures. Lafont finds the problematic of the world-disclosure in terms of *Dasein*'s existential structure (particularly its mode of Being as understanding), since it creates a symbolically structured world.[52] She argues that the *a priori* perfect, *always already*, in world-disclosure undermines Heidegger's project carried out in *Being and Time*. Heidegger's concept of the worldhood of the world denotes the Being of the ontical condition or the pre-predicative manifestness of beings (as what-being and how-being) which makes it possible for entities to be discovered within the world.[53] However, his analysis of the meaning of equipment shows that it is the context that determines the meaning of things. The ground for our understanding the meaning of things lays in an intelligibility based on the prior-structures, which provide their meaning with a concealed-structure. The intelligibility, which refers to itself for the understanding of the meaning of things, is described in terms of readiness-to-hand, presence-at-hand and *Dasein* that constitute the elusive modes of Being.[54]

The serviceability of equipment opens up truth of another context, which determines the truth of the equipment. In the essay, beginning with the words "And yet," Heidegger describes the serviceability of the one of the piece of equipments, namely the shoes painted by van Gogh.[55] In this description the essence of the piece of equipment is revealed. The essence of the shoes consists in their serviceability; they are what they are in their utility. It is the utility that shows the transcendental, ontological nature of the Being of the piece of the equipment, shoes. For Heidegger, revealment is at work in the work of art. Van Gogh's painting has *spoken* to us, revealed to us what the pair of peasant shoes truly *is*. The work reveals a pair of shoes, its truth comes-in-to-pass. Disclosure is the happening of truth. It is the essence of truth. Art is truth at work.[56] When we look at the painting, it takes us away from it and leads us to some other realm (field, work etc.) which is opened to us, called the disclosure of beings. In the above description of the shoes many of the traits of a peasant's life are exposed to sight. In Heidegger's description, the Being of the peasant-shoes opens up the world of a peasant woman to whom these shoes belong; the truth of Being of these equipments relate essentially to the world of a peasant woman in which they are what they are. Even though observational findings do not constitute the Heideggerian truth, he interprets the equipment in order to reveal the traditional concept of the equipment-being. Derrida criticizes the observational truth of the painting because it can be reinterpreted and equally applied to many instances. Any assertion of the painting is false since the thing (shoe-equipment) and its truth, the meaning of it, are incommensurable. It should be noted that neither Heidegger nor Derrida argues for the objective nature of truth of a thing, instead they stand for an origin of the unsettling force of meaning.[57] There are thinkers like pattison, Kockelmans who defend Heidegger's position of the description of the painting, through which Heidegger explains only the essence of work in the tradition view.[58]

b. Reliability and the essence of the equipment

With regard to the essence of equipment, reliability is more important and essential than serviceability. In the essay on the work of art Heidegger explains the concept of reliability as one of the fundamental aspects of the truth of equipment in order to create a more profound basis for the understanding of the truth of the work of art. Reliability is handed down in a given culture and community; it is formed through our faith, habit and customs and practices. It is because of reliability, one uses equipment in daily life even without thinking of its usefulness. For example, the peasant woman wears the shoes when she goes out into the field and takes them off when she comes back without being aware of them. Reliability rests on equipment; that is why she takes off her shoes at night and again puts them on at dawn without reflecting upon them. Because of the reliability of the shoes she is sure of her world. Even though usefulness and reliability constitute the essence of equipment, Heidegger says that equipment has a distant source, deeper origin, other than its usefulness. What equipment *is* in truth can be finally discerned only in its reliability.[59]

The essence of work of art

There is an old saying: art for art's sake. It implies the centrality and importance of art for our experience and understanding of things. For Heidegger, the essence of work consists in its self-disclosure. Pattison maintains that the Heideggerian truth is not the discovery of a finished product, but its very disclosedness involves its prior state of concealment. He points out the dynamic character of revealment.[60] Art as bringing-forth denotes the dynamic and the ambivalence of truth. Heidegger defines art as "truth setting itself to work"[61] and anything that reveals itself in truth performs this function is called work of art. To set here means to bring to *stand*, or to determine a thing on the basis of fundamental principle. For example, even if he does not know where the shoes *stand*[62] or their subject, to which they belong, he describes them from the unitive background. In the work of art by van Gogh, a pair of shoes comes to stand in the light of its Being. In other words, the essence of the work is that it lets this being (a pair of shoes) emerge in its Being; the truth of painting is revealed. Here Heidegger's concept of disclosedness shows how art and truth are mutually related. The mode of Being characteristic of work of art is that it discloses a world, which all people share. In work of art, truth is at work and therefore, it (work of art) unifies people by providing them determinative understanding of beings. He says that the origin of the work of art as the truth of beings setting itself into work has some kind of *unfamiliar* source as its origin,[63] this *unthought* origin is explained in terms of truth as self-disclosure and poetry. There is no 'origin' in the sense that it is or it was. Instead truth as disclosure is a process of uncovering what is still concealed and which never reaches to an end.

a. *Self-disclosure and the origin of the work*

Heidegger's analysis of artistic production exposes how truth comes-to-pass as some*thing* in the work. The important aspect of the work of art is that it has its own self-subsistence; in the work the truth itself is ultimately responsible for the origin of truth (revealment), it comes-to-presence by its own. The openness is brought about not by an agent from outside, but by truth itself. In the question of the origin Heidegger subordinates both artist and work to art. The artist is only an agent of the happening of truth, the important element of it is truth itself; the character of truth consists in bringing itself about in and through works or beings. If truth by nature is self-disclosure, what then is truth? Art is the setting-into-the work of truth and it is the happening or the non-concealment of truth by its own. Art as the origin of both an artist and the work, is an event (primal or propriative event), a movement in the sense of bringing forth of truth.[64] The essence of the work of art does not confine itself to the relationship between artist and work, for it is the (Platonic) Idea or look, which enables him to be an artist. Beyond all the limits, the thought of the Greeks flows and overflows. The Greek philosophy is the great work of art, which gives us the shared values of those times. The beginning of great art in Greece is remoulded and reformed through the works of art of different centuries, which represent in turn the common meaning and understanding of those times. The spirit that flows underneath all throw the centuries is basically one and the same: metaphysics of presence. In C.F. Meyer's poem, *Roman Fountain*, Heidegger finds that the essence of works of art is always pre-given, the spirit of metaphysics, which originates from the Greek and flows to the West.[65] Truth happens historically; different systems of thought from the early Greeks to the modern era are to be considered as different forms of one fundamental origin, the spirit that rests and flows, reveals and conceals. Art is the embodiment of socio-culture of the given time. Gethmann-Siefert and Pattison argue that in Heidegger the truth of *Dasein* and the philosophy of the work of art cannot be separated from his socio-political views.[66] Can we attribute subjectivism to the Heideggerian truth? Among his critics Derrida is the prominent one who argues that he detects the furrows in Heidegger through which this spirit unceasingly flows.[67]

The meaning of Being as *physis* has the meaning of art.[68] The act of bringing forth of the truth of beings is a form of uncovering, of letting something come from hiddenness into non-concealment.[69] The term bringing-forth of the essence of work is truth, revealing.[70] In work of art the origin of the truth rests and moves, conceals and reveals. *A*, the first Greek syllable of *a-lētheia,* is a negation of concealment. Truth is the absence of concealment. The original meaning of truth, therefore, means to be unconcealed.[71] It implies a negation or privation that brings entities to appearance; *a-lētheia* is translated as un-concealment or disclosure, truth. Truth as disclosedness is the possibility and power of Being, in which something can appear. It is what happened in art. Self-disclosure of beings is truth of art, which happens in and out of concealment. This self-disclosure of being cannot be reduced to presence.

Truth is a privation. The essence of truth as correctness is only a privative attainment to disclosure. The alpha-privative, the *a* of *a-lētheia,* denotes that truth as revealment is to be determined along with the hiddenness, since it permeates in the essence of beings.[72] Truth is the revealing which takes place in and out of hiddenness. Then, can truth be then rightly thought of correctness? Heidegger's answer to it is a negation: truth as revealement has nothing to do with correctness.[73] From the very beginning the very essence of truth remains unthought. His question of the meaning of Being is an inquiry into this unthought, pre-philosophical understanding of *a-lētheia*; truth is the uncovering, emergence from hiddenness. The 'truth of *Dasein*' and the truth of the work of art open up the *other* realm of the hiddenness of truth, another context, and give importance to the essence of truth as disclosedness which holds good both concealment and unconcealment alike. In *Introduction to Metaphysics* he mentions that the aim of *Being and Time* is the disclosedness of Being, it is to be disclosed or unveiled from its coveredness: "Disclosedness means: the openedness of what the oblivion of Being closes off and conceals."[74] The Greek term *a-lētheia* denotes unhiddenness that is related to hiddenness. The Greek experience of truth as unhiddenness involves at the same time the aspect of hiddenness of things.[75] Truth as uncoveredness involves the unveiling of coveredness. Heidegger retrieves this aspect of truth in terms of the 'disclosure of *Dasein*' and the 'truth of the work.'

b. *Unconcealment and the concept of poetry and language*

Philosopher and poet hunt for the truth; philosophy and poetry are the composition of the truth. In other words, the truth is something that is composed by philosopher and poet. Heidegger's concept of poetising makes explicit how truth of beings comes-to-pass in the work of art. The essence of poetry consists in the bringing forth of the non-concealment of beings. "*All art*, as the letting happen of the advent of the truth of beings, is as such, in *essence*, *poetry*."[76] The essence of poetry is the appearance of being, which also the function of the truth of the work of art, i.e. the unconcealment from the concealment. The term poem or saying does not have the meaning of reflexivity or self-consciousness, which constitutes the identity of a literary work, but it (poetical language) signifies the ontic-ontological difference whereby things become present *as such*: beings in their Being. All artistic productions such as architecture, music, painting, sculpture, literature; etc. are examples of art in the sense that they are in essence poetry, in which truth comes-into-fore: poesy. Pattison holds the view that Heidegger's concept of language and poetry has the meaning of the Greek understanding of art in the sense of mode of knowing things.[77] In short, like the work of art, in language too there is an opening up of the world. Heidegger says that art breaks open a region or an open-place in work and it is in this opening that things are revealed.[78] Dreyfus opines that art in general embodies the background practices of our culture and tradition, into which we are socialized and on the basis of which we direct our thought and actions. It is called clearing, in which things and people can show up as meaningful for us.[79] Richard Wolin identifies truth of the Heideggerian poetizing with a mere empty generality, in and through which entities come-to-be as what they are.[80] Entities are emerging in their immediacy. Clark opposes this argument by saying that Heidegger's poetry is not the disclosure as such, but it is the differing itself of the ontological difference. The dialectic of language does not present, but it gives presence without representing any objective value: withdrawal of Being.[81] It gives Derrida impetus to reduce the philosophical values to that of literary.

Heidegger uses poetry as a synonym for art and language. There is a poetic element in language in the sense that language brings into its own the unconcealment of beings.[82] In language the content precedes the external means of expression and the possibility of signification arises out of this content of entities. "Language is the house of Being. In its home man dwells."[83] Here language is understood as the appropriating power of Being, i.e. Being is thought of language or *vice versa*. Prior to any conceptualization, language preserves within itself what it *gives* us from itself. It gives us familiarity of house to understand things, i.e. we understand things through the known way, through Being.[84] Everything, including human beings, is disclosed or first opened to us as what they are in language. We are in Being or in the midst of it, in other words, it is not we but the Being, which is the necessary condition for our understanding of beings, accomplishes everything. The meaning of beings is manifested in Being, which is mainly the function of language. In relation to art, particularly to Heidegger's famous phrase, world-opening, one can say that a thing revealed as something is already disclosed for a historical linguistic community, is mainly the function of language. Entities can appear in a given culture as something what they are because of the pre-reflexive understanding which is the essential function of language.[85] Lafont criticizes the world-disclosing function of language. She argues that Heidegger's concept of language in *Being and Time* leads to a sort of linguistic relativism and even to the reification of language (i.e. the reduction of the functions of language to the world-disclosing function), since everything is achievable to human understanding only in and through the prior understanding of it. Disregarding the irreducibility of ontological difference, the difference between Being and beings, in language entities are disclosed to us only through the higher level of understanding of them. Things can be *meaningfully* connected and articulated in and through the language.[86] But, in my point of view, her attribution of normative significance to the ontological difference is to be criticized, since in Heidegger there is no agreement between the truth of language and that of entities disclosed by it. The truth of poetry and that of work of art are essentially ontic-ontological, i.e. the being that emerges in the space or region opened up by them cannot be taken in any objectifying manner. The meaning of disclosure in poetry and in the work of art denotes the prior giving of truth of an entity on account of that an entity appears *as* what it is, in the sense that its truth is at issue.

Let us consider some of the conflicting elements in the Heideggerian language and world-opening. Lafont criticizes the transcendental status in the Heideggerian language. In his famous dictum: 'Language speaks,'[87] she finds the internal logic and speaks of the reification of language in him.[88] The transcendental status of language is the ground for our understanding of things. Timothy Clark too observes that Heidegger's dictum denotes not merely a relationship between language and human understanding of things, but it signifies the precedence of language itself; i.e. language is not merely an effect of human speaking.[89] The ontic-ontological structure of language is the ground and possibility through which entities come to light and stand in the openness of presence. "...language alone brings beings as beings into the open for the first time. Where there is no language, as in Being of stone, plant, and animals, there is no openness of beings..."[90] As we have already discussed the essence of language and that of poetry is the bringing forth of beings in works, for they let open region, in and through which beings come into the fore. This linguistic and poetic function is to be understood as clearing, the nothingness or absence (i.e. Being) in which things can present themselves. Language brings beings to appearance and it withholds itself, which is the very nature of language.[91] Entities that are revealed in and through language lack objective value because of the function of withdrawal. In language there is a relation between the 'opening' or the coming-into-presence of entities, and human culture. Taylor interprets the opening up as the world of culture and practices, in which entities attain specific content. In language the idea or content of entities precedes their naming or external expressions. Language inaugurates a world and gives to things their appearance and meaning. As a work of art language unifies the people by giving them the common understanding or meaning of entities in a particular culture and time.[92] In language the ontic (pertaining to beings) and the ontological (pertaining to Being) are interlaced, gathered together. Language is the metaphysical mode of beings because in and through it (language) things stand revealed in their Being.[93] Disclosure of entities as what it is, is the forgetfulness of difference between Being and being, which is the characteristic of Being itself; Heidegger calls it the withdrawal of Being, Being *as* Being. The essence of language in Heidegger indicates the truth of Being *as* such, Being as *nothing*; at the moment Being reveals as beings, it conceals. He calls it the *as*-structure.[94] Derrida accepts the meaning of withdrawal of the meaning of beings and speaks of the force of effacement in a text, which obliterates the objective value of representation. Language does not have the instrumental function, since it as referent or sign does not refer to anything, other than itself, which has the force of self-effacement. Derrida reduces philosophy to literary in order to deconstruct the precedence of the presence and the meaning of representation.[95]

By articulating the *how* of things, the meaning of entities is made manifest and made to stand through the language. Being initiated into the belief and the language of our culture, we understand things in a determinative way. We are carried away by the pre-ontological understanding of *how* things are in general. Heidegger says that language is projective in nature, i.e. the unconcealment of beings from out of their hiddenness.[96] Poetry as the projective saying denotes the unconcealment of beings. This projective, linguistic function of poetry is called by Heidegger poesy, which brings things to the fore, to the world. Poesy as a mode of presencing has the meaning of *physis*, bringing-forth.[97] In other words, it is in and through language that entities come-to-the-fore and stand in the openness of presence. The operation of art and language is *projective* in the sense that it gives entities their meaning. Language is the instrument of transcendental mode of understanding things, i.e. *a priori* linguistic experience of the world. It reveals the meaning of entities which is already come to light on its own accord. Language is not like an entity in the world, but it is that stage, that space, in which alone things become apparent. The mode of Being of language and the truth of Being are similar in the sense that they open upon the *other*. The openness to the *other* or the heteronomy is the essence of language and that of Being. Derrida develops a form of literary, heteronomic writing that manifests the force of otherness in any theoretical text.[98] The truth of language is the unconcealment, the pre-predicative manifestness of beings, in which the two different aspects: the opening up of the world and the understanding of thing, which constitutes the ontic-ontological difference.[99] The linguistic function, which has essentially the meaning of art, does not possess any normative value. It is the hallmark of the philosophy of later Heidegger.[100]

There is a relationship between language and the unconcealment of beings. In language beings first disclose themselves to man in a meaningful way.[101] "Because the fate of language is grounded in the particular *relation* of a people to *Being*, the question about *Being* will be most intimately intertwined with the question about *language* for us."[102] Meaning and values are transferred in a definitive manner through the culture and the history of people. The question of the meaning of entities is concerned with the meaning of Being; beings are disclosed to people by means of language. Since everything is understandable to us within language, there is no way to get out of it to get some objective reference.[103] The question concerning the Being as such is the same as the inquiry into the structure of our understanding. "Truly poetic projection is the opening up of that into which human being as historical is already cast. This is the earth and, for a historical people, its earth, the self-secluding ground on which it rests together with everything that it already is."[104] The poetic projection denotes the truth of Being as the withdrawal, it opens up the truth of prior context. The self-secluding earth of historical people can be compared to the projective fore-structures (fore-having, fore-sight, and fore-conception) of understanding in *Being and Time*.[105] Our understanding of a thing is always controlled by the understanding of ourselves and our situation. Interpretation and understanding are not something new, but they are always already given. They are taken as an unfolding of our lived self-understanding, *something we have in advance*.[106] Dorethea Frede opines that every *Sicht* (or *Licht*, clearing, world-opening) takes place in darkness of *Vor-sicht*.[107] In the fore-structures, the meaning of *Dasein* is not property of its own, but its meaning appears within "the formal existential framework of the disclosedness which belongs to understanding."[108] The truth of *Dasein* is the *other*.[109] The structure of the truth of *Dasein* as Being-in-the-world sheds light upon our understanding of how things are interconnected such that the world hangs together with them in a meaningful way as a whole. The fore-structure is the inseparable element which constitutes the truth of a thing.[110] What is the truth of *Dasein*? The *Da* of *Dasein*, the *there*, is the articulation of *Dasein*'s existence as Being-in-the-world. The entire history of metaphysics defines the truth as revealment, ignoring the poetical nature of truth.[111] Each epoch of the history of metaphysics ignores the poetical implication of truth, and thus grounds the origin of truth in revealment of beings. For Heidegger art as poetry means that the origin of truth is not revealment, but the 'strife,' which is the pivotal point in the essay on the work of art.

Truth as the strife

The truth of the work of art is explained in terms of the originary strife, which denotes an opposition in the essence of truth that subsists between 'clearing' and concealing.[112] The term *origin* of the work of art implies that the very revealment involves concealment. The origin of truth as the strife, which is unfamiliar in the history of metaphysics, is the essence of the Heideggerian truth. He explains this strife as the battle between the world and the earth or revealing and concealing. In view of the fact that the world has been called the open and the earth that which is self-secluding, one might be inclined to believe that revealment or truth is to be identified with the world and concealment or untruth with the earth. Heidegger does not make such identification and claims that to the open, opened up in the clearing, there belongs a world as well as the earth. The world opened in the work is the shared practices into which we are socialized. The world is the clearing of the paths of the essential guiding directions with which all human decisions must comply. But, on the other hand, any such decision is founded on something that is not mastered, something that is concealed and confusing: the earth.[113] Thus the essence of truth is a strife means that the world and the earth, which together constitute the origin, are always intrinsically and essentially in conflict with each other. In order to explain the origin of truth as originary strife between the world and the earth, these two aspects of truth, the setting up of the world and the setting forth of the earth are to be examined.

The notion of the world and the origin of the truth

Generally, work of art manifests or shows the meaning represented by it. In her essay on *Martin Heidegger und die Kunstwissenschaft*, Siefert refers to K. Bauch who argues that a work produced in particular place and time reflects the historical meaning and the general vision of the people.[114] In the works of art the truth happens by the opening up of the world, which deals with the inter-subjective meanings that unite people of given community. Like the linguistic function, the world in Heidegger is to be understood as the totality of possible references and meaning handed down in a culture. It is also called clearing, which implies that entities are antecedently given or revealed in a fixed way in accord with the practices of a community or culture, by the very fact of that the truth of the entities revealed is arguable.

This revealing function of the work of art is also called the dwelling of the historical people, in the sense of poetizing which draws on tradition, culture, belief etc. A thing is what it *is* only in the world, in truth. For example, the painting of van Gogh opens up the world of a peasant. It is a work of art since it brings the hidden truth into open; it tells us about life of a peasant woman, her anxieties and works in the field. Traditionally, most general view of art is that it is a way of representing things. According to Pattison, Heidegger's phenomenological description of the painting does not belong to the traditional categorical truth that is based on intuition, but it deals the Heideggerian concept of origin, which he explains in terms of 'strife' between world and earth.[115] In order to explain how the coming-to-pass of the truth of beings occurs in the work of art Heidegger selects yet another example, a

Greek temple, which has no character of representation.[116] Since the temple portrays nothing, one cannot think its truth in terms of correspondence theory. How is truth at work in temple, even if it does represent in fact nothing at all? According to him, it is in and through the temple, which is constructed by the people of that time using materials such as stone, wood, metal, colour, etc., that the values of that generation come-to-the-fore. Since man's knowledge about himself and his relation to the world depends and varies from age to age, the world opened up by the temple represents the state of knowledge of a particular time and culture. The temple is a work of art since it discloses or brings to realization of what is definitive of a people's form of life. The nature of a work of art implies setting up a world, which means that it helps us to understand the meaning and values of the historical community.[117] Great works of art represent the meaning and value of the historical community, which have also the founding function. Work of art as founding denotes the defining task for the future. According to Heidegger, the founding or beginning of the Western philosophy took place in Greece, which gives the present generation the guidance. 'Art let truth originate' and it happened for the first time in Greece; what is in the future to be called Being was set into the work in a way which set the measure for what is to come. Heidegger calls the works of art in different epochs *preservers* since they carry forward what was originated at the dawn of Western civilization. The truth is thrown or projected towards the coming preservers, i.e. toward a historical human community. The word *origin* literally means *leap*.[118] He opines that the entire history of Being is the history of forgetfulness of Being, since it springs from the very first, primordial origin and passes through the darkness of forgetfulness. Each new era or the new dawning of humanity is nothing other than the repetition of the first beginning, the Platonism. Heidegger, followed by him Derrida, argues that foundational rule does not allow one to articulate particular truth, since there is contradiction within its grounding, which is explained by Heidegger by means of work of art. In terms of literary language, Derrida too outlines this contradiction within the foundational moments of Western philosophy.[119]

The word *origin* in Heidegger's essay on *The Origin of the Work of Art* indicates the world defining function of the Greek philosophy. The 'first beginning' took place in Greece, but in each and every epoch of the history of philosophy 'truth establishes itself in the work,'[120] i.e. the values and practices of the particular community in a specific time are preserved and carried forward in and through the work. Greek temple is an exemplar or an outstanding example for the unarticulated values and norms of that time. Annemarie Gethmann-Siefert, having analyzed the essence of art as happening of truth, argues that Heidegger's philosophy of work of art too reflects the social, cultural phenomena of the German people, particularly under the reign of National Socialism.[121] Dreyfus calls work of art the 'cultural paradigm,' which is better defined as originary strife between world and the earth. Work as cultural paradigm unifies the people of particular community since it collects the scattered practices of a community, defines and dictates how things can be understood for a community.[122] The work of art opens up a world of particular sort, in which entities become intelligible and evident as what they are. "The temple, in its standing there, first gives to things their look and to men their outlook on themselves."[123] The bringing forth into what is present belongs to the characteristic nature of the essence of truth of work. In other words, the truth of work demands an opening up of a world and lets it abide and endure, i.e. in the opening up of the world we understand entities as what they are. The temple manifests the people's world; it opens up a fore-structure. Being based on the rocks of the earth, i.e. on the domain of culture, belief and tradition of the Greeks, the magnificent towering of the temple makes visible the invisible air, the world of full meaning and beauty. Siefert speaks about the communicative function of the work. The manifestation of god in temple is the opening up of the Greek world, its culture and belief in and through the great work of art. The world is the realization of the self, the meaningful aspect of the work.[124] Kockelmans holds the view that the temple opens to us today the meaning of the ancient Greek world. "Thus the concrete historical world of the Greek colonists is gathered by and through the temple insofar as the temple lets the god become manifest. This world must thus be disclosed to the members of this people before they can relate meaningfully to the beings and the events that are to appear in it."[125] It is only in the light of the world opened that we can understand what things are. Thought on the basis of Greek sense of setting up (*thesis* = to place, to set), the truth of work of art means the placing in the sense of *bringing forth* into what is present.[126] It is the metaphysical implication of the truth of the work of art. The work belongs uniquely within the domain that itself has opened up and the truth of work is present only in this opening. Work of art is not merely a symbol, but it produces a shared understanding, gives us the meaning and practices of a community: the opening up of the work. Pattison provides three features of the concept of the world discussed in the essay: (1) the work of art does not predeterminate the world with mathematical precision, but it allows the world to be opened up, so that entities appear as what they *are* in truth; (2) It does not open up a particular world, but a world in general, the world of the people, e.g. the public faith and practices of Greek people or that of Germans; and (3) the world of an object remains together with its materiality. In work of art, materiality plays more important role than that in equipment.[127] The self-secluding earth is the unavoidable aspect of the world, and therefore, truth of work of art as revealment includes concealment.

In order to understand the transcendental nature of the origin of truth and to know how truth is at work in the work one also has to look into the concept of world given in other writings of Heidegger, particularly in *Being and Time*. The world is the precondition of *Dasein*'s truth. John Haugeland compares the world-opening to the chess play or game, in which each pieces and positions are meaningfully discovered.[128] Game or play is directed by rules that are necessary to produce opening to the *other*. The world is not a corporeal or physical thing, but the non-objective and non-actual to which we relate as long as we live as *Dasein* (Being-in-the-world).[129] The world is the field of practical involvement, within which human concerns are already implicated. According to Dreyfus, our concern and practical involvement with things let things, people, institutions, etc. come-to-the-fore *as* some particular thing.[130] *Dasein* is *worldly* because its existence discloses to it such a phenomenon as world. *Dasein* is at the centre of the world, since it consists of relationships which are, ultimately, *Dasein*'s relationship to itself. In our everyday concern with ontic and ontological things we have already let things have their involvement in the world. World as a whole is not a being, it does not have any essence; rather it is *Dasein*'s pre-reflexive involvement, which allows things to *be* as what they are.[131] Krell remarks that *Dasein*'s concern about ontic and ontological beings and their mode of Being constitute *Dasein*'s worldliness, its *way* of existence or the *Da* of *Dasein*, the *there*, which has the equally original ontological structure of three ecstatic temporality: future, having-been and present. *Dasein*'s essence as the temporalization in the unity of three ecstasies deconstructs the traditional ontology's understanding of Being as presence. The rapture in the heart of 'now' leads to the destruction of ontology.[132] Früchtl holds the view that the equi-primordiality of truth of *Dasein* in relation to its temporalization constitute the unspeakable and unexplainable nature of the meaning of *Dasein*. The essence of *Dasein* is its temporality; it *will be* (future) what it *was* (past). *Dasein* is caught up in the circularity of time, in such a way that Früchtl speaks of the leaping out of the past to the future or the future-past, i.e. *Dasein*'s past is continually re-visiting or re-entering into its present.[133] Früchtl and Derrida differ in interpreting the meaning of the equally original ontic-ontological structure of *Dasein*'s temporality; Derrida ascribes nature of present to the *now* of *Dasein*,[134] whereas Früchtl finds the equally original ontic-ontological structure of *Dasein*'s temporality leads to the meaning of manyness and un-decidability.[135]

Heidegger's revised notion of the world appeared in his book On *the Essence of Ground*, where he describes the transcendental phenomenon of the world, i.e. that conception of the world which is constitutive to *Dasein*'s transcendence. He focuses at first on the oldest Greek conception of the world as cosmos. For the Greeks, cosmos or the world does not designate the things themselves; it considers world as the mode of Being of things or the *how* of the beings rather than these being themselves. This *how* defines beings in their totality of the meaning, *how as a whole*, and at the same time it is the possibility for the *how* of every being. This *how* of the beings taken as a totality is *a priori*. But this *how* is relative with respect to human *Dasein*.[136] Although the world encompasses all beings, it is, however, true that the world, strictly speaking, belongs to the human *Dasein*. Taken in its fundamental sense the world aims at explaining human *Dasein* in its relationship to beings as such and taken as a whole.[137] The world is considered as the totality of possible references and meanings handed down in a culture and tradition. He refers to Immanuel Kant to explain the transcendentality of the truth of the world. "The concept of world is accordingly that idea in which the absolute totality of those objects accessible in finite knowledge is represented a priori. World thus means as much as 'the sum-total (Inbegriff) of all appearances.'"[138] The characteristic of *Dasein* is that it *transcends*. We have the ability and character to transcend every experience with entities, which we encounter. The transcendence of *Dasein* is the essence of its Being, which constitutes the world, in the sense that it lets world happen. Through the happening of the world *Dasein* provides an original view, a view of the pre-structure of beings. The transcendentality of the truth of entities can be conceived as a pre-view and model for all manifest beings, including *Dasein* itself. The beings could never become manifest, if they could not find the opportunity to enter a world; entering into the world is the event which happens with the beings.[139] Interpreting Kant's epistemology, Heidegger says that knowledge or the discoveredness of things is possible only through the transcendental idea, the syntheticall unity of thought: idea and thing. Beings can manifest themselves only in this aboriginal happening. The beings that come-to-pass exist as Being-in-the-world, and their existence has the character of transcendence.[140] In other words, the world has no essence in itself; it belongs to *Dasein*, since the disclosure of the world is *Dasein*'s exsistence and the whole chain of referential relations connecting the beings in the world refers to *Dasein* itself.

In *Being and Time* Heidegger explains the transcendental character of equipment in order to describe the world as the possibility for the appearance of things. The non-objective or non-actual implications of world are expounded in the analysis of the meaning of equipments, which cannot be theoretically grasped. Strictly speaking, there is no equipment, since a piece of equipment functions as a part of the total context of things. Heidegger's world denotes the mode of Being, rather than being.[141] The world is the primordial mode in which things appear to us as ready-to-hand. The equipment-being of equipment depends upon the totality of equipment; therefore it is a form of reference that constitutes its Being. Meaning of a thing derives from the context. *Dasein* means to exist as Being-in-the-world. In short, the truth of *Dasein* derives from the prior-structures, and therefore, it has no meaning of the presence of a moment.[142]

In the essay on the work of art, the revealment of the holy environment of the temple indicates the ontological nature of its truth. The temple is a work of art since it opens up a non-objective world; it represents the world of the historical people, their belief and their culture.[143] The Temple opens up the truth of other context, the historical culture of the Greeks. The world is the totality of possible references and meaning handed down in a culture. It is "the clearing of the paths of essential guiding directions with which all decision complies."[144] The work of art, providing the guiding directions and tasks of a community, unfolds its future-directed, life-orienting function. The opening up of the world is the clearing in which entities become accessible and intelligible for people. The temple is not a mere structure constructed by the people, but it is the work of art because it held up to the Greeks what was important: by holding together the shared experience of their lives, such as, victory and disgrace, disaster and blessing, the temple provides them meaning and direction to their lives. Manifesting the moral space of gods, heroes and slaves, the practices of the Greek people comes to the fore in and through the temple and provides direction and meaning to the their lives.[145] It is a work of art since it reveals the truth by concealing it. It is the art that opens a world of beauty and lets the truth of beings come-to-pass. The truth of temple has the meaning of infrastructure, which is here explained as the world of the Greeks, the anterior context, opened up by it. However, what the temple opens up is *nothing* or non-actual.[146]

The notion of the earth and the origin of the truth

Even though work of art manifests the collected experience or the common meaning of a community, which dictates each one the norms to be followed, Heidegger opines that it cannot be stated as a fixed criterion or rules in accord with each individual case can be determined. Even though the shared paradigm is prior to the truth of a concrete situation, it cannot be always strictly reduced to or equalized to the truth of each and every single element. In short, the earthy aspect of work of art resists any kind of generalization or rationalization. "Heidegger calls the way the artwork solicits the culture to make the artwork explicit, coherent, and encompassing the *world* aspect of the work. He calls the way the artwork and its associated practices resists such totalization the *earth*."[147] The world-aspect of the work makes explicit the meaning of entities for a given people, the earth-aspect of it resists and shows what is at stake in our understanding of beings in a given culture. Since the world and the earth are inseparable in the work of art, culture's understanding of beings is inexhaustible or it cannot be fully revealed. Truth of work of art remains unsettled. Even though the Greek temple manifests the values and practices of that era, it, as a thing, resists any such rationalization. Temple, being a man-made thing, resists any kind of meaningful representation of moral and social values. As Dreyfus understands, "All those aspects of a cultural paradigm and the practices it organizes that resist being rationalized and totalized are included in Heidegger's notion of the earth."[148] Work of art articulates what is *already there* as the necessary condition for our understanding of beings, such as customs and practices of a particular community, which unite the people in a determinative way. Even if the earth is the basis of which our actions can matter to us, it is at the same time the self-secluding element.

Work of art cannot be a totalizing paradigm, which makes everything clear. In the example of the Greek temple, as a work of art it signifies people what they stand for, but at the same time there is concealing aspect of things that withdraws and does not allow to be articulated. In Heidegger, work of art is the struggle between the two opposing elements: revealing and concealing. In every revealing there is a concealing aspect. In other words, the very origin of truth there is an ambivalence of truth and untruth since the earth co-emerges in everything that emerges.[149] The earth and the world are the integral part of the truth of the work of art; without the earth there is no possibility for the world.

In Heidegger the earth is the concealing dimension of the truth, which has very deep and hidden meaning varying from the meaning of 'matter' of the work to the pre-Socratic meaning of self-emergence, *physis*. Let us first examine the co-emergence and the self-secluding nature of the earth. A work of art is made out of some material. There is a difference between the material of a piece of equipments and that of a work of art; in equipment the material usually disappears in the usefulness and the serviceability of the equipment. For example, no one thinks about the steel when the knife cuts well. But the work, by opening up a world, does not cause the material to disappear, but rather causes it to come forth as such; the rock bears and supports the temple, the colour of the temple remains to glow etc. The temple, being rooted on the rock, rises itself up into the sky. Thus the work sets itself back into its material.[150] The earth is understood as the mattering, *on the basis of which* we understand things meaningfully. The earth means that our cultural practices, which are unarticulated, unmastered, and concealed, but at the same time, gives us today directions to our decisions and thought.[151]

The setting-forth of the earth must happen in such a way that the work must set itself back into it. It denotes the self-secluding character of the earth. Here we have to ask what the meaning of earth is.[152] Let us consider a stone as earth. A stone is heavy. One can measure its heaviness; but heaviness is not stone. Even if we break it into pieces, its pieces still do not show us anything that has so been opened. Any amount of scientific discovery is thus inadequate to say what a stone is. The same holds good for colours, metal, etc. Thus the earth shatters every attempt to penetrate into it. In other words, the very nature of earth cannot be disclosed. The work achieves the setting forth of the earth as it sets itself back into the earth. The earth is that towards which the original emerging brings back and shelters everything that emerges; in particular it is into which the work of art sets itself back as that which shelters and conceals. In everything that emerges the earth co-emerges as that which gives shelter and conceals.[153] In the example of the temple Heidegger tries to show that the truth of the work of art consists in the interrelationship between revealing and concealing. The temple opens up a world of divinity and at the same time sets this world again back on the earth (rock) of historical past. "That into which the work sets itself back and which it causes to come forth in this setting back of itself we called the earth."[154] The earth, into which a work sets itself back, is non-objective. The work of art makes the earth itself move into the open of a world and it (the earth) remains there. Thus the work lets the earth be an earth for the people. The self-secluding earth co-emerges in everything that emerges as that which comes to the fore and gives shelters and conceals at the same time. Our culture and beliefs direct our thoughts and activities and make our lives meaningful insofar as they (culture and beliefs) are and stay unarticulated, i.e. as long as they stay the soil out of which we live. "Every decision, however, bases itself on something not mastered, something concealed, confusing."[155] Even though man bases his 'dwelling' upon the earth, the self-secluding earth shatters any kind of proper understanding of it; it is what grounds by raising itself up through the world. In other words, our meaningful lives draw on the unarticulated background beliefs and practices. Our meaningful lives are rooted deeply into self-closing earth. Those who see a work of art (here the temple) are not aware of the hiddenness of the earth, but see only the world, the holy environment of the temple. Culture and society are not human creation, but they are the embodiments of human spirit, which is circulating in and through the works of art in different epochs.

In the absence of man as creator they become the voice of no one, a voice of the impersonal *They*, *das Man*. Culture and practices are identical with man, who is not present, the unconscious man, i.e. the absence of subject.

Again in the essay on *The Thing* Heidegger describes the earth in relation to the possibility of the 'dwelling' of people. "Earth is the building bearer, nourishing with its fruits, tending water and rock, plant and animal."[156] Everything emerges or springs out of the earth. It is that which supports lives that arise from it. Here we have an obviously naturalistic, although non-objectified earth; it is an earth within which man dwells prior to any theoretical reflection. As the 'building bearer' the earth is the foundation (i.e. constructive support), upon which man dwells. It is only on and out of the earth that man can dwell at all. Heidegger's earth always denotes the non-objectified, non-actual element, which supports the world by providing meaning of beings.[157] And on this earth man constructs his dwelling means that it is only within a particular mode of dwelling that the world receives content. By earth, in this context, he means essentially what he meant by *physis*.[158] When we recall that the word *physis* is usually translated as 'nature,' to mean the upsurge of beings in their self-emergence. For the Greeks *physis* means the emerging and rising itself and within the whole, and it is that on which and in which man grounds his dwelling. "In the emerging of *physis* the earth comes-to-present and abides (*west*) as that which shelters."[159] The earth that co-emerges and shelters everything is to be understood as the native ground of particular people. The hidden aspect of the truth, from which a thing emerges as what it is, causes the originary strife.

The originary strife as the essence of the meaning of Being

Reflecting on Reiner Schürmann's book, *Heidegger on Being and Acting: from Principles to Anarchy*, Gasché maintains that Heidegger's inquiry into the 'origin' is carried out with the purpose of freeing it from its systematic covering-ups. The term 'origin' is taken here not as a *pricipium* or foundation but as coming-forth, *oriri*, which implies the meaning of multiple presencing or the 'origin' in the sense of *there*, the 'ahistorical, always instantaneous emergence of presencing.'[160] Heidegger interprets truth as revealment in terms of the strife between the world and the earth in order to explore the original Greek meaning of Being as *polemos*. Traditional philosophy discarded this aspect of truth, and what is missing in it is precisely the implications of *physis,* earth. In *The Origin of the Work of Art* the term earth is to be understood as non-metaphysical and non-historical equivalent of the Greek term *physis*.[161] Heidegger's analysis of Heraclitus' Fragment 123 intends to show *physis* is a non-metaphysical concept to the extent that the essence of it is concealment: "Nature loves to hide,"[162] which is considered as *a-lētheia* itself. It seems that the notion of earth designates the meaning of *physis,* which does not have the meaning of revealment, but it is the dark, concealed, unexplored and subterranean, from which beings emerge as what they are and upon which humans dwell.

In order to explain the essence of truth Heidegger explores the meaning of *logos* in accordance with pre-Socratic thinkers. They viewed Being from within itself, as a unit of discord, from which everything unfolds. He finds the meaning of Being as *physis* in terms of warlike conflict, which holds everything in unity. The first principle, *polemos*,[163] for Heraclitus, is the strife or confrontation which causes unfolding in the form of oppositions, through which everything comes to presence.[164] The origin of truth is understood as the confrontation, which does not destroy unity, but it lets the entities—gods and humans, free and servile-appear. The gathering together of all beings in warlike confrontation covers the pure presence of entity.[165] The irreducible nature of the meaning of beings is dealt in the essay *On the Question of Being*, in which Heidegger deletes the *is*, the meaning of Being.[166] On the basis of Heraclitus' Fragment 123, Heidegger understands the truth of Being as a strife of revealing and concealing. The originary strife implies the concealment in the unconcealment of entity, which constitutes the basic structure of the essence of truth.[167] The truth as unconcealment implies the meaning of the *other*, which is concealed in it. By reason of *physis* beings become un-concealed, hence *physis*, is equivalent to *alētheia*. According to Heidegger, the world, in and through which beings first come to being, implies the provenance of concealment.[168] Therefore, beings that are revealed cannot be reduced to the single moment of presence. *Physis* is the inscrutable, irreducible unity of motion and rest, which the Greeks struggled to think over.

For the Greeks Being means *physis*, *alçtheia* or *logos*.[169] The meaning of *logos* is found in the Fragments (especially in Fragment 53) of Heraclitus, in which it means *gathering* in the sense that, e.g., one gathers wood or *bringing together* entities into a unity.[170] The Greeks understood beings in their Being. Originally, *logos* is the gathered-togetherness of beings.[171] Heidegger finds the fundamental meaning of *logos* in *gathering together*, an irreducible unity which does not mean presence. The truth of Being as *gathering together* denotes both truth and untruth. Heidegger's retrieval of the truth of Being consists in the re-discovery of the Greek meaning of Being in terms of *physis* and *logos*, even if the Heideggerian notion of truth is not identical with them.[172] The truth of *Dasein* and the truth of the work of art elucidate the happening of truth as the aboriginal fight between closure and disclosure.

a. *Difference at the origin of the truth*

For Heidegger the essence of truth is the strife; at the origin of truth of the work the world appears to be opposed to the earth. By initiating a strife between the openness or the intelligibility of the world and the withdrawal of the earth, work of art has a particular capacity to disclose the truth of Being. The world and the earth are not separate; they are linked in a mutual strife, which itself characterises the truth of the work of art.[173] The nature of the work of art is an inward strife, through the process of erecting the world and of setting forth the earth "The work-being of the work consists in the instigation of strife between world and earth."[174] The strife between world and earth (openness and concealment) is the happening of truth. Erecting a world and producing the earth, the work accomplishes the strife in which the disclosure of all that is, i.e. truth, is accomplished. All this is but another way of saying that truth and untruth (disclosure and concealment) belong together; truth is the unit of opposites. The setting-up of a world and the setting-forth of the earth, which constitute the essence of the truth of work, are held together in the origin of truth of the work. Earth and world are different from each other, but they are never separated. Opening and withdrawal are the two important aspects of truth.[175] Setting up of the world denotes the movement in which an epoch within the history of Being is brought into open; the setting forth of the earth marks the counteracting movement of withdrawal, i.e. the effacement of the present epoch in the happening of truth. Truth is dialectic or polemic in the sense that opening and withdrawal or clearing and concealing play together at the origin of the truth. The world, which is grounding itself on the earth, has no existence independent of earth and at the same time, the earth cannot be there without the world to be opened.

In Heidegger the origin of truth is the unit of the opposition of world and earth in the form of mutual striving. This striving has nothing of disorder and destruction. The essence of the work of art is not an empty unity of opposites; rather in the strife the opponents raise each other into the self-assertion of their essential natures.[176] The opposites are needed for the raising of each other; earth cannot be there without world to be open, and *vice versa*. The truth of the work denotes the truth of infrastructure, which do not yield the truth of moment. In the originary strife the opposites belong to one another; the origin is the confluence of truth and untruth.

b. *Truth as self-disclosure*

The objective of Heidegger's inquiry into the meaning of Being is to think of Being; in other words, to avoid thinking it in terms of beings. Thinking that orients itself by being is metaphysics or Platonism. The term *alētheia* as un-concealment is unthought in the history of philosophy underlies our familiar conception of the essence of truth as correctness. "The truth is the essence of true... The essence is discovered in the generic and universal concept, which represents the one feature that holds indifferently for many things."[177] According to Aristotle, a proposition is true if the cognition articulated in it has the conformity with the actual, with what is in truth.[178] Thus a thing must itself already be in some way unconcealed. Prepositional truth is pre-predicative in the sense that it is already there before we make a judgement. In other words in all our propositions we always remain within unconcealment. "Propositional truth is rooted in a *more originary* truth (unconcealment), in the pre-predicative manifestness of *beings*, which may be called *ontic truth*."[179] The truth of a proposition here is the correspondence. Conforming to something means that the truth has already come-to-pass in unconcealment. It is impossible for us to judge the correctness of a proposition, unless the unconcealment of beings had already exposed us to, and placed us in that cleared realm in which every being stands and from which it withdraws.[180] Before we come to know a being we have access to it in advance by means of Being. But when Heidegger speaks of truth as *alētheia*, he does not take the literal translation of the Greek term *alētheia* as non-concealment. What then is truth? Heidegger explains the truth of Being as unconcealment in terms of *Dasein*'s existence as Being-in-the-world (thrownness) and of the strife as the truth of the work of art, the openness or clearing (as unconcealment).[181]

i. The equiprimordiality of the truth of Dasein

Being influenced by Duns Scotus' doctrine of the *intentionality* of the nature of all objects, Heidegger argues that the meanings of things are to be sought in human understanding, which is also the pivotal point for Brentano's conception of intentionality and also for Husserl's *transcendental subjectivism*, i.e. it is the subject (Self or Ego) that provides the conditions for all determinations of the objects of experience and thought. Dorothea Frede opines that in *Being and Time* Heidegger shares Husserlian transcendental subjectivism and modern anthropologism in order to expose the question Being, the essence of entities.[182] In it he deals with question of Being through an analytic of *Dasein*'s pre-reflexive access to a world. However, it must be remembered that Heidegger's purpose of the question of Being is to overcome the subject-centred ontology. Since he does not accept consciousness or Self as the self-evident starting point for the account of any reality, the analytic of *Dasein* is essential to bring to light the conditions for the intelligibility of entities in general. The essence of *Dasein* lies in its existence and the existential (concrete, local or specific) meaning of *Dasein* is its disclosedness: "*Dasein is its disclosedness.*"[183] *Dasein*'s disclosedeness as Being-in-the-world denotes the irreducible structure of its truth, which cannot be explained in traditional philosophical terms.

Apart from *Dasein*'s disclosedness, its relation to the world, *Dasein* cannot be understood, and like wise, without *Dasein* the world too has no separate existence. For their existence they are mutually dependent. Heidegger's exposition of the truth as *Dasein*'s disclosedness as 'exsistence' denotes that human being's way of Being is an issue for it. The analytic of *Dasein* '-care, thrownnes, projection and falling-' provides its basic character that it is in truth as well as in untruth.[184] Its structure of truth helps him to avoid all associations with common philosophical terminologies and sheds light on the meaning of the uncoveredness of entities within-the-world. Intra-worldly things can be understood *as* something or they can be discovered only because of the prior disclosedness. The antecedently given world is the possibility and the necessary condition for the uncovering of the phenomena, which have been covered up from the beginning of Western philosophy. In short, disclosedness makes discoveredness possible.[185] *Dasein*'s analytic is designed to expose the theory of truth as unhiddenness.

Heidegger's question of the meaning of Being indicates that our understanding of a phenomenon is always a pre-understanding of it. Things are already revealed to us because of its interconnectedness and involvement to the world in a meaningful way. We understand such things as what they are by virtue of their relation to the world; things are meaningful by virtue of their *in-which*. Thing's involvement and interconnectedness to the world is the power of its signification. Particular things can be taken to signify (*be-deuten*) something by virtue of the understanding that we have of the relational structure of significance within which they shows up and with reference to which we interpret them.[186] The relational structure of significance of a thing can be explained by Heidegger's concept of the world of equipment. To the Being of equipment belongs a totality of equipment, in which any equipment is something in-order-to and it is this form of reference that constitutes the Being of equipment.[187] In our everyday dealing with things we have some pre-understanding of what things are all about. In *Being and Time* one can detect the ontological priority, which is given to *Dasein*'s practical activity and understanding. "Meaning is that wherein the intelligibility (*Verständlichkeit*) of something maintains itself."[188] Entities become intelligible as something by means of meaning that we bestow on them in our understanding.[189] In other words, meaning of things that we articulate in and through language is always already given to us. Language has the structure of the truth of equipment, i.e. it is ontologically grounded in the totality of equipment.[190] Then 'to be' means that 'to be already understood as' something. Christina Lafont argues that Heidegger's world-disclosure has a quasi-transcendental status and a *normative* significance, since meaning defines things as what they are.[191] In ontological difference she observes a kind of constitution, in which the ontological determines and constitutes the ontic. She argues that the meaning of *Dasein*, which is already dependent upon a world, undermines the ontic-ontological structure of *Being and Time*.[192] However, I would like to refute her criticism in reference to the Heideggerian truth because the truth of *Dasein* opens up anterior context, which cannot be taken as a system of relation between Being and beings. Ontological difference denotes the difference between Being and beings, rather than their peaceful structural unity, in which things are determined ontologically.

The structure of the origin of the truth of entities that unfolds in the analytic of *Dasein* that comprises two levels of human existence: ontic and ontological. In order to uncover the origin of truth he introduces two terms: *existentiell* to denote the ontic level of the factual for human existence, which is open to observation and *existentiale*, which denotes ontological level of human existence that underlies the ontic level of existence.[193] Lafont questions the putting-together of the ontic (factual or empiric) entities and ontological (symbolical meaning that exists 'always already') into the existential structure of *Dasein*, since it entails the quasi-transcendental nature of world-disclosure.[194] But I uphold the view that *Dasein* as Being-in-the-world cannot be understood as the ontological determination of its ontic, factual existence. According to Frede, even though the pre-understanding, the disclosedness of the world, underlies *Dasein*'s basic structure, Heidegger knows that any *bracketing* of *Dasein*'s factual world would be mistake.[195] In short, the truth of entities is to be understood in terms of the undecidability of the infrastructure. In the concept of Being-in-the-world, what is primordial is the clearing of entities in equipmental context in the sense that they emerge-into-presence in and through their reciprocal interdependence. Even though Being-in-the-world is the primordial structure, the *a priori* ground, of *Dasein*'s truth of Being, it does not constitute the metaphysical meaning of existence. There is no ultimate ground for *Dasein*'s existence as Being-in-the-world. For Heidegger the meaning of Being is the absence of ground (*Abgrund*, abyss).[196] *Dasein* as 'Being-in something' constitutes the infrastructural, transcendental character of its existence. *Dasein* is a kind of being or entity whose mode of Being is exsistence, 'to be-in-the-world;' the truth of *Dasein* is to be sought in its natural and social context; it is the Being-with and *Dasein*-with.[197] For Heidegger individual is embedded with his culture and society and *Dasein* as Being-with is the essential structure of human beings. *Dasein* is lost in its world; its state of Being is such that it is in untruth. To *Dasein*'s state of Being belong care (i.e. *Dasein* as Being-in-the-world as well as Being alongside with entities with-in-the-world), *thrownness*, (i.e. humans as thrown into an open space, *Da-sein*, or there-being; when man steps forth, or exists, he becomes the *there* for Being. *Dasein* always finds itself thrown into a concrete situation and attuned to a cultural and historical context where things already count in a determinative ways in relation to a community's practices. This prior thrownness into the medium of shared intelligibility, disclosed in our moods, makes up *Dasein*'s 'facticity,' which does not, however, constitute any nature of *Dasein*), projection (i.e. *Dasein*'s potentiality-for-Being, *Seinkönnen*, which is related to our understanding. It is the temporal interpretation of the structure of our Being-in-the-world), and falling (i.e. our day-to-day preoccupation or our worldly existence as 'average everydayness,' *Dasein* as 'any one' or *They*).[198] Falling means the human situation of anxiety, care, resolve, death, guilt, etc., that he experiences in three temporal dimensions -past, present, and future- enable *Dasein* to project itself upon Being.[199] *Dasein* as *They* knows only the 'public norms,' in and through which it is deprived of its responsibility for what it does. In other words, preoccupied with things, human *Dasein* is absorbed in the things. Frede makes clear the transcendental meaning of beings that entities have meaning in their Being; they can have meaning only if they belong within the 'project' that we make of ourselves.[200] Meaning of a thing as well as our understanding is directed and controlled by the past. Temporality in *Being and Time* denotes the temporal structure of the truth of *Dasein*: it is extended to past, present and future.[201] The world constitutes the existential situation of human beings, in which *Dasein* is always already thrown. Pattison describes man's thrownness as a part of larger story which exposes the truth of beings in their truth. By the term thrownness Heidegger means that human being is thrown by itself into the truth of beings. There is a relationship between the truth of Being and that of human beings. Thrownnees and falling mean that *Dasein* is not the ground of its existence.[202] The truth of *Dasein* does not allow to ask *what* is the ground of Being. *Dasein*'s transcendence is the result of double movement of projection of the world in the sense that the being which projects, i.e. *Dasein*, is itself *always already* (past) governed by this world before the act of projection. Therefore, the world and *Dasein* are equi-original,[203] which results in the dislocation of the centrality of Self or consciousness, the subject-centred metaphysics. In this context, what is human *Dasein*, what is its nature or who is *Dasein*? It is not a being or a Self, a subject with a substantial self or enduring identity of fixed qualities so that there can be no possibility for the objective experience and measurement of the truth of *Dasein*. Its Self is to be conceived only as a *way* of Being of this entity. *Dasein* cannot be understood as something present-at-hand.[204] The truth of human *Dasein* and that of entities are given in Being. "Truth (uncoveredness) is something that must be wrested from entities. Entities get snatched out of their hiddenness."[205] Since entities are what they are only in their Being, in hiddenness, the essence of revealment is to be critically examined. *Dasein* as Being-in-the-world is an *entity* which is the Being with *others*.[206] In relation to world and temporality, the truth of *Dasein* *is* as it is *already was*.[207] Having analysed *Dasein*'s thrownness and falling in relation to the world and the temporal distinctiveness -past, present and future-, Früchtl argues that the meaning of 'now' is essentially an anticipatory disclosure in the sense that *Dasein*'s Being, the current situation of the *there*, is ultimately its self-revealment. *Dasein* understands itself or it is self-understanding. Früchtl describes *Dasein*'s temporalization is the anticipatory disclosure, which makes its mode of Being an issue, in the sense that it does not maintain the nature of presence.[208] Heidegger's human *Dasein* denotes the notion of absence, instead of subject-centred metaphysics.

In everyday existence *Dasein* is not given, it is understood as a *self* which is not truly its own. Its *givenness* is to be understood as self-disclosure in which it is co-determined and dominated by *others*, the public in general. The subject of everyday being-in-the-world is characterized by *das Man* (it is translated as *They*),[209] which denotes our mode of living and self-understanding in compliance with the general standard. For example, *Dasein* speaks means that *one speaks* or *we speak*, which denotes the 'forgetfulness of Being' in and through our everyday absorption in the world. All kinds of different forms of alterity, such as law, ethics, belief, politics, religion, international diplomacy institutionalized pedagogy, etc. exert on us the obligation, which is to be carried out for the *other*.[210] *Dasein* is an entity which is basically Being-with, which is the existential character of *Dasein* as it is Being-in-the-world. The Self and world belong together in the single entity of *Dasein*. Equiprimordiality is the basic characteristic of the truth of *Dasein*; it *is* and at the same time it *is not*. "Being-in is Being with Others."[211] The Being with *other* determines *Dasein*'s truth of Being which is an issue for *Dasein* in its very Being. *Dasein* itself *is* not, it is *nobody*; the *who* of everyday *Dasein* or Self of *Dasein* is no particular Self, but a neuter, *They*, (*das Man*). *They*, or *das Man* is nothing definite, but has its own *way* in which it *can be*.[212] The Being of *Dasein* is constituted by its Being among others; it is the possibility of becoming concrete as something characteristic of *Dasein*.[213] Gethmann claims that *Dasein*'s existentialle-existential constitution builds the intersubjectivity, which attains the quasi-transcendental meaning of Being. However, he adds that it cannot be described in terms of the transcendental truth of Scholastic philosophy of St. Thomas, but it should be explained in aporia, since there is no defined way to explain *Dasein*'s truth: it is and at the same time it is the *other*.[214]

Dasein's truth is always a 'Being-in,'[215] which is the necessary *a priori* condition of *Dasein*'s way to be. *In-sein* or Being-in stands for *Dasein*'s self-disclosure as Being-in-the-world, a disclosure of the spatiality as the Being of the *there*. The existence of *Dasein* as Being-in something makes its truth equiprimordial. It is a Being *in-between*.[216] It *is* and at the same time it *is* not. The *there* (*Da*) in the name of *Da-sein* (*there*-Being) indicates this self-disclosedness of an entity. The term *there* indicates a *here* and a *yonder*, *Dasein*'s existential spatiality or the location of its Being-in-the-world. In-*sein* refers to *Dasein*'s truth as *betweenness*, its awareness of openness towards its existential-ontological structure as Being-in-the-world. Michael Zimmerman finds Heidegger's indebtedness to divine mysticism particularly in his concept of human existence as clearing, openness or nothingness, in which things come-to-be as what they are. In order that a thing 'to be' it must disclose or present itself that can only take place in the clearing, or in an opening, or in emptiness, or in nothingness, or in absencing.[217] In other words, presencing is possible in absencing or the truth of Being is withdrawal; the *Da* of *Dasein,* which is cleared or present as something, is something that does not occur or take place. The *there* is *Dasein*'s inner light; its openness towards the *other*, it is the illumination or coming-to-pass of an entity. Being-in of *Dasein* is an inner light, which makes possible *Dasein*'s way of to be *there*, i.e. as Being-in-the-world it is cleared. Its self-disclosure happens in and by itself; in disclosure *Dasein* itself is disclosed to itself, *Dasein* itself is *there*. Being-in stands for self-disclosure, which is the essential character of *Dasein*'s Being as Being-in-the-world. All discovery of beings is grounded in the structure of *Dasein*'s Being-in, i.e. in the disclosure of the world that happens necessarily with the existence of a *Dasein* that is the *there* (*Da*). The analysis of the Being of *there* shows the in-*sein* as *Dasein*'s existential constitution, its equiprimordial constellation of the involvement with the world. *Dasein* is its own disclosure through its components of mood, understanding and discourse that form its existential constitution *there*.[218] Along with Lafont, Gasché and Clark too argue that "*Dasein*'s pre-reflexive understanding remains part of a subject-centred metaphysics," since it is "through *Dasein*'s various moods and concern that a world light up and things appear as what they are."[219]

The fore-structure, from which the truth of *Dasein* originates, is called the earth. "This is the earth and, for a historical people, its earth, the self-secluding ground on which it rests together with everything that it already is, though still hidden from itself."[220] For the historical people the earth is poetizing, what is revealed from the hiddenness of the past. In this sense, disclosure of a work and that of *Dasein* are mutually interrelated. The truth of the work of art as unconcealment of beings is the disclosure of that into which *Dasein* as historical is already thrown. It describes the meaning of Heidegger's dictum: unconcealment occurs in concealments or Being presents itself in a concealed form.[221] "In Heidegger's view, world is the total meaningfulness into which a man with his contemporaries finds himself thrown in each epoch of history. World is the concrete totality of meaning as which Being's truth comes-to-pass to him as the '*Da*' of Being in given epoch."[222] The *Da* of *Dasein* is structural. The meaning of Being is related to the Being of humanity. The Being of humanity is the *Da-sein*, (*Being-here*), the site for the opening up of Being.[223] Wolin argues that Heidegger's question of Being provides him with conceptual support for Hitler's politics, as a result of which he wilfully sacrifices differences and plurality, his concept of Being.[224] The *Dasein* of historical humanity is an incident, a fall-between in which the truth of Being confirms itself in works as *history*, as finite manifestation.[225] Richardson interpreted the Being-*there* of Heidegger thus: "If Being makes an appearance, so that non-concealment (truth) comes-to-pass, then there must be some 'place' (*Stätte*) where this happens, some breach in the darkness, some sudden irruption, or incident (*Zwischenfall*) where Being opens-up in light. This 'place,' where truth takes 'place,' is precisely what Heidegger understands the 'There' of Being and in so far as it is, sc. is a being, it is called with all justice 'There-being.'"[226] The *Da* of *Sein* is the opening up, *Dasein*'s transcendence and relatedness to the *other*, which constitutes the structure of the truth of Being; *Da* is qualified as an irruption, a happening of truth of infrastructure, which *is* and at the same time *is not*. Non-concealment is regarded as the irruption of that which is already given and the truth of a thing thus comes to the fore as the *Da* of *Sein*. In the essay Heidegger explains the truth of the there-being as disclosure, clearing.

ii. Clearing and the truth of the work of art

The concept of clearing explains the meaning of entities, the emergence. Disclosure means clearing of beings, an openness, a breach, within which (opening) all entities come to *be*. Dreyfus and Harrison opine that in early Heidegger the clearing of entities is based in human *Dasein* or understanding; in later Heidegger it involves the structure of strife.[227] The *Da* of *Dasein* means 'here' or 'there' and *Sein* means the verb 'to be.' *Dasein* is the place or the openness in and through which beings occurs. The truth of disclosedness unfolded in and through equipment and *Dasein*, and the truth of the work of art shows the meaning of clearing that has the *a priori* structure of revealment, the element of the hiddenness of truth.[228] A being that appears presents itself as something other than what it is. Art as the setting-itself-into-work means that truth as revealing always comes from hiddenness, from the self-secluding earth, and as a result of that everything is concealed even in the clearing.

In the clearing of beings truth itself establishes in the strife, for the clearing truth hides or covers the untruth, the prior structure of the primordial darkness. Clearing is the bringing forth of being in an open region by removing darkness. Therefore, the truth of a being that is cleared is always in-between: truth is untruth. It is the meaning of *technē*, bringing-forth.[229] "The establishing of truth in the work is the bringing forth of a being such as never was before and will never come to be again."[230] The clearing is the unfolding of the originary unity of Being, which holds the opposites, truth and untruth; this is just another way of saying that self-disclosure is the coming to the fore (truth) of beings in a very special way. Disclosure as clearing has the complexity of pre-structures than self-manifestation. For example, what the painting of van Gogh (shoes) or the Greek temple make manifest is thus not a particular isolated being that is correctly represented. The truth that happens in van Gogh's painting and in the Greek temple does not represent or correspond to some particular being; what they manifest is the non-concealment in regard to the beings as such and taken as whole. Thus in the work truth itself is at work (*am Werk*), not just something that is true. In other words, the shoes and the temple come to the fore as what they are in their modes of Being. "Truth happens in van Gogh's painting. This does not mean that something at hand is correctly portrayed, but rather that in the revelation of the equipmental being of the shoes beings as a whole—world and earth in their counterplay—attain to unconcealment."[231] The painting of van Gogh and the Greek temple as well as painting, a piece of pottery, etc. show the way in which Being conceals itself, becomes illuminated and enters the clearing. In *Nietzsche* Vol. I, with the title *The Will to Power as Art* Heidegger says that 'art is worth more than the truth.'[232] With regards to the origin of truth, art is more important than truth because art provides us with a critical view on the meaning of things revealed in the world.[233] Truth is possible only by eliminating the original difference between Being and beings. By eliminating the difference between Being and beings, work of art makes public (reveals) something other than itself; it manifests something else other than itself.[234] According to Heidegger, truth happens in the work of art as an originary conflict between clearing and concealing; the earth towers up into the world and the world grounds itself on the earth in so far as truth happens as a result of this primal conflict. The presence of the twofold in the work of art is the very nature of truth, the primal conflict, which brings beings as a whole into unconcealment.

The entire discussion in *Being and Time* and in *The Origin of the Work of Art* revolves around the question: how does being appear in Being? In traditional philosophy, from Plato to Hegel, that which is illuminated becomes the essence of truth and, as a result, it is known as the philosophy of presence since it suppresses or discards the aspect of the hiddenness (i.e. prior structure) of the meaning of beings. The shining which in this way becomes a constitutive part of the work is the beautiful according to traditional philosophy. But in Heidegger's critique the concept of beauty as shining or revealing constitutes only one of the aspects of truth; the retrieval of the concept of beauty takes place in his emphasis on unconcealment *in a particular way*: the truth in the work of art occurs in concealing denial which denotes that the "opposition in the essence of truth which subsists between clearing and concealing." The essence of the work of art is not something true; at the same time the claim, "the essence of truth is untruth," does not mean that truth is always false from its beginning.[235] What Heidegger's phenomenological investigation into the meaning of Being stresses is the fact that concealment belongs to unconcealment as clearing. The retrieval of the truth of Being consists in the analysis of the structure of the truth, which opens up prior structures. It shows pure present impossible; the result of his philosophy is the undecidability of the truth of Being, which destructs the entire history of philosophy from Parmenides to Nietzsche. Siefert argues that truth in Heidegger's essay does not have the meaning of correctness, which is the hallmark of traditional philosophy, his very search for the origin, however, entails the possibility for the theory of work of art.[236]

Since beings conceal themselves in their very unconcealment, Heidegger wants to inquire into the nature of truth as unconcealment. He sets aside all traditional concepts of metaphysics and initiates a new origin of the essence of truth as revealment. His recollection of the essence of truth in Platonism aims at the destruction of metaphysics and he undertakes a new originary origin of truth for the purification of metaphysics.[237] Heidegger's question of the meaning of Being is not only a critique of metaphysics but results positively in the overcoming of metaphysics. His works on the meaning of Being inaugurate the new originary origin, which can hardly be understood in terms of any philosophical concepts.[238] *Dasein*'s truth and the primal strife at the essence of truth of the work denote the irreducibility of the meaning of being. Even though Derrida accepts Heidegger's critique of metaphysics and his works as a beginning of a new era, he says that Heidegger has not gone far enough in deconstructing metaphysics of presence. In *The Truth in Painting*, Derrida criticises Heidegger's overcoming of aesthetics and comes up with his own originary origin of the truth.

References

1. The term 'origin' (*der Ursprung*) means that from which something originally springs forth (*Entspringen*). *Ursprung* means originary

leap from, source, beginning, origin. This springing forth is described as originary strife, which is the origin or the essence of the truth of Being. *The Origin of the Work of Art* is an inquiry into the question of the essence of truth as the coming-to-presence of 'something,' i.e. the other, in the work of art. Martin Heidegger, *The Origin of the Work of Art*, 143-44. Martin Heidegger *Introduction to Metaphysics*, 6-7.

2. Martin Heidegger, *The Anaximander Fragment*, 50-51.
3. Martin Heidegger, *On the Essence of Truth*, 151.
4. On 13 November 1935 Heidegger delivered a lecture *On the Origin of the Work of Art* to the Art-Historical Society of Freiburg-im-Breisgau. He expanded and developed it into three lectures, which he presented on various occasions. In this essay he uses some new terms to explain the concept of the truth of the Greeks, *alētheia*. He uses the words like *earth, world and battle*, in order to explain how truth occurs, when truth sets itself into the work of art. With these terminologies he explains how truth is at work in art works. The title of the essay refers to both 'Origin' as well as 'Art.' However, he deals with the work of art in order to explain its origin. He subordinates both artist and work to the art and searches for its origin. The German text for the translation is, Martin Heidegger, *Der Ursprung des Kunstwerkes*, ed. H.G. Gadamer, Stuttgart, Philipp Reclam Jun. GmbH & Co. 1960. Albert Hofstadter translated Heidegger's essay *Der Ursprung des Kunstwerkes*, in *Poetry, Language, Thought*. Martin Heidegger, *The Origin of the Work of Art*, in *Poetry and Language, Thought*, trans. Albert Hofstadter, New York, Harper & Row, 1971. In *Basic Writings* David Farrell Krell accepted his translation with some minor changes.
5. Martin Heidegger, *Addendum* to *The Origin of the Work of Art*, in *Basic Writings*, ed. David Farrell Krell, London and New York, Routledge, 1993, 210. However it is to be noted that Heidegger himself speaks about the turn that happened after *Being and Time*. It is the change consists in the shift away from fundamental ontology, with its focus on *Dasein* as the source of the intelligibility of things, to the project of thinking the history of Being. After the *Kehre* he concentrates on the happening of the truth of Being, the event of manifestation or how things come *to be*.
6. *Phenomenon* in Greek means that which shows itself.
7. Vincent van Gogh was born in Holland in 1853. He worked in Brussels, Paris and London. Being influenced by impressionism his paintings are very outstanding. He died on 17 May 1890 in Auvers-sur-Oise.

8. Martin Heidegger, *The Origin of the Work of Art*, 152. Ref. George Pattison, *The later Heidegger*, 47-48.
9. Martin Heidegger, *Being and Time*, 26, 29, 61. Martin Heidegger, *The Basic Problems of Phenomenology*, 19.
10. Being (*das Sein*) is not any*thing*. It is the most self-evident and universal concept, extending to any and everything; it unavoidably presents itself in all particular concepts. It is the highest generality. Being as discussed by the history of philosophy always names what beings show up *as*, what Heidegger calls 'beingness,' However, the understanding of Being or the concept of Being does not show up directly, it is not beingness. The concept of Being denotes *how* beings in their beingness become available to us or *how* we come to understand what it mean *to be*. "The question of Being, in this sense, inquires into the happening, the event, in which all beings become accessible and understandable to us as beings." The understanding of Being as presencing has the implication of *how* entities show up, not of *what* makes it possible for entities to show up or to present. For Heidegger, the clearing that makes presencing possible necessarily 'withdraws.' Ref. Martin Heidegger, *Introduction to Metaphysics*, xi, 42-43. Whereas, being (*das seinde*), for example, a piece of chalk can be understood in two ways: (1) *das Seinde* as the Greek *to on*, means *what* at any time in being, i.e. a particular thing in such and such a way, for example a piece of chalk as white, light, breakable mass. Beings literally means what is,' or that which is.' (2) The second implication of *das Seiende* means that which makes a particular thing a being instead of nonbeing (*nichtseiend*); being, in other words, means "that which makes up the Being in the being, if it is a being." The Greek word *to on* means the second meaning of being, i.e. *das Seiende* is not that particular thing, *what* is in being, but rather "'the in-being, beingness (*Seiendheit)*, to be in being, Being.'" In the first meaning of being, names the things themselves that are in being, but always in reference to these things, not in reference to their beingness, *ousia*. In this respect *to on* designates *ta onta* (*entia*). In the light of second meaning things in reference to their beingness (that which characterizes beings as beings in general) is called *to einai* (*esse*). Martin Heidegger, *Introduction to Metaphysics*, xi, 33.
11. Martin Heidegger, *Being and Time,* 23.
12. *Ibid.*, 58-63.
13. Martin Heidegger, *The Origin of the Work of Art*, 148. Before the question concerning the essence of things is discussed, we have to ask what a thing is in our normal way of understanding. Every*thing* can be called a *thing* (thing is ὄν =*res* =*ens*= being). The beings like stones, lumps of earth, furrows in the field, wells, jugs, water, milk,

clouds, etc., are some of the examples of things. They are things-in-themselves (*Ding an sich*), because they do not themselves appear or show. Things-in-themselves and also things-that-appear, i.e. 'all beings that in any way are, are called things. Things can be divided into two: the inanimate things of nature and the inanimate man-made things. Inanimate things such as the stone, the piece of wood, etc. are "mere" (*bloße*) things. Equipments and works of art are the inanimate man-made things. There is stone in a work of architecture. Man uses mere things for works of art, e.g. there is wood in sculpture, colour in painting. There are sounds in literary works, tones in a musical composition. *Ibid.*, 145-47. Martin Heidegger, *The Thing*, in *Poetry, Language, and Thought*, trans. Albert Hofstadter, New York, Harper & Row, 1971, 172-73.

14. For Hegel Plato's Idea is the essential truth behind intellectual concepts and material entities. Idea occurs beyond the limit of historicism and gives history a trans-historical teleology. Ref. William de Vries, *Hegel's Logic and Philosophy of Mind*, in *Routledge History of Philosophy* Vol. 6, eds. Robert C. Solomon and Kathleen M. Higgins, London, Routledge, 1993, 235-36.
15. Martin Heidegger, *Nietzsche*, Vol. III and IV, 108-09.
16. George Pattison, *The later Heidegger*, 88-89. Intentionality is the structure of lived experience as such, by which one is able to bridge the gap between subject and object.
17. Timothy Clark, *Derrida, Heidegger, Blanchot*, 21-22.
18. Martin Heidegger, *The Origin of the Work of Art*, 149.
19. George Pattison, *The later Heidegger*, 86-87.
20. Martin Heidegger, *The Thing*, 175-79. *Nearness* or proximity implies the co-belonging of man and Being. The principle of proximity (or of identity, of Being, of presence) is for Heidegger the condition of the possibility of the philosophy, which ultimately yields the truth of structural principle. The infrastructure of the truth in Heidegger and Derrida denotes the origin as withdrawal.
21. *Ibid.*, 175.
22. *Ibid.*, 166.
23. *Ibid.*, 178-79.
24. Immanuel Kant, *Critique of Pure Reason*, trans. J.M.D. Meiklejohn, Mineola and New York, Dover Publications, INC, 2003, 44-87.
25. Martin Heidegger, *The Origin of the Work of Art*, 151.
26. George Pattison, *The later Heidegger*, 90-91.
27. Martin Heidegger, *The Origin of the Work of Art*, 151. Ref. Daniel Bonevac, *Kant's Copernican Revolution*, in *Routledge History of*

Philosophy Vol. VI, ed. Robert C. Solomon and Kathleen M. Higgins, London and New York, Routledge, 1993, 51.

28. Martin Heidegger, *The Origin of the Work of Art*, 152. Ref. Aristotle, *Metaphysics, Books Z and H*, Z, 1038 b20- 1041 b28.
29. Martin Heidegger, *The Origin of the Work of Art*, 154. Heidegger describes the *hylemorphic* structure and the serviceability of a piece of equipment, e.g. shoes, as follows. Everyone knows what belongs to a shoe as such. If they are not made of wood they will have leather soles and uppers, joined together by thread and nails. Everyone knows the serviceability of the shoes. Shoes serve to protect one's feet. Their matter and form will differ, depending on the use to which shoes are to be e.g. the use of shoes in work in a field, use of the shoes in dancing. The matter and form of a thing depend on its serviceability or usefulness. On the use of van Gogh's shoes Heidegger says that the farmer's wife wears her shoes in the field; only in the field are they really are. She walks and works in them; that is the way shoes are actually used; that is the way they actually serve her. It is in this very fact of the usefulness of a piece of equipment that we must try to discover the truth of the Being of equipment. *Ibid.*, 158-59.
30. The term 'equipment' denotes Heidegger's word *Zeug*, which has, however, no precise English equivalent. For the most part Heidegger uses the term *Zeug* as collective noun, which means instrument or tool, equipment. Ref. Martin Heidegger, *Being and Time*, 97, see footnote 1.
31. Martin Heidegger, *The Origin of Work of Art*, 154-55. *Being and Time* deals with readiness-to-hand in order to explain the kind of Being an equipment possesses. It has a Being "in which it manifests itself in its own right." Martin Heidegger, *Being and Time*, 98.
32. In Heidegger the usefulness of equipment does not mean utilizing, using up or exploitation, instead it denotes the transcendental meaning of entities, it (usefulness) lets a thing be *what* it is and *how* it is. Ref. Hubert Dreyfus, *History of the Being of Equipment*, in *Heidegger: A Critical Reader*, eds. Hubert L. Dreyfus and Harrison Hall, Oxford and Cambridge, Blackwell, 1992, 176.
33. Martin Heidegger, *The Origin of the Work of Art*, 154.
34. Hubert Dreyfus, *History of the Being of Equipment*, 174.
35. Martin Heidegger, *Being and Time*, 63-64. The world in *Being and Time* is the network of relations into which can be fitted the systems of equipmental totalities with their internal relations (or references). Ready-to-hand things have their place in such a world.
36. *Ibid.*, 97.

37. *Ibid.*, 97-98, 176, 265. Ref. John Haugeland, *Dasein's Disclosedness*, in *Heidegger: A Critical Reader*, eds. Hubert L. Dreyfus and Harrison Hall, Cambridge and Oxford, Basil Blackwell, 1992, 31.
38. Martin Heidegger, *Being and Time*, 244
39. *Ibid.*, 189, 192-93, 200. Ref. Rodolphe Gasché, *Joining the Text: From Heidegger to Derrida*, 156-60.
40. Heidegger's term *Welt* is translated as the 'world,' which denotes the characteristics of *Dasein*'s existence. It is not ontic; its structure is ontological, *Dasein*'s going beyond. The noun *Weltlichkeit* and its adjective *weltlich* have the English translations worldhood or wordliness and 'worldly' respectively, which denote the ontological concept of *Dasein*'s necessary mode of Being (*existentialia*). The 'world' essentially belongs to *Dasein* and its ontic-ontological relatedness is an essential quality of all beings in the world. Martin Heidegger, *Being and Time*, 91, footnote 1. Martin Heidegger, *On the Essence of Ground*, 108-23.
41. Martin Heidegger, *Being and Time*, 98-99.
42. John Haugeland, *Dasein's Disclosedness*, 31-32.
43. Heidegger defines meaning as that in terms of which something becomes intelligible *as* something. It has the fore-structure of understanding wherein intelligibility of thing maintains itself. Ref. Martin Heidegger, *Being and Time*, 192-93.
44. Hubert Dreyfus, *History of Being of Equipment*, 180.
45. Martin Heidegger, *Being and Time*, 101-02, 104-05. Presence-at-hand (*Vorhandenheit*) is Heidegger's articulation for objectivity (*Gegenständlichkeit*). It means that we can understand an object (beings) as something if it is already discovered in its universal terms, i.e. categories of beingness, Being. We know things, which are thematized. *Ibid.*, 121.
46. Hans-Georg Gadamer, *Hermeneutics and Logocentrism*, 51.
47. Martin Heidegger, *Being and Time*, 114.
48. Equipment-structure and sign-structure have a similarity because their specific character consists in showing or indicating. Indication is a reference; reference is a relation. Through its relational character *Dasein* signifies to itself beforehand its Being-in-the-world as something to be understood in 'in-which' and 'with-which.' *Ibid.*, 108, 121.
49. *Ibid.*, 106.
50. *Ibid.*, 115.
51. *Ibid.*, 120.

52. Christina Lafont, *Heidegger, Language and World-disclosure*, trans. Graham Harman, Cambridge, Cambridge University Press 2000, 15-28.
53. *Ibid.*, 18. Martin Heidegger, *Being and Time*, 121.
54. Hubert Dreyfus and Harrison Hall, *Introduction* to *Heidegger: A Critical Reader*, ed. Hubert Dreyfus and Harrison Hall, Oxford and Cambridge, Blackwell, 1992, 4.
55. Martin Heidegger, *The Origin of the Work of Art*, 159. Derrida criticizes the description of the shoes as an example of his return to the metaphysics of presence. The critique of Derrida and Schapiro is given in Chapter 3 and my critical evaluation of it is given in Chapter 4.
56. Martin Heidegger, *The Origin of the Work of Art*, 161.
57. See Chapter 4.
58. Joseph J. Kockelmans, *Heidegger on Art and Art Works*, Dordrecht, Martinus Nijhoff 1985, 125-31; George Pattison, *The Later Heidegger*, 85-86. See Chapter 3.
59. Martin Heidegger, *The Origin of the Work of Art*, 159-61.
60. George Pattison, *The later Heidegger*, 50-51.
61. Martin Heidegger, *The Origin of the Work of Art*, 162.
62. *Ibid.*, 159.
63. *Ibid.*, 146-50.
64. Heidegger understands that the philosophy of aesthetics sets the work of art up as an object against the subject, who has an experience of the object (sensuous apprehension). The subjective experience of things constitutes only one part of the truth. In his philosophy of the work of art, he does not preserve this subject-object dichotomy. His concepts of the artistic production and of the poetry hold together the antagonism. Art as the origin of the truth is to be understood as strife, war, *polemos*. The meaning of Being is an event of the coming-to-pass of the truth, which cannot be reduced into a single moment of truth as presence. Martin Heidegger, *Addendum* to *The Origin of the Work of Art*, 211.
65. Martin Heidegger, *The Origin of the Work of Art*, 163.
66. Annemarie Gethmann-Siefert, *Martin Heidegger und die Kunstwissenschaft*, 251-55. George Pattison, *The later Heidegger*, 26-27, 35, 40.
67. Of primary concern to Derrida, then, in his confrontation with Heidegger is locating the attachments or holds of metaphysics on his philosophy. See Chapter 3.

68. Martin Heidegger, *Introduction to Metaphysics*, 18.
69. The Greek word *technē* derives from the root word *tec*, which means "to make something appear, within what is present, as this or that, in this way or that way." The verb *tikto* means to bring forth or to produce, in terms of letting appear. The Greeks called an artist and a craftsman *technitēs*, who brings forth beings through production. Art and craft (*technē*), means the essence of knowing, *alētheia*. For the Greeks the essence of knowing consists in the revealment of beings. Martin Heidegger, *Building Dwelling Thinking*, 157. Martin Heidegger, *The Origin of the Work of Art*, 184.
70. Martin Heidegger, *The Question Concerning Technology*, 317-318. The Greek terms *lath* means to be concealed and *A-lētheia* means *das Entbergen*, the disclosure.
71. George Pattison, *The later Heidegger*, 49.
72. Martin Heidegger, *Plato's Doctrine of Truth*, 171.
73. Martin Heidegger and Eugen Fink, *Heraclitus Seminar*, 161.
74. Martin Heidegger, *Introduction to Metaphysics*, 21.
75. Martin Heidegger, *Plato's Doctrine of Truth*, 172. Martin Heidegger, *The Essence of Truth*, 9.
76. Martin Heidegger, *The Origin of the Work of Art*, 197.
77. George Pattison, *The later Heidegger*, 49.
78. Martin Heidegger, *The Origin of the Work of Art*, 197.
79. Hubert L. Dreyfus, *Heidegger on the Connection between Nihilism, Art, Technology, and Politics*, in *The Cambridge Companion to Heidegger*, ed. Charles B. Guignon, Cambridge, Cambridge University Press, 1993, 297.
80. Richard Wolin, *The Politics of Being: The Political Thought of Martin Heidegger*, 121. Ref. Timothy Clark, *Derrida, Heidegger, Blanchot*, 42.
81. Timothy Clark, *Derrida, Heidegger, Blanchot*, 42.
82. *Ibid*., 28.
83. Martin Heidegger, *Letter on Humanism*, 217, 237.
84. Timothy Clark, *Derrida, Heidegger, Blanchot*, 118, 123.
85. *Ibid*., 27. Ref. Joseph J. Kockelmans, *Language, Meaning and Ek-sistence*, in *On Heidegger and Language*, ed. Joseph J. Kockelmans, Evanston and Illinois, Northwestern University Press, 1972, xiii, 9.
86. Christina Lafont, *Heidegger, Language and World-disclosure*, xii-xiii, 7. Martin Heidegger, *Being and Time*, 25.
87. Martin Heidegger, *On The Way to Language*, trans. Peter D. Hertz, San Francisco, Harper & Row, 1982, 124.

88. Christina Lafont, *Heidegger, Language, and Wolrd-disclosure*, xii.
89. Timothy Clark, *Derrida, Heidegger, Blanchot*, 27.
90. Martin Heidegger, *The Origin of the Work of Art*, 198. Ref. Martin Heidegger, *Introduction to Metaphysics*, 47.
91. Martin Heidegger, *On the Way to Language*, 81.
92. Charles Taylor, *Heidegger, Language and Ecology*, in *Heidegger: A Critical Reader*, ed. Hubert L. Dreyfus and Harrison Hall, Cambridge and Oxford, Basil Blackwell, 1992, 252.
93. Timothy Clark, *Derrida, Heidegger, Blanchot*, 34.
94. Martin Heidegger, *Logik, Die Frage nach der Wahrheit*, in *Gesamtausgabe*, Vol. 21, V. Klostermann, Frankfurt, 1976, 127 ff. Ref. Rodolphe Gasché, *Joining the Text: From Heidegger to Derrida*, 159-60. Martin Heidegger, *Being and Time*, 199.
95. Timothy Clark, *Derrida, Heidegger Blanchot*, 108-10. Ref. Jacques Derrida, *Force and Signification* in *Writing and Difference*, trans. Alan Bass, London and New York, Routledge, 1978, 13. Derrida's philosophy of textuality, see Chapter 4.
96. Martin Heidegger, *The Origin of the Work of Art*, 198.
97. Martin Heidegger, *The Question Concerning Technology*, 317.
98. Timothy Clark, *Derrida, Heidegger, Blanchot*, 17, 28-29.
99. *Ibid.*, 41.
100. George Pattison, *The Later Heidegger*, 5.
101. Martin Heidegger, *The Origin of the Work of Art*, 199. Martin Heidegger, *Letter on Humanism*, 217.
102. Martin Heidegger, *Introduction to Metaphysics*, 54.
103. Martin Heidegger, *On the Way to Language*, 134.
104. Martin Heidegger, *The Origin of the Work of Art*, 200.
105. Martin Heidegger, *Being and Time*, 193.
106. George Pattison, *The later Heidegger*, 109. Ref. Martin Heidegger, *Being and Time*, 191.
107. Dorethea Frede, *The Question of Being: Heidegger's Project*, 63. Martin Heidegger, *Being and Time*, 171.
108. Martin Heidegger, *Being and Time*, 193.
109. *Ibid.*, *27*. See footnote 1. John Macquarrie and Edward Robinson translate the noun *Dasein* as 'Being there,' or 'existence.' The verb *dasein* means 'to be there.' Heidegger hyphenates the term *Da-sein* to mean Being-there; *Da* is the *site* of the opening up of Being (*Sein*). The prefix *da* means *there, here*, and *then*; and *Sein* means the characteristics of a phenomenon, the way of Being of a human being which is *there*, is thrown into time and space, in which unconcealment

happens. In traditional German philosophy *Dasein* means any kind of Being or existence. Heidegger's concept of *Dasein* provides the deeper understanding of the truth of the Being of entities. One of the important characteristics of the ontological existence of *Dasein* means that its Being itself is an issue, i.e. *Dasein* is not its own, it has no self. *Dasein* as Being-in-the-world points to a general *one*, the indefinite pronoun *man. Dasein*'s transcendence constitutes its *selfhood*. Although Heidegger says that *Dasein* refers to human beings, he insists that it does not have an anthropological, psychological concept, because the question of *what* cannot be applied to *Dasein*. Its truth is always a question. *Dasein* is to be understood as a possibility or "condition into which human beings enter, either individually or collectively, at a historical juncture when Being becomes an issue for them." In this sense he often speaks of "historical *Dasein*," "our *Dasein*," "human *Dasein*," or "the *Dasein* of the People." *Ibid.*, 32. Martin Heidegger, *Introduction to Metaphysics*, xi-xii.

110. Heidegger's concept of language exposes the structure of the truth of entities.
111. Martin Heidegger, *The Origin of the Work of Art*, 201.
112. *Ibid.*, 180.
113. *Ibid.*
114. Annemarie Gethmann-Siefert, *Martin Heidegger und die Kunstwissenschaft*, 255-56.
115. George Pattison, *The later Heidegger*, 98-99.
116. Martin Heidegger, *The Origin of the Work of Art*, 162. Heidegger selects the example of the Greek temple in order to describes how truth comes-to-pass in the work of art, which has no character of the truth of representation. It is the temple of Neptune (Poseidon) in Paestum (originally Poseidonia) in the ancient Greek city of Lucania, Italy, about 30 miles south of Naples. The city of Paestum was first founded by Sybaris in Acadia in 600 B.C., and the Greek colonists had built the temples of Athena, Hera, and of Neptune. The city was later conquered by Lucanians and they gave it the name of Paestum. Ref. Joseph J. Kockelmans, *Heidegger on Art and Art Works*, 141-42.
117. Jonathan Loesberg, *Aestheticism and Deconstruction*, New Jersey, Princeton University Press, 1991, 67.
118. Martin Heidegger, *The Origin of the Work of Art*, 167, 202.
119. Jonathen Loesberg, *Aestheticism and Deconstruction*, 7. See Chapter 4.
120. Martin Heidegger, *The Origin of the Work of Art*, 187.

121. Annemarie Gethmann-Siefert, *Martin Heidegger und die Kunstwissenschaff*, 251, 254-56. Otto Pöggeler too asserts the relationship between Heidegger's political involvement to the National Socialism and his philosophy. Ref. Richard Wolin, *The Politics of Being: The Political Thought of Martin Heidegger*, 2-10.
122. Hubert L. Dreyfus, *Heidegger on the Connection between Nihilism, Art, Technology, and Politics*, 298.
123. Martin Heidegger, *The Origin of the Work of Art*, 168.
124. Annemarie Gethmann-Siefert, *Martin Heidegger und die Kunstwissenschaft*, 262-63.
125. Joseph J. Kockelmans, *Heidegger on Art and Art Works*, 142.
126. Martin Heidegger, *Addendum* to *The Origin of the Work of Art*, 207.
127. George Pattison, *The later Heidegger*, 99.
128. John Haugeland, *Dasein's Disclosedness*, 28.
129. Martin Heidegger, *Being and Time,* 78. The hyphenated term 'Being-in-the- world' indicates that all these words are not separable from each other. They function as a unitary, organic, structural whole. The Being of *Dasein* cannot be separated from the 'world' in which it exists or it *is*. *Dasein*'s as Being-in-the-world is a unit of the continuous whole of interconnected relationships, which constitutes the structural totality of *Dasein*'s Being. *Ibid*., 78, 252.
130. Hubert Dreyfus and Harrison Hall, *Introduction* to *Heidegger: A Critical Reader*, 3.
131. Martin Heidegger, *On the Essence of Ground*, 121.
132. David Farrel Krell, *The Perfect Future: A Note on Heidegger and Derrida*, in *Deconstruction and Philosophy*, ed. John Sallis, Chicago and London, University of Chicago Press, 1987, 114-16.
133. Josef Früchtl, *Zeit und Erfahrung: Adornos Revision der Revision Heideggers*, in *Martin Heidegger: Innen-und Außenansichten*, eds. Forum für Philosophie Bad Homburg, Suhrkamp, 1989, 307.
134. Jacques Derrida, *Ousia and Grammç: Note on a Note from Being and Time*, 31-67.
135. Josef Früchtl, *Zeit und Erfahrung: Adornos Revision der Revision Heideggers*, 291.
136. Martin Heidegger, *On the Essence of Ground*, 111-12. The world is related to *Dasein* and it belongs to it. In the early Christian writings of John and Paul (e.g. Prologue of John's Gospel, 1.1-10; St. Paul's First letter to the Corinthians and Galatians) presented the world as a mode of Being of *Dasein* itself, the quality of being human itself in contrast to divinity.

137. *Ibid.*, 114, 121.
138. *Ibid.*, 117-18.
139. *Ibid.*, 123.
140. *Ibid.*, 119. Martin Heidegger, *Being and Time*, 101.
141. Christina Lafont, *Heidegger, Language, and World-disclosure*, 30-31.
142. Martin Heidegger, *Being and Time*, 107.
143. Martin Heidegger, *The Origin of the Work of Art*, 167.
144. *Ibid.*, 180.
145. Hubert L. Dreyfus, *Heidegger on the Connection between Nihilism, Art, Technology, and Politics*, 296. Martin Heidegger, *The Origin of the Work of Art*, 167.
146. Martin Heidegger, *The Origin of the Work of Art*, 169.
147. Hubert L. Dreyfus, *Heidegger on the Connection between Nihilism, Art, Technology, and Politics*, 300.
148. *Ibid.*
149. *Ibid.*, 302.
150. Martin Heidegger, *The Origin of the Work of Art*, 171.
151. Hubert L. Dreyfus, *Heidegger on the Connection between Nihilism, Art, Technology, and Politics*, 296.
152. The very notion of earth appeared in Heidegger's later thought. The topic is elaborated for the first time in *The Origin of the Work of Art* (1935-36). In *Introduction to metaphysics* and in *The Origin of the Work of Art* the concept of earth is to be understood in terms of *physis* which is translated as nature; *physis* and nature now understood as *alētheia* itself, i.e. the very process of manifestation which has the character of concealment. In Hans-Georg Gadamer's famous *Introduction* to *The Origin of the Work of Art*, he points out that Hölderlin's poetry provides Heidegger the background for new concept of the earth. Hans-Goerg Gadamer, *Zur Einführung* to *Der Ursprung des Kunstwerkes*, Martin Heidegger, Stuttgart, Philipp Reclam Jun. GmbH & Co., 1960, 99. Johann Christian Friedrich Hölderlin (1770-1843) was a German lyric poet who resolved to solve antagonism of philosophical thought, the distinction between subject and object, by means of the dialectical exposition of poetry. Ref. Peter Fenves, *Hölderlin, Jahann Christian Friedrich*, in *Encyclopaedia of Aesthetics*, Vol. II, ed. Michael Kelly, Oxford, New York, Oxford University Press, 1998, 415.
153. Martin Heidegger, *The Origin of the Work of Art*, 168, 172-73.
154. *Ibid.*, 171.

155. *Ibid.*, 180.
156. Martin Heidegger, *The Thing*, 176.
157. Martin Heidegger, *The Origin of the Work of Art*, 171.
158. See Chapter 1.
159. Joseph J. Kockelmans, *Heidegger on Art and Art Works*, 145.
160. Rodolphe Gasché, *Like the Rose-without why: Transcendentalism and Practical Philosophy*, in *Diacritics*, Fall-Winter (19.3-4) 1989, 106. Ref. Reiner Schürmann, *Heidegger on Being and Acting: from Principles to Anarchy*, trans. Christine-Marie Gros, Bloomington, Indiana University Press, 1987, 130.
161. Martin Heidegger, *The Origin of the Work of Art*, 171.
162. Martin Heidegger and Eugen Fink, *Heraclitus Seminar*, 45.
163. By the term *polemos*, Heraclitus means the Greek meaning of the athletic character of warlike elements, which exists in a collective purpose. In Greek thought, the athletic character preserves and discloses everything that fight together. *Polemos* is the battle which is to be thought as a movement in which gods and men, free and servile, come forth into the shining appearance of their being. Since *polemos* holds together all conflicting elements, their Being itself is an issue. Martin Heidegger, *Elucidations of Hölderlin's Poetry*, 185.
164. Martin Heidegger and Eugen Fink, *Heraclitus Seminar*, 23-24. *Polemos* or strife here means the father and king of all things. It is the ultimate principle of dialectic movement which causes appearance and also relatedness, something that is brought together. See also, Martin Heidegger, *Introduction to Metaphysics*, 64-65.
165. Martin Heidegger, *Elucidations of Hölderlin's Poetry*, 185.
166. Martin Heidegger, *On the Question of Being*, 321.
167. Martin Heidegger, *Introduction to Metaphysics*, 121.
168. *Ibid.*, 64.
169. *Ibid.*, 138.
170. Martin Heidegger and Eugen Fink, *Heraclitus Seminar*, 24. Martin Heidegger, *Introduction to Metaphysics*, 65. William J. Richardson, S.J., *Heidegger: Through Phenomenology to Thought*, New York, Fordham University Press, 2003, 261.
171. Martin Heidegger, *Introduction to Metaphysics*, 135-36. Martin Heidegger, *The Principle of Reason*, trans. Reginald Lilly, Bloomington and Indianapolis, Indiana University Press, 1996, 107.
172. Joseph J. Kockelmans, *Heidegger on Art and Art Works*, 153.
173. Strife is to be understood in the sense of Heraclites' *polemos*. This strife or conflict is the original separation and mutual opposition of all that is, through which beings first obtain separation and opposition.

What is here opposed is gathered into a unity. The unity itself emerges only in the separation in which all is joined in a harmony of opposites. This joining or gathering or collection is the function of *polemos* as *logos*. Artistic *polemos*, the world and the earth, brings things to a stand, gives them status and presence, makes them appear, and thus brings about disclosure, truth, Being.

174. Martin Heidegger, *The Origin of the Work of Art*, 175.
175. *Ibid.*, 173-75.
176. *Ibid.*, 174.
177. *Ibid.*, 175.
178. Aristotle, *Metaphysics*, Gamma VII, 1011b, 107, Gamma, V, xxiv, 1024b, 148-49 and also IX, x, 1051b, 280-81.
179. Martin Heidegger, *On the Essence of Ground*, 103.
180. Martin Heidegger, *The Origin of the Work of Art*, 177.
181. Martin Heidegger and Eugen Fink, *Heraclitus Seminar*, 161-62.
182. Dorothea Frede, *The Question of Being: Heidegger's Project*, 50-53. For Duns Scotus things are intentional objects of acts of comprehension. The meanings of things are based on the general structure of our understanding. Brentano's conception of intentionality describes all phenomena as objects of or contents of different types of acts of consciousness. In other words, an object is grasped by an act of comprehension in consciousness. Husserl also shares this view since he argues that if we want to know the essence of an object, we have to analyse the consciousness itself. It is the human consciousness or Ego that provides to all disciplines with the *a priori* conditions of the cognitions. Dorothea Frede holds the view that in *Being and Time* Heidegger shares Husserlian transcendental subjectivism and the modern anthropocentrism in order to attain the meaning of Being.
183. Martin Heidegger, *Being and Time*, 171.
184. *Ibid.*, 160, 265.
185. *Ibid.*, 117, 175, 264-65, 342-43.
186. *Ibid.*, 120.
187. *Ibid.*, 97.
188. *Ibid.*, 193.
189. Knowing occurs because of the openness of human existence in three temporal dimensions: past, present and future, which hold open the horizons on which entities may manifest themselves in determinative way. The so-called Self or consciousness is subjected to temporal constitution, which is constitutive of human understanding. Thinkers like Derrida, Zimmerman, etc., ascribe the *a priori* nature to the

temporality of human existence. Ref. Michael E. Zimmerman, *Heidegger, Buddhism, and deep ecology*, 243; Jacques Derrida, *Ousia and Grammē: Note on a Note from Being and Time*, 29-68.

190. Hubert Dreyfus, *History of the Being of Equipment*, 180-181. Ref. Martin Heidegger, *Being and Time*, 121.
191. Christina Lafont, *Heidegger, Language and World-disclosure*, xiii.
192. *Ibid.*, 18.
193. Martin Heidegger, *Being and Time*, 32-33, 70. George Pattison, *The later Heidegger*, 35-36.
194. Christina Lafont, *Heidegger, Language, and World-disclosure*, 18-19. See footnote nr. 11.
195. Dorothea Frede, *The Question of Being: Heidegger's Project*, 56.
196. Martin Heidegger, *Being and Time*, 194 footnote 1, 149-68.
197. *Ibid.*, 149.
198. *Ibid.*, 82, 264.
199. George Pattison, *The Later Heidegger*, 11.
200. Dorothea Frede, *The Question of Being: Heidegger's Project*, 64.
201. Martin Heidegger, *Being and Time*, 370-71.
202. George Pattison, *The Later Heidegger*, 9.
203. Martin Heidegger, *On the Essence of Ground*, 123, 125.
204. Martin Heidegger, *Being and Time*, 153, 164.
205. *Ibid.*, 265.
206. Our presuppositions or the fore-structures of the truth of an entity make its total disclosure impossible. There is no full disclosure or closure. For Heidegger the essence of truth is the happening of truth, the self-disclosure of *Dasein* as Being-in-the-world. The truth of *Dasein* is a dialectic process, which is based on its character of transcendence; truth *is* and it *is not*. In each disclosure, truth and untruth or disclosure and concealment inevitably occur together. He does not accept the Greek meaning of truth as unconcealment, but rather finds the 'other' in truth. Truth is undecidable because it is the unconcealment of this concealment, the presence of the 'other' in the presence, a difference at the origin, what he calls the 'more original' origin, or the other beginning of a new philosophical era. Ref. Martin Heidegger, *Introduction to Metaphysics*, 41.
207. Martin Heidegger, *Being and Time*, 372-73.
208. Josef Früchtl, *Zeit und Erfahrung: Adornos Revision der Revision Heideggers*, 291. Martin Heidegger, *Being and Time*, 373.
209. Martin Heidegger, *Being and Time*, 150, 153-54.

210. It can be compared to the concept of alterity and the responsibility for the other in Derrida. He explains the voice of the other in Abraham's mind to sacrifice his son Isaac on the Mount Moriah. Ref. J. Hillis Miller, *Derrida's Others*, 163-64.
211. Martin Heidegger, *Being and Time*, 155-57, 225-74.
212. *Ibid.*, 160-64.
213. Even though *Dasein* is described as nothing, *Dasein*'s *Miteinandersein* is regarded as its positive constitution of its own way of Being. "*The 'they' is an existentiale; and as a primordial phenomenon, it belongs to Dasein's positive constitution.*" *Ibid.*, 167.
214. Carl Friedrich Gethmann, *Heideggers Wahrheitskonzeption*, 118-19.
215. Martin Heidegger, *Being and Time*, 169-224. The expression *in* of Being-*in* derives from *innan (in-an), wohnen*, which means to dwell, to reside. *An* means 'I am familiar with.' The term Being-in is entity, which means I am (*bin*) myself. *Bin* is related to *bei* to mean that I dwell alongside the world. It is the *existentiale* or the existential expression for the Being of *Dasein*. To be-in-the-world means to dwell in the truth of Being, which constitutes the essence of man. *Ibid.*, 79-80. Ref. Günter Figal, *Martin Heidegger-Phänomeology der Freiheit*, Frankfurt am Main, Athenaeum 1988, 78.
216. *Ibid.*, 170-71.
217. Michael E. Zimmerman, *Heidegger, Buddhism, and deep ecology*, 241-43.
218. Martin Heidegger, *Being and Time*, 170-71.
219. Timothy Clark, *Derrida, Heidegger Blanchot*, 26-27. Ref. Rodolphe Gasché, *The Tain of the Mirror*, Cambridge and London, Harvard University Press, 1986, 85.
220. Martin Heidegger, *The Origin of the Work of Art*, 200.
221. Martin Heidegger, *Being and Time*, 178, 206, 208-09.
222. Joseph J. Kockelmans, *Heidegger on Art and Art Works*, 153.
223. Martin Heidegger, *Introduction to Metaphysics*, 219-20.
224. Richard Wolin, *The Politics of Being: The Political Thought of Martin Heidegger*, 44. Wolin even argues that Heidegger feels the need to avoid the *Dasein* because of his failed involvement in Nazi politics and begins to think in still another way on the problem of Being, which is called the later Heidegger. Ref. *ibid.*, 133.
225. Martin Heidegger, *Introduction to Metaphysics*, 174.
226. William J. Richardson, S.J., *Heidegger: Through Phenomenology to Thought*, 266.

227. Huber Dreyfus and Harrison Hall, *Introduction* to *Heidegger: A Critical Reader*, 8.
228. Martin Heidegger, *The Origin of the Work of Art*, 178.
229. *Ibid.*, 184-86, 197.
230. *Ibid.*, 187.
231. *Ibid.*, 181.
232. Martin Heidegger, *Nietzsche* Vol. I and II, trans. David Farrell Krell, San Francisco, Harper and Row 1979-1987, 75. Here Heidegger gives five important points on art and artist: (1) The meaning of art is grounded in the activity of the artist; (2) art manifests will-to-power in the sense that it embodies the artists' will to communicate his vision to the audience; (3) art represents the basic occurrence of beings the sense that the truth of art depends on the world opened; (4) Art is the counter-movement to nihilism; and (5) Art is more important than truth.
233. George Pattison, *The later Heidegger*, 80.
234. Martin Heidegger, *The Origin of the Work of Art*, 152.
235. *Ibid.*, 180.
236. Marrianne Siefert-Gethmann, *Martin Heidegger und die Kunstwissenschaft*, 279.
237. Martin Heidegger, *Plato's Doctrine of Truth*, 182.
238. Martin Heidegger, *Letter on Humanism*, 265.

3

Derrida's Critique of Heidegger's Philosophy of the Work of Art

Derrida's essay *Restitutions*,[1] in *The Truth in Painting*, is concerned with the deconstruction of Heidegger's essay *The Origin of the Work of Art*. Deconstruction is a reading of text in terms of its marks. In *Restitutions,* Derrida deals with the correspondence between Heidegger and Schapiro, and the description of van Gogh's painting in order to raise the question of painting and the problem of restitution.[2] He claims that he finds the irreducible alterity in the essay and speaks of 'undecidability' of truth, which is the aim of his reading of many other philosophical texts too.[3] In the correspondence, Schapiro accused Heidegger of determining one of the paintings of van Gogh; even though Heidegger is well aware of the fact that van Gogh painted such shoes more than once, he described the one of his paintings as a pair of peasant shoes without exactly mentioning the painting that he had in mind.[4] By contrast, analysing the situation and life of the artist, Schapiro attributed the painting, "The Old Shoes with Laces," to the artist himself. Derrida criticises the concept of restitution of the truth of van Gogh's painting. Does a painting correspond with an actual thing which it can be said to refer to? Derrida observes that the shoes in the painting are separated from the subject;[5] therefore, each interpreter can tie the untied laces of the abandoned shoes to himself or to any other subject he wants. In order to deconstruct the essay he criticizes Heidegger's description of the shoe-equipment and argues that the meaning of interpretation reflects self-reference and subjective consciousness. Art is a way in which each interpreter discovers himself within his world. In

Restitutions, he discusses the concept of the origin of truth that manifests itself in the work. He tries to show that even though Heidegger clearly raises the question of the meaning of Being of beings, his essay on the work of art is not devoid of the metaphysical determinations of things. This chapter is Derrida's critical hermeneutics of one of the paintings of van Gogh in the context of Heidegger's essay on the work of art which sets the shoes, these beings, in relation to Being. Origin of truth, for Heidegger and Derrida, is the ambivalence of true and false, something unspeakable and unthinkable. Derrida, however, having accused Heidegger of the determination of the painting, speaks of relativity and undecidability of the meaning of the Being of beings as against the philosophy of identity or logocentrism.

The concept of the restitution of the work of art

Work of art, taken in the sense of metaphysics of presence, manifests the essence or the meaning of beings. Restitution deals with the problem of the determination of the truth or essence of work of art. Derrida uses the French word *rendere* to denote the concept of restitution of the truth of the work of art. The word *rendre* means *to render*, *to give back*, *to restore*, or *to give restitution.*[6] The question in *Restitutions* is to decide to whom and to what do the shoes of van Gogh return?[7] Derrida engages in processes of restitution of the shoes made by Heidegger and Schapiro and examines their consequences in the context of Western aesthetic tradition. Does Heidegger overcome in his essay on the work of art the aesthetics of Western philosophy? According to Derrida, the concept of restitution shows how the onto-theology still operates in Heidegger's work of art. The main concern in Derrida's thought is to deconstruct the meaning and absoluteness, which is the construction of human thought.[8]

In the essay, Heidegger describes the painting of van Gogh in the particular context in which he is explaining the relation between *Thing* and *Work*. It should be remembered that in the essay Heidegger himself opens the discussion of defining the truth of a simple thing in its truth, which is for him an assault upon it. Derrida wants to ignore the context of the essay on work of art in order to expose again some relevant metaphysical questions. In *Restitutions* he shows how truth occurs in Heidegger's description of the shoes, by showing relationship between thing and the truth of the work. *Restitutions* deals with the metaphysical question: Whose shoes are these? In the painting of van Gogh, "The Old Shoes with Laces," the laces of the shoes are untied that open the space of indeterminacy.[9] Does the picture represent the shoes of a peasant woman and that of the artist? In other words, what is the problem in describing a simple thing in terms of its *other*?

The way of the disclosure of the truth has to do with the important motivation of Heidegger's treatise on work of art as well as his entire philosophical investigation. In *Restitutions* Derrida is concerned with these untied shoes in order to show how truth is revealed in traditional metaphysical sense in Heideggger's treatise on van Gogh's painting. The restitutions of the unlaced old shoes disclose the truth as something external to them: in Heidegger's essay the external *other* is a peasant woman and in Schapiro it is the city dweller, namely van Gogh.[10] In both cases the determination of the painting means that it shows itself as what it is in phenomenality in general. When the painting shows itself as something, it reveals itself, true in the sense of correctness.[11] Siefert refers to Kurt Badt to indicate how the determination of the painting deals with the correctness of the communicative function of the work, which is challenged by Heidegger in the essay.[12] The laces of the shoes function like a copula which couples the things to the accidents: they can be tied either to the feet of a peasant or to that of the artist. By determining the painting both Heidegger and Schapiro restitute the truth of the painting to its owner.[13]

Derrida's criticism of the restitution of the truth of the work of art

In the essay, *The Origin of the Work of Art*, Heidegger tries to show how the truth of equipment comes to the fore through the work of art. For that purpose he selects one of the paintings of van Gogh. Having explained the phenomenological structure of the truth of thing, Heidegger describes the van Gogh's painting and thereby brings to life the world of a peasant. His description of the shoes shows us *something* of a given piece of equipment; what it *is* in truth.[14] In this context Derrida criticises Heidegger's handling of the work of art and says Heidegger himself committed the very same error of traditional philosophy, i.e. the determination of thing by the fundamental principle that he wants to avoid in his essay.[15] Loesberg maintains that Derrida's reading of philosophical texts indicates the conflicting necessities that those who try to ground thought and knowledge invite the negation that include within the ground of thought.[16]

Derrida bears in mind that it is Heidegger who brings forward the question of the meaning of Being in order to reach the original, pre-historical realm of beings by overcoming all pre-given, metaphysical determinations. But he criticises Heideger that even though he is well aware of the fact that metaphysical determinations dominate the entire sphere of the history of philosophy, his treatise on the work of art is not free from the same domination. Derrida acknowledges Heidegger's position that the determination of thing on the basis of pre-given truth is the assault upon the meaning of simple thing. This long familiar mode of thought forces a certain preconception on all immediate experiences of beings which makes any serious reflection on the Being of beings impossible. Derrida accepts Heidegger's argument that this conception of the thingness of thing still dominates every theory of art and all aesthetics today, but even including Heidegger.[17]

The recognition of the being of work of art is indeed, according to Derrida, the very act of the restitution of truth of art. The determination of the shoes of van Gogh as peasant's shoes or artist's shoes is in effect the restitution of the truth of art that rests upon some sort of pre-given conceptions or determinations. "To whom and to what do the 'shoes of van Gogh' return in their truth of painting? What is a desire of restitution if it pertains to (*a trait á*) the truth in painting? The opportunity here was given by a sort of duel between Heidegger and Schapiro."[18] Derrida examines the correspondence between Heidegger and Schapiro, and argues that they restitute and determine the truth of the work of art as *something that is* on the ground of the pre-given, subjective projection. He finds the truth of textuality in both Heidegger's and Schapiro's determination of the product in the painting *as* a pair of peasants' shoes or *as* artist's shoes. Every determination of a thing *as* a specific thing, *as something*, comes from a distant, prior context; every text presupposes a pre-text or pre-conditions. "The border between this text (in the usual and supposedly strict sense of a thing printed in a book) and a general textuality (with no absolute edge) here comes away (*s'y enlève*)."[19] In general textuality or in the system of differential relations nothing can be ultimately originated.[20]

In his essay *The Still Life as a Personal Object—A Note on Heidegger and van Gogh*, Schapiro detects the error made by Heidegger in his description of the shoes as peasant shoes. In contrast to Heidegger, Schapiro argues that these shoes, beyond any doubt, belong to van Gogh himself. Derrida follows these different attributions made by the two famous professors and with particular interest analyses the correspondence between them about the issue of the determination of the shoes. Those who tell us the truth of the painting owe us the very truth. "And when both of them say, basically, 'I owe you the truth' (for they both claim to be telling the truth, or even the truth of the truth-in painting and in shoes), they also say: I owe the shoes, I must return them to their rightful owner, to their proper belonging: to the peasant man or woman on the one side, to the city-dwelling painter and signatory of the painting on the other."[21] In Derrida's view, everybody who determines the shoes in the painting tries to own them and thereby owes us the truth of the painting, because its truth is determined by his or her own subjective projections and experiences with the particular objects.

a. *Schapiro's criticism of Heidegger's determination of the painting of van Gogh*

In *The Origin of the work of Art*, Heidegger selects one of the paintings of van Gogh to show the equipmental quality of equipment: "We choose as example a common sort of equipment—a pair of peasant shoes."[22] Schapiro rejects Heidegger's determination of the painting of van Gogh as a pair of peasant shoes. "Professor Heidegger is aware that van Gogh painted such shoes several times, but he does not identify the picture he has in mind, as if the different versions are interchangeable, all presenting the same truth."[23] Since Heidegger did not specify the painting that he described in the essay on the work of art, Schapiro verifies the reference studying van Gogh's pictures of shoes recorded in *De la Faille*. He published the results of his study together with Heidegger's answer to his letter. In his article *The Still Life as a Personal Object—A Note on Heidegger and van Gogh*, Meyer Schapiro denies Heidegger's description of the shoes as peasant shoes. "In reply to my question, Professor Heidegger has kindly written me that the picture to which he referred is one that he saw in a show at Amsterdam in March 1930. This is clearly *de la Faille's* 225."[24] After having verified the catalogue and examined the correspondence with Heidegger about the description of the particular painting, Schapiro writes: "There was also exhibited at the same time a painting with three pairs of shoes (6 no.250), and it is possible that the exposed sole of a shoe in this picture inspired the reference to the sole in the philosopher's account. But from neither of these pictures, nor from any of the others, could one properly say that a painting of shoes by van Gogh expresses the being or essence of peasant woman's shoes and her relation to nature and work. They are the shoes of the artist, by that time a man of the town or city."[25] Schapiro challenges Heidegger's determination of the painting arguing that the concerned painting represents van Gogh's own shoes. Here Schapiro understands Heidegger's essay in a traditional way: art as imitation. There are thinkers who argue that the aim of Heidegger in the essay is not at all the issue of the ownership of the shoes. Pattison, for example, argues that Schapiro's view jeopardizes the value of Heidegger's philosophy of the work of art that overcomes the general understanding of art as imitation and likeness. Pattison maintains that it is not the treatise on the shoes of van Gogh that makes the truth of work of art *qua* work of art, but the conflict of world and earth that he explains also in terms of Greek temple and of disclosure.[26]

Schapiro calls Heidegger's restitution of the shoes a projection.[27] He examines Heidegger's description of the painting and comes to the conclusion that here is a case of self-deception, because in his description everything was first imagined from his own personal experiences and then projected into the picture.[28] Schapiro conducted a thorough inquiry into the details of Heidegger's claim of the painting as peasant shoes and also into the circumstances of van Gogh's life especially during his stay in Paris (1886-1888), where he painted the picture in question. He established with certainty that during the period of his stay in Paris van Gogh had not had any contact with a farmer's or peasant's world; the shoes he painted during this period were not peasant shoes but his own. On this basis Schapiro argues that Heidegger's description of the painting as a pair of peasant shoes can be considered as the results of his own previous experiences with the farmers and fields in Black Forest.[29] However, the shoes in painting do not represent a pair of peasant shoes. Schapiro also points out that the shoes in the picture carry some relevant marks of their ownership; Heidegger overlooked the artist's own signature in the painting and his presence in the work.[30]

b. Derrida's critique of Schapiro's criticism on Heidegger

As far as Derrida's concept of restitution is concerned, Schapiro's criticism of Heidegger's determination of the painting is valid, in so far as Heidegger attributes his own experiences to the shoes in the painting. But Schapiro is not right with regard to his argument concerning the identification of the picture.[31] Derrida says that Schapiro's criticism of Heidegger's description of the painting makes the real problem much simpler than what Heidegger really thereby had committed. He did not give enough attention to the real context of Heidegger's essay. He seems not to have realised that it was Heidegger's intension to go beyond all metaphysical determinations of the thing, the framed picture.[32] Schapiro considers the picture to be a copy, and "ignores an elementary structural law in inferring relations of property in the 'reality' external to the painting."[33] The real problem in Heidegger's essay on work of art is not the determination of painting, but the determination of thing in terms of the *other*.[34] "No doubt he simplified. No doubt he misrecognized the necessity of the argumentation, the lacing movement of its coming and going and the abyss of its *fort:da*. No doubt he ignored its more than philosophical scope."[35] Schapiro does not give attention to the philosophical problems of attribution or determination in the context of ontic-ontological difference. The problem of Heidegger's restitution of the painting from the point of view of his inquiry into the meaning of beings is more far-reaching than what Schapiro considers in his analysis of the painting, regarding the ownership of the shoes.

Derrida's critique of Schapiro's criticism of Heidegger's essay of the work of art is mainly centred on the usage of the word *illustration*: he refutes Schapiro's argument that Heidegger interprets the painting in order "to illustrate the nature of art as the unveiling of truth."[36] Such kind of understanding again is an oversimplification of the matter because here Heidegger deals with the essence of equipment. To facilitate the description or the illustration of truth of equipment he selects a common sort of a product, a pair of peasant shoes.[37] Having explained the domination of equipmentality of equipment that dominates the history of Western philosophy, he selects one of the paintings of van Gogh to overcome encroachments of all kinds of metaphysical determinations.[38] Even though the painting does not contribute to a better visualising of what a piece of product is, Heidegger's illustrative exemplification helps us to understand what the truth of product is.[39] He intends to show it through the intuitive presentation of the picture; even if it does not help anyone for the same he says that 'everybody knows what is proper to shoes:' the serviceability of shoes. Even though the picture does not serve to get better intuitive sensations, Heidegger points out that everybody knows *already* the serviceability of the product, in which its truth resides.[40]

Derrida argues that what we *already* know is something prior to any painting, which is Platonism.[41] He points out that in the example of the shoes Heidegger breaks the distinction between sensuous and spiritual, external and internal; he determines the truth on the basis of a truth *beyond*. Everybody knows the usefulness of shoes before they are painted. For the moment Heidegger leaves the wooden-shoes, he leaves the particular shoe-picture (in terms of its representation to peasant-shoes) and turns his attention to the essence of the product which resides in its usefulness.[42] Heidegger does not mention any reference number to the particular painting of van Gogh because he does not describe the picture to illustrate the nature of art as representation of some particular being. He is concerned only with the being-product of the product that cannot be reduced to any particular determination. His intention was not at all to describe its singularity: he is describing not a picture but the product, shoes.[43] Derrida's critique of Schapiro's criticism of the Heidegger's work of art is based on the fact that Heidegger's intention in dealing with this picture is to overcome all forms of aesthetic determinations.[44] Heidegger is well aware of the consequence of the phenomenological description of the truth of an equipment, which is based on categorical structure that has origin in intuition and self-consciousness. However, Pattison maintains that Heidegger needs to describe the painting in order to go further into the more originary aspect of origin, which is given by the example of Greek temple.[45] In this sense, being based on their own presuppositions and purposes, both Schapiro and Derrida hurry to judge Heidegger's concept of origin.

The truth and the usefulness of shoes in the picture or in canvases and that of the actual product that man wears in the city or in the fields are not the same. The shoe-product in canvas that Heidegger describes by means of a picture is interchangeable; it can be equally applicable to a city man or to a peasant. The description of the shoes after the words "And yet," is not at all a description of the picture. It goes beyond the traces and marks of the particular picture; Schapiro uses this description only to identify the particular picture.[46] Here both Derrida and Schapiro do not recognize what Heidegger means in and through the phenomenological description that begins with 'And yet.' Pattison, having explained Heidegger's view of phenomenological truth that is based on intentionality, i.e. the act of consciousness which is to be explained in Aristotelian-Kantian categories, concludes that Heidegger's description of the shoes does not belong to the truth of traditional categories, but to the new schema which he explains in terms of *earth* and *world*.[47]

Schapiro's criticism of Heidegger and his attribution of the shoes to the artist belong to the traditional understanding of aesthetics of representation, which Heidegger tries to overcome in his essay on the work of art. Derrida distinguishes three basic thoughts in Schapiro's understanding of the shoe-painting: first and foremost, Schapiro believes that the painting can be restituted to a real, identifiable subject. Secondly, the shoes in the painting are shoes which are what they are. According to the theory of adequation they are fit to feet. And finally, feet belong to a body proper which means that the attribution of the shoes in the painting to a particular person is possible only within a particular system of thought. On the basis of these convictions, according to absolute systems of traditional thought, Schapiro detaches the shoes from the feet of one person and again reattaches them to the feet of the artist. All these assumptions are valid in so far as one thinks of the shoe-painting in terms of the philosophy of aesthetics.[48]

The truth of the shoe-picture in Heidegger's description holds the same truth as any other shoe-picture does. In presentation the truth of shoes in painting is the *product* in general. With regard to the attribution of the shoes, Schapiro is mistaken, says Derrida, since Schapiro considers the pictorial function in them; the Heideggerian art, however, as putting to work of truth is not an imitation.[49] Schapiro considers the picture of van Gogh as an art of reproduction which represents the particular truth of being, whereas Heidegger does not. In *Restituions*, Derrida cites a paragraph from Schapiro in order to show how Schapiro contradicts his attribution of the shoes to the artist. Schapiro's reply *nowise* to the question concerning the picture in Heidegger's essay as copy of the real disqualifies his own argument that the shoes are artist's shoes.[50] A thing can be known only in the *usual view*, in which we know it is always *already* in advance. In his effort to break the usual view of understanding thing, Heidegger resorts an oscillating procedure between the painted shoes and the actual shoes worn by the peasant woman. Here Pattison warns the readers of the possibility for the disorientation.[51]

In terms of the implications of his concept of restitution Derrida finds that Schapiro's criticism of Heidegger is equally applicable to his own description of the shoes, in which he attributes them to the artist.[52] The painting does not provide sufficient internal evidences to anyone so that he can attribute it strictly to an external subject. Also external reasons like date, place of the origin of the picture and the verification of catalogue cannot prove that van Gogh could not paint peasant shoes in Paris and that they are clearly the artist's own shoes.[53] In the same manner that Schapiro criticizes Heidegger's determination of the shoes as his projection, Derrida says that Schapiro's attribution of the shoes to the artist in turn can be his projection and hallucination. Derrida criticizes both Heidegger and Schapiro because both of them restitute the truth of the painting as *something*, thus making the point that both belong to the representatives of the philosophy of traditional aesthetics.[54] However, Heidegger's error is regarded as more serious than what Schapiro digs out from his description of the painting as peasant shoes because even though he tries, he fails to overcome the metaphysical determination of the question of the meaning of Being.

Derrida's critique of Heidegger's philosophy of the work of art

The aim of Derrida's reading of different philosophical texts consists in discovering the contradiction in the founding moment of truth. He claims that Heidegger's essay is an example of the 'usual view' of work of art and objects, the perception of entities on the basis of subjective reflection. The perception in this sense is the pure act of mind like, as Loesberg puts it, "Husserlian transcendental acts of pure perception in the absence of outside objects perceived." The truth of empirical perception is grounded upon "the moment of pure reflection within a subject's unmediated consciousness."[55] In his essay on Restitution Derrida mentions truth of the re-establishment of the proper subject of the work of art. He accuses Heidegger of the subjective interpretation of the meaning of the painting by tying the laces of the abandoned shoes that have no structure of relationship with any external subjects to peasant women. In order to describe the undecidability of origin of truth Derrida mentions the truth of many origins. After the subject of the shoes has been announced by Heidegger, one of the other subjects of the shoes i.e. van Gogh, whose signature is still there on the shoes, began to return and question the truth of Heidegger's restitution.[56] The process of the restitution of the truth of the work of art announces different origins, because it deals with the determination of 'mere' thing (in Derrida's term 'detached shoes') on the basis of lived experience or intentionality. In *The later Heidegger*, Pattison describes, referring to Heidegger's concept of perception of thing and intentionality, how a *mere* thing is perceived *as* something that it is from out of our lived out experiences.[57] Derrida observes that van Gogh's shoes in the picture are abandoned, unlaced and are detached from the feet of their subject; the possibility for attributions arises out of the state of detachment. "...the problem of the origin of the work of art might well pass through these lace holes, through the eyelets in the shoes (in painting) by van Gogh."[58] The origin of the work of art can be in this instance compared to the eyelets of the shoes, through which everybody—Heidegger, Schapiro or any one—who wishes to interpret the shoes, can let the lace pass through them in order to tie the shoes to a particular subject. By attaching the abandoned shoes to the feet of a peasant woman or to the artist, the truth of restitution, thus provides answer to the unresolved problem of the origin of the truth of the work of art. Derrida's aim in deconstructing each philosophical text is to question the purity of foundation of the truth; there is incoherence within the grounding moment of truth.[59] Both Heidegger and Derrida argue that a thing that is understood in traditional point of view is to be detached from the 'thingly' character.

Heidegger's essay on the work of art is very important with regard to his question of the meaning of Being. But in the essay, as Derrida reads, there occurred the aesthetic determination of thing, the very element that he wants to avoid. Derrida holds the view that the product-being of the product in Heidegger's essay is determined by its usefulness.[60] Derrida considers the interpretative mode of Being of the product *shoes* in picture in terms of the truth of their usefulness as an error on the part of Heidegger insofar as he makes an effort to critically analyse the entire system of determinations which in the tradition one has superimposed on the thing.[61]

a. *Heidegger's description of the shoes and the truth of product*

In the essay, *The Origin of the Work of Art,* Heidegger explains the traditional concepts of thing, equipment and that of the work in order to overcome the aesthetic determination of the meaning of Being. At the very beginning he describes three modes of interpretations of thing, that shackle the true reflection on the Being of any given being.[62] From these prevailing thing-concepts he moves towards the equipmental character of equipment. He asks himself about the relationship between thing and work. In order to make clear the relationship between them Heidegger selects as an example a common sort of equipment, a pair of peasant shoes.[63] The peasant-shoes are things that we can encounter and experience them in our everyday life. At the same time they are not mere things, they are made by human beings, an example of a piece of equipment. The example of a pair of peasant shoes serves to illustrate Heidegger's discussion of equipment and further the equipmentality of equipment which resides in its serviceability and reliability. These peasant shoes serve a peasant woman, whom Heidegger goes on to describe them in some details. He describes the shoes in relation to the serviceability, to the context in which they are worn. Even though the worn out condition of the shoes does not provide enough resources for any precise description, he writes: "From the dark opening.... This equipment belongs to the earth, and it is protected in the world of the peasant woman. From out of this protected belonging the equipment itself rises to its resting-within-itself."[64] The shoes are what they are only in the world of the peasant; they are protected in it. Heidegger speaks of two different aspects of the truth: 'protected-belonging,' i.e. the truth of shoe-equipment belongs to the realm of the concealment (earth) and at the same time they are what they are in revealment (world). In the shoes there is the silent vibration of the 'call of the earth,' the meaning of the equipment arises out of itself. It *gives* itself out of itself. The things are 'what they are' only in truth, out of which they come to be *as* something. In the example of the painting there is a coming of the *other* into the simple thing. Heidegger's ontological difference denotes the structure of appearance, how something comes to be. It has the meaning of 'step-back,' the meaning of the equipment comes to the fore out of itself and shows itself in the world of the peasant woman. Here the origin of truth takes place as an originary leap into the presence in which the truth of the thing present is a gathering-together: fort-da, which is not reducible to an objective truth. Pattison opines that the description of painting and the Greek temple, etc. are to be taken as examples to show the thingly element in them. For Heidegger, work of art is a thing and the particular description provides the thingly aspect of art.[65]

Unlike Pattison, Derrida finds in Heidegger's description of shoes a suitable opportunity to deconstruct the essay. Derrida criticises Heidegger's description of the shoes more severely than that of Schapiro's description. Schapiro's argument and determination of the painting are based on the law of representation and adequation, whereas Heidegger's description of the painting reveals more originary nature of truth in painting, the unveiling or revealment of truth. Both Schapiro and Heidegger speak of the picture in accordance with some law: Schapiro in accord with the theory of adequation and Heidegger the truth as revealment.[66] The following is Derrida's criticism of Heidegger's description of the shoes.

i. The usefulness of the product: subjective projection

In his essay on the work of art Heidegger states that the product-being of product consists in its usefulness. The peasant woman uses the shoes in the fields. She may not think of these shoes, or even feel them. She stands and walks in the shoes. This is how the shoes are of service. Through the process of using the product the essence or what the product in truth is, is bound to come to meet us.[67] Derrida draws a distinction between the usefulness of a real product and the usefulness of a product in the picture. The truth of the usefulness of the product in a picture is primarily that of subjective projection.

Even though the truth of equipment consists in its usefulness, the understanding of the usefulness of shoes in a picture is a different matter. In the picture one has to project the meaning of the usefulness of the shoes in order to describe what a woman supposes to do with her shoes. "But perhaps it is only in the picture that we notice all this about the shoes. The peasant woman, on the other hand, simply wears them."[68] Heidegger distinguishes well the usefulness of simple equipment (shoes that a woman wears) and the usefulness of the shoes in a picture. According to Siefert, the source or origin of the interpretation of the painting is based on the subjective experience of the interpreter. In the essay the meaningful aspect of the work is revealed through the description, which is the self-projection, the source of the truth of painting.[69]

The traits in the picture detach the object from its real milieu.[70] Being detached from their actual context, the product-being of the shoes in the picture cannot be determined in terms of their actual usefulness. Heidegger's descriptions of the shoes in the picture are not the actual usefulness of the shoes, but the truth or being of the usefulness of the shoes. Referring to Heidegger's description of the use of shoes in picture, Derrida opines that the truth of the usefulness in painting and the truth of the product are not one and the same. In a painting the truth of the usefulness of the product is transformed from its actual field to a painter's canvas. The truth of the usefulness of a product (being of beings) in painting is interchangeable. In painting the usefulness of the product and its truth are displaced and misplaced.[71]

The product-being of the product, the description of the shoes in the picture is evocative and deliberate. The truth of the usefulness of the product in the picture originates from subjective experience. The meaning of the work of art is intimately related to the personal experience of the beings that revealed what they are in the world, in a particular culture and practice. Heidegger's interpretation of the shoes originates from his experience and therefore, his description of the shoes is only an evocative thought rather than the representational or the reproductive nature of the work of art.[72] Derrida too is at this moment liable to the same criticism, because he makes all these arguments from his own personal resources. Pattison maintains that one cannot accuse Heidegger's essay of the truth of representation, because he wants to describe van Gogh's shoes in order to give a general view of art as representation before going deeper into the critical realm of artistic value, which is given in terms the truth of Greek temple.[73] Therefore, he feels the need to describe the truth of representation, which he does not accept as the origin of truth. However, Pattison upholds the fact that the truth of work of art in Heidegger also represents his political views, even though he considers the National Socialism as one of the technological products of the time like: Communism in Russia or Americanism.[74]

Heidegger, who is well aware of the indeterminate character of the painting, declares that the painting is useless for any research.[75] In this context Derrida criticises Heidegger for describing the un-laced shoes after the word 'And yet.' "In this phase of the argumentation, Heidegger puts the emphasis on the un-; the un-laced, the unstrictured, detachment, abstraction. Later, the process of reattachment, the always already begun restricturation will come, after the 'And yet,' to put this double uselessness to work, to make use and surplus value of it in a certain way."[76] After the term 'And yet' he describes a new paragraph out of his subjective imagination and then he says: "But perhaps we see all this only on shoes in picture."[77] Derrida makes use of these two words, *And yet* and *perhaps*, to denote Heidegger's deliberate intention to go beyond the particular picture; the shoes are determined in terms of traditional metaphysics. Like the frame of inside-outside formed by the movement of the laces of the shoes, his description binds his experiences and imaginations together with the object, shoes. Heidegger's description is not limited to van Gogh's picture; it goes beyond its frame and ends up in the sphere of subjective projection. What he describes as the usefulness of the shoes in the picture after the words "And yet," is to be considered as the uselessness of the useless shoes in the picture, because what he describes comes originally from his imagination and projection, and this surplus value is not the truth of the undeterminable shoes of van Gogh. Derrida calls this particular approach of Heidegger to the picture as symptomatic contradiction. For Heidegger says, even if the picture is useless, that it is a pair of peasant shoes and describes the peasant world. Thus he provides these shoes in the picture with external values based on the general principle of usefulness, loaded them and laced them around the peasant's life.[78]

ii. The reliability and the truth of product

In the essay Heidegger describes still another factor of surplus value, reliability, which goes beyond usefulness of a thing constituting an even more fundamental basis for the truth of a product.[79] Reliability involves our experience with things that provides us with fidelity to restitute things faithfully, in this case, the shoes. The reliability of the product or fidelity predates every system of thought and as it belongs to world and earth, it gives foundation or stability to the world. The silent call of the earth of the product is heard and understood in the description of the shoes. Derrida examines the French translation of *reliability* of shoes to explain how it gives security to the world of a peasant and freedom to the earth. "...thanks to the solidity of the product, she is soldered to her world (*ist sie ihrer Welt gewiss*). For her, and for those who are with her like her, world and earth are only there in this way: in the product...for it is only the solidity of the product which gives to this so simple world a stability all its own, in not opposing the permanent flow of the earth."[80] Here the term reliability is translated as solidity by means of which the peasant woman is soldered to her world. The reliability of the shoes gives solidity or protection to the world of the peasant woman. It is the soil or solid *ground* which makes every description of shoes possible; it is the solidity of a product.[81] It is on account of reliability or solidity that the usefulness resides in the shoes. Since reliability is prior to any concept of usefulness or determination of product, it can be considered as the ultimate condition for the possibility of any reattachment. It is the ground for attribution, for the coming-to-pass of truth. It is the condition for the possibility of the reattachment of a product to its usefulness, to its subject. The concept of reattachment is ultimately related to the reliability, to the preoriginary gift. Reliability is not only prior to all theories of matter-form, of usefulness, of production, of subjectivity, of objectivity, of symbol, and law, etc., but it also causes a regression into the simple trust.[82] Reliability is acquired, it has the quality of *had*: we have already learnt from others about what a product is, or we have experienced it. We have confidence in the usefulness of a product because of the reliability. Heidegger's descriptions of shoes and peasant world reveal his subjective projections based on the principles of reliability. It is a contradiction to the main stream of the thought of Heidegger's essay. Derrida observes that Heidegger questions the fundamental principle that provides stability to the traditional concepts by indicating the combat between world and earth.[83]

b. *The origin of truth as the surplus value*

Derrida bears in mind that Heidegger analyses the modes of Being of things to show how the metaphysical determinations become an assault upon mere things all through the history of philosophy till today. Van Gogh's shoe-painting manifests how equipment, the formed-matter, has its origin in its truth, in terms of usefulness and reliability. In his description of the shoe-picture Derrida mentions the combination of different modes of things in shoes. Heidegger's description of the shoe-picture is in fact the determination of truth of a thing on the basis of higher value, which is beyond the thing itself.[84] Derrida criticizes Heidegger's description and determination of the painting because he fails to keep the distinction between beings and Being, which is the very purpose of the essay itself.[85] Thinkers like Kockelmans and Pattison, etc. defend Heidegger's position saying that in the essay he is well aware of the determination of mere things on the basis of the *other*, the external values. For them, it is very evident at the very beginning of the essay, as Heidegger asks of the essence of the work of art, he says work is not a mere thing, but a bearer of meaning functioning as an allegory, which manifests the something other.[86] Pattison argues that one cannot have an adequate understanding of the truth of art, unless at first the three dimensions of thing that have dominated in Western metaphysics are explained.[87] Heidegger's description of the painting denotes the thingly dimension of the work of art; from there he begins to explain the truth of work of art as never ending conflict between concealment and unconcealment.

Indeed the useless, abandoned, and unlaced shoes in the painting are undeterminable. The interpretation of the abandoned, useless shoes is a mistake on the part of Heidegger, because he interprets the undeterminable *things*, shoes, on the basis of its serviceability. The determination of pure thing *as* something constitutes the core of the philosophical inquiry into the meaning of Being by way of substraction. The interpretation of a thing in terms of matter and form takes place in the context of traditional metaphysics, e.g. medieval or Kant's transcendental philosophy.[88] Heidegger calls such kind of superimposition of matter-form, which aggressively falls upon thing, an assault.[89] Derrida mentions that at the very moment Heidegger turns towards the picture he is interested in the truth of the product. Heidegger's description of the shoes manifests the presence of a peasant woman, the truth in the painting, the shoes *as* something. The interpretation of thing as *something* by means of serviceability or informed-matter is still prevalent today.[90]

The irreducible structure of the truth of product

Derrida criticizes Heidegger's task to determine the undeterminable shoes by weaving together different moments of truth. The undetermined painting being determined says something to us. The shoes in painting are a discourse on painting.[91] In other words, the origin of the painting is the truth itself, i.e. the shoes or more clearly a pair of peasant shoes that comes-to-the-fore and resides in the painting. Here Derrida indicates how Heidegger violates his own argument on the unpresentable origin of truth. Derrida uses Heidegger's weapon to attack him by exposing the force of withdrawal in his essay, which obliterates of objective value of the discourse on shoes. The laces of the shoes that bind together many lyers of truth, the *other*, constitute a meaningful discourse of the undeterminable painting, and thereby, reduce the irreducible character of the structure of truth of the painting by determining the *Da* of *Sein* of the shoes, the truth in painting. In order to expose the undecidability of the truth in painting, Derrida discusses the logic of the laces of the shoes, the determination of the *Da* of *Sein* and the truth of the painting.

The differential structure of truth of the painting: the logic of the laces

The restitution process ties the laces of the shoes to the feet of the definite person and thereby provides a peculiar form and meaning to the abandoned shoes. The identity of the subject of the shoes remains outside the painting: in the field, the peasant women or in the city, the artist. The work (*ergon*) marks an otherness on the shoes through the peculiar movement of laces and the structure of the in-formed shoes are called *parergon*.[92] It means what remains outside the work. Derrida argues that with the determination of a subject of the work in Heidegger it acquires the self-sufficient presence, by way of gathering together of what remains the *outside of the work*. The inside-outside relationship of the shoe-product is *parergonal* in fashion; since its outside is assigned in the inside, it has the structure of irreducibility. He makes use of an example of a cobbler, who makes shoes out of different materials, to show how Heidegger ties together different modes of thing in his interpretation of the picture.[93] The lacing movement of the shoes that binds together various elements of shoes—simple thing, usefulness and reliability—constitutes a definite form to the irreducible structure of the shoes. It denotes again the origin of truth of the painting in its surplus values.[94] The laces of the shoes tie together the *other*, what is not there. The truth of the in-formed shoes is marginal to work. In order to identify what is proper to work, one has to search it outside of the work. The truth of work of art is irreducible. However, Pattison does not accept Derrida's criticism that Heidegger's concept of the truth of the work violates the irreducibility of the ontological difference, because his concept of truth does not provide the world with mathematical precision.[95]

The truth of the shoe-product is constituted by the interlacing function, binding the inside to its outside, adding the *other* to its inside. Derrida compares the shoes in the picture to a blank check, which offers possibilities to people to own or to wear them by putting their name and signature upon it. The blank check welcomes others into it, makes it possible for others to possess it. Likewise, the detached, undetermined shoes allow Heidegger and Schapiro to be owned by them; the shoes are owned by the *other*. Originally the shoes are undeterminable, beyond any determination; it is this detachment or undecidable character of simple thing that allows both professors to determine the painting. In his essay, Derrida calls the determination of undeterminables (simple thing) re-mark or over-mark.[96] Determination of the painting entails re-mark, the irreducible process of opening-closing relation to the *other*, i.e. the meaning of withdrawal in the sense that the painting attains its meaning in reference to the *other*, the peasant woman. Re-mark opens and at the same time closes the meaning of the painting. Derrida mentions the artist's signature upon the picture, which has the meaning of re-mark: the meaning of the painting does not rest in itself, but its origin is something outside of it, i.e. the person who signed the picture. For him the object of the representation (in this case the peasant woman or the artist) renders the value of literary text, i.e. their objective appearance is to be understood as withdrawal. In his essay on *Force and Signification*, he explains that in a text a thing is determined by the force of its own effacement.[97] The so-called origin is to be grasped as the non-origin, which is made clear in the textual character of the truth of shoe-painting: the laces pass through the eyelets and bring the *other* together.

The function of the laces, which constitutes the essence of the shoes, represents the logic of *différance* which holds together the outside-inside, not by eliminating (*sublating*) oppositions and differences. Derrida calls the traditional philosophical terminology and logic the logic of cut because they define things by eliminating ontic-ontological differences. Derrida's deconstructive thought keeps together the different forces in a particular way so that a thing cannot be determined in terms of pure presence. The determination of the subject of the shoes, however, can be explained in accordance with the underlying principle of the traditional philosophy, which overpowers and controls the truth of a thing. In Heidegger's interpretation, says Derrida, the unlaced, detached shoes have (an out-going) representative mission.[98] They are not simple things, but they stand for something else. The shoes with the subject, to whom the laces tie them together, are the truth in painting: "We, the shoes, are bigger than the frame and the incorporated signature. The picture is in the shoes that we are."[99] Determination of anything entails its *other*, in the sense of the unity between sensible and intelligible in Kantian thought. The description of the shoes in the picture is formed by the traits of laces which overflow the frame of the painting and consequently they cause the frame of the work to explode, since the thing determined cannot remain in itself. In Heidegger's description, the shoes are bound together with their origin that is marginal to them. For Derrida, any discourse on the picture belongs to the fact of this surplus value, which is formed by the play of traits and laces, goes beyond its frame.[100] The very origin of the shoe-product stems out from the surplus values of the shoes which are found beyond the frame of the picture. It constitutes the ambivalence of the truth in painting. Timothy Clark argues that Derrida follows the meaning of the Heideggerian poetry to develop the complex nature of text, in which everything can be in its effacement. In this instance the shoe-product can be what it is, only by denying itself in the complexity of textuality.[101] Even if in Heidegger there is no place for the meaning of representation, Derrida accuses him of the truth of representation in his treatise on the painting. Derrida attacks him with his own argument and at the same time upholds the same Heideggerian position, i.e. the irreducible difference at the origin.

a. *The* Da-Sein *of the painting in Heidegger's restitution*

In Heidegger's essay on the work of art the truth of van Gogh's painting is manifested in the revealing of truth itself. In his words, 'the painting has spoken'[102] in the sense that its truth is revealed in the nearness of the work. In his thought the value of proximity plays a decisive role for the understanding of the truth of product. Derrida looks through the implications of Heidegger's concept of proximity and says that *near* or proximity in Heidegger does not simply mean distance or far way; it is to be rather understood both in ontic and ontological senses; proximity of work means its truth as '*Da* of *Sein*.'[103] In the determination of the painting, a thing is defined in terms of its *other*, in other words, the ontic is determined by ontological factor that undermines Heidegger's purpose in *Being and Time* as well as in the essay.

The truth in painting is related to the concept of nearness of the work. The concept *nearness* or *proximity* of the work reveals the meaning of the painting as the truth of a 'text,' as difference, since it is defined and determined by the *other*. The truth in painting is constituted by the differential movements of the laces of the shoes which inscribe the inside with outside reality (peasant woman or artist) and thus constitute a textual meaning to the shoes. A text presupposes pre-texts. In contrast to the traditional concept of the text, which has a unity and coherence of truth, Derrida argues difference and cleft that divide the unity or centre of it.[104] In the restitutions by both Heidegger and Schapiro something external to the shoes constitutes their truth: the truth of beings, the truth of these shoes that comes back from the fields or from the city, and resides in shoes in painting and the presence of this external truth in the painting constitutes the *Da* of *Sein* of the shoes as something that what is, which is an issue for its objective value.[105] Derrida advocates the indeterminacy of text, by explaining the many origins of the painting: a peasant woman as well as the artist. The subject of the shoes differs and distances itself from the painting; the pre-textual structures of the painting make it impossible to get closer to the determined meaning of the shoes.[106] Heidegger's description of the shoes simplified the philosophical implication of "...the lacing movement of its coming and going and the abyss of its *fort:da*."[107] *Fort-da* is the *belonging togetherness* of Being and beings, the truth of ontological difference. Here the laces of the shoes that bring together various levels of truth mean, then, the meaningful discourse of the shoes by laying of the different elements side by side according to some sort of pattern. It is this *belonging togetherness*, this side by side character of the many-layered structure of truth that gives rise to the sense of *physis* and logos.[108] If Heidegger's description deals with a 'pair-shoes,' with the question of the *belonging togetherness* of the two shoes, his concept of the *belonging togetherness* of Being and beings should also be questioned. Because, as Silverman thinks, in the example of peasant-shoes Heidegger is working on the relation of beings to Being: "The van Gogh painting is an example of 'what is there' *(Da)*, a being, the what is, the 'that' which is present, namely, *Da*—here or there (*Da/Fort—Fort/Da*)."[109] *Fort-Da* denotes a relation that belongs together: beings are given in relation to Being. Heidegger calls this relation the ontological difference. Derrida opines that if in Heidegger's description of the painting the shoes is revealed as something, he "was committing himself heavily,"[110] because he is thereby falling back to the line traditional metaphysics, which he wants to overcome.

Since the essence of *Da-Sein* of the shoes involves the *other*, any arbitrary determination of its truth *as* something is regarded as a contradiction.[111] The pictorial text, which is formed by the peculiar movement of laces by inside-outside relationships, implies Heidegger's whole discourse on *fort-da*. The truth of the painting can be called *fort-da*, namely the shoes of somebody (peasant woman or city man). Here the relavent questions such as, where do the shoes start from and to whom do they return, belong to the context of traditional metaphysics. But the truth of *Dasein*, which is the very essence of the shoes in painting, involves the notion of external subject, the *other* and therefore, any effort to restitute the shoes in painting is a violation to the question of meaning of beings. "And the whole path of thought, for Heidegger, leads back, by a dis-stancing, to a *Da* (thus the *Da* of *Sein*) which is not merely close, but whose proximity lets the distance of the *fort* play within it.

The relation is not one of opposition; each notion offers an eyelet to be traversed by the other, to the figure or the size (*pointure*) of the other. *Fort:Da.*"[112] The truth of *there-being* or *da-fort* of shoes in painting originates from the necessity of speculating on *other*, lacing across the line of both directions: ontic and ontological, inside, outside. Even though Heidegger argues that such kind of bringing-together causes the forgetfulness of the meaning of beings, he falls back, as Derrida evaluates, to the same pit fall. By developing the difference at the origin of the shoes, Derrida argues for meaning of withdrawal and irreducibility of the meaning of beings, something that Heidegger stands for.[113]

b. *Truth in Heidegger's philosophy of the work of art*

According to Heidegger's philosophy of art, the product-being of the shoes is found not in a description or an observation of the use of shoes, but by placing ourselves in front of van Gogh's painting.[114] In revealment the work of art has given us to know *what* the pair of shoes is in truth. In his philosophy of art, the truth of equipment and that of the work are mutually related. More concretely, by means of the work by van Gogh, one can understand the product-being of product. The work tells us what the shoe-product in truth is. The essay on work of art makes it clear that the particular work of van Gogh does not serve us to understand what the product is in truth, but its pictorial presentation helps us for the same, because it is only through the work and only in the work that the truth of the product comes-to-pass (comes to its appearing). "What is at work in the work? Van Gogh's painting is the disclosure of what the equipment, the pair of peasant shoes, is in truth."[115] The painting of van Gogh discloses what the product is in truth. In painting being comes (in van Gogh's painting beings mean the shoes) into non-concealment in its Being. The Greeks called it *alētheia*.[116]

Derrida criticises the above-mentioned Heidegger's philosophy of art as worse than the subjective projection. In fact Heidegger selects the picture as an example for the truth of product, which does not relate to a particular person or a particular thing, but it pertains to an object in general.[117] If the painting speaks, if it reveals something *as*, it is no more an example, but the truth of the product, i.e., "some particular pair of shoes sequenced into their determination as peasant's shoes."[118] Even though Heidegger selects one of van Gogh's pictures as an example of a common sort of product, he suddenly determines it as a pair of peasant-shoes.[119] In his treatise on work of art, the painting is the revealing of what equipment is in truth, a pair of peasant shoes.[120] Derrida says that it would be worse if the truth in painting were peasanthood of shoes, and not merely their product-being.[121] The disclosure of the painting as a pair of peasant shoes is the truth of the Being of beings. In Heidegger's treatise on van Gogh's painting the truth of the Being of being is very ostentatious, namely the revealment of the truth of product as the shoes and further as a pair of peasant shoes. "It is indeed *this* pair in this painting which opens to the truth of the being-product. But which opens to it in its unveiled-unveiling presence, letting itself be traversed."[122] By determining the truth of product as a pair of peasant shoes, Heidegger lets the painting be traversed through the history of metaphysics. His description sets the shoes, these beings, in relation to Being. Derrida criticizes that *this* being-product (the presence of peasanthood), is the concept of non-revealment or truth in Heidegger's essay on the work of art.

The artist sets his subjective projection, 'truth,' in work. Van Gogh says, "When I say that I am a painter of peasants, it is indeed truly so and will get a better idea from what follows that it is there I feel in my element." And as far as the subjectivity of van Gogh is concerned, "Peasant and *artisanal* 'ideology' in painting, concern for truth in painting..."[123] At the very outset of the essay *Restitutions*, Derrida cites van Gogh's declaration that in painting he is a cobbler.[124] By the selection of the picture, motivated by his own subjective projection, Heidegger finds the cobbler van Gogh in it. The truth of art is constituted by subjective projections. On the one hand Heidegger realizes the presence of a peasant woman in the shoes, but on the other hand, Schapiro sees in them the presence of van Gogh. Schapiro, the man from great city, sees the presence of the artist in the painting. "No more detachment: the shoes are no longer attached-to-Van-Gogh, they *are* Vincent himself, who is undetachable from himself. They do not even figure one of his parts but his whole presence gathered, pulled tight, contracted into itself, with itself, in proximity with itself: a *parousia*."[125] The painted shoes not only are real but equal to be the person, peasant woman or van Gogh. The shoes are van Gogh's self-portrait. His face is hiding in the painting; the old leather is his old, wrinkled skin, which bears the marks of his weariness and experiences. The presence of the subject of the work is so near to the work that it never can be detached. These shoes are inseparable from the body, from the whole person.[126] The proximity or nearness of the work reveals the presence of *other* in picture. According to Heidegger, the proximity or nearness of the work reveals its truth *as* something, as a pair of peasant woman, whereas in Schapiro's restitution it is revealed *as* the artist himself. The truth of the shoes *as* something is the determination of the *Da* of shoe's *Sein*.

Heidegger mentions the picture by van Gogh in order to ask the question: what is the being of the existent? Wherein does the Being of existent consist, which enables us to say that the existent *is*? He speaks of this picture as "one of the examples of what *is there* (*da*), of the existent, of what *is present*, hence *there* (*da*)."[127] Van Gogh's painting is an example of 'what is there;' the *Da* of a being means what *is*, that which *is* present in presencing (*Da-fort*). The Being of the existent is not existent, it is nothingness. In order to understand the Being of existent, one has to think or experience the non-existent or nothingness. The Being of existent comprises both presence and absence; nothingness is there without being there. The shoes are there, there are two painted shoes: *es gibt*.[128] The determination of the undetermined shoes in the picture as a pair of peasant shoes, and all other descriptions revealing the presence of something are considered as an error in Heidegger's essay, in his endeavour concerning the question of the meaning of Being. By exposing the element of truth in Heidegger's work of art, Derrida argues that he could not overcome the very problem that he grappled with in his essay on the work of art. However, Pattison holds the view that the truth that is revealed in the description of the painting shall not be taken as a concrete, particular fact with mathematical precision, but it is the opening up of the public, the world of the people, in which entities are what they *are*. The essence of art consists in the opening up of the world, in and through which entities come to be. He argues that the world opened up in the description of the painting does not have the truth of beings or particular peasant, but it reveals the world of peasant by bringing the hidden truth into the fore. The truth revealed in work of art does not have the meaning of truth as correctness since concealment too is the integral part of it.[129] The origin of the work of art deals with Heidegger's concept of originary strife between world and earth: truth is untruth in the sense that it is concealed-revealment.

Restitutions: Derrida's concept of undecidability

Derrida begins his essay *Restitutions* with Cezanne's[130] declaration of the debt of the truth in painting: "I owe you the truth in painting, and I will tell it to you."[131] By making use of different objects, colours and canvas he renders the truth in painting and shows us something other than the materials and objects that he used up. What he uses in painting to produce a work of art are only some kind of materials, but what we perceive in his work of art is not only materials, but also some theoretical truth of beings; we perceive the truth of the Being of beings in his work of art. Therefore he tells us that he owes us the truth in painting.[132] To return to van Gogh, he restores the essence of the shoes by rendering them in a particular way in his painting. Heidegger takes away that essence by attributing the shoes to a peasant woman. Schapiro does owe us the same in restitution. Derrida says that both Heidegger and Schapiro, who determine the painting of van Gogh as something, owe us the truth. By restituting the truth of the painting, they put the shoes of van Gogh on their own feet;[133] they take possession of them by defining them according to their own subjective experiences. Like Cezanne both Heidegger and Schapiro ought to tell us that they owe us the truth in painting.

Even though Heidegger observes that the picture itself is of no use he describes the shoes, speculating on their usefulness and thus making two shoes in the picture *a pair*. Derrida finds that both Heidegger and Schapiro "bound them together in order to bind them to the law of normal usage."[134] The concept of *pair* denotes Heidegger's concept of ontic-ontological difference, which is also regarded as *relationship* or *belonging togetherness* of Being to beings. It gives an answer to the origin of the work of art as the truth in *shoe* sizes, as the shoes of a peasant or of the artist. In painting truth discloses itself as truth in *shoe* sizes: a pair of shoes of a peasant woman or that of the artist, and it can happen only in the work, in art.

The indefinite space of the shoes, the uncertainty of to what they belong, provides the process of restitution with the possible reference to many worlds. The same shoes in painting open up different worlds at the same time, the world of a peasant woman and that of the city man. The world of a peasant is substituted by the world of the artist; the location of the product has been changed from field to city. The worlds and the equipmentality can be changed, but the thing remains the same. However, van Gogh's shoes cannot be the same as the peasant woman's shoes. "How can the truth of a work which discloses a world be the same truth if it discloses something different?"[135] Derrida's philosophy of deconstruction suggests that the shoes in painting are undecidables. Being extracted from their actual fields and set into the canvas, the shoes have an uncertainty of the contexts; there is an indefinite space. There is nothing to which they could belong. There is no centrality or fixed origin out of which the shoes emerge; the interchangeability of worlds, from peasant world to artist world suggests the character of origin of the work of art. The two worlds that are interchanged denote the very worlds of Heidegger and Schapiro. They possess the shoes and tell us the truth of the shoes which is that they are the truth of the painting. In order to mention the underlying substantial meaning of the work, Siefert refers to Panofsky who identifies it with the truth of the culture and the tradition of the people.[136]

The *belonging togetherness* of the shoes and their subject raises the question of meaning of Being of beings. The relationship of beings to the truth of their Being does not yield the judgement upon them. The same shoes in the painting reveal different worlds, contexts and objects. The same shoes in the painting can be tied to the feet of different people.[137] The world of a peasant woman can be substituted by the artist's world. In restitutions, the world has changed; the context of peasant woman is substituted by the context of the city; the same shoes are revealed as different objects, as man's shoes and as woman's shoes. The undetermined shoes do not let anyone to do justice to their truth. Question concerning what is proper to the work of art, its origin, its relationship to the artist and art, etc. are the metaphysical quest for the meaning of Being of beings. Derrida's *Restitutions* show not only how Heidegger belongs to the group of traditional philosophers with his effort to do justice to the truth of the shoes in the painting but also suggest the impossibility of doing justice to the truth of shoes in painting. Heidegger interprets van Gogh's shoes in relation to the equipmentality of actual shoes of a peasant and thereby brings about the truth of Being of beings. Derrida criticizes Heidegger's interpretation of the shoes as an error that happened in the context of his philosophical endeavour to overcome traditional aesthetics. His rigorous reading of Heidegger's essay is to be criticized since he does it from the standpoint of another presupposition. Culler, Norris and Gasché consider Derrida as a rigorous transcendental philosopher. 'From the dark opening' of the shoes Heidegger observes a hidden subject, the truth based on a hidden, distant realm. Derrida too reads Heidegger's essay and evaluates it from the dark *opening* of the shoes. Norris says that he is to be treated as a transcendental philosopher in the Kantian tradition because he digs out presuppositions in Heidegger's essay.[138]

References

1. Derrida first published his essay on the exchange between Heidegger and Meyer Schapiro in the art journal *Macula*, no. 3 with the title *Martin Heidegger and the shoes of Van Gogh*. The expanded version of this essay was republished in the book entitled *La Vérité en peinture* in 1978. This book was translated into English as *The Truth in Painting*. Jacques Derrida, *Restitutions*, in *The Truth in Painting*, trans. Geoff Bennington and Ian MacLeod, Chicago and London, The University of Chicago Press, 1978, 256.
2. Meyer Schapiro left Germany in 1933 and became professor of Art at the University of Columbia in 1936. In his article, *The Still Life as a Personal Object—A Note on Heidegger and van Gogh*, he criticises Heidegger's determination of the painting of van Gogh. This article was first published in the journal *Macula* under the title *The Still Life as a Personal Object—A Note on Heidegger and van Gogh*. It is a criticism of Heidegger's description of van Gogh's shoes as it is given in *The Origin of the Work of Art*. Schapiro dedicated his article to the memory of Kurt Goldstein, who was the first, writes Schapiro, to draw his attention to the particular issue in Heidegger's essay, *The Origin of the Work of Art*. Schapiro's essay is published in *The Reach of Mind: Essays in Memory of Kurt Goldstein*, ed. M. L. Simmel, New York, Springer Publishing Company, 1968; Ref. Derrida, *Restitutions*, 256, 271.
3. Dominique Janicaud, *Presence and Appropriation*, in *Jacques Derrida: Critical Assessments of Leading Philosophers*, Vol. II, eds. Zeynep Direk and Leonard Lawlor, London and New York, Routledge, 2002, 24.
4. Jacques Derrida, *Restitutions*, 309.
5. *Ibid.*, 258-61.
6. *Ibid.*, 348-49.
7. *Ibid.*, 259.
8. Eve Tavor Bannet, *Structuralism and the Logic of Dissent*, Hampshire and London, The Macmillan Press LTD., 1989, 186.
9. Jacques Derrida, *Restitutions*, 258.
10. *Ibid.*, 260.
11. Timothy Clark, *Derrida, Heidegger, Blanchot*, 24.
12. Annemarie Gethmann-Siefert, *Martin Heidegger und die Kunstwissenschaft*, 262.
13. Jacques Derrida, *Restitutions*, 260-61.
14. *Ibid.*, 319-21.
15. *Ibid.*, 284.

16. Jonathan Loesberg, *Aestheticism and Deconstruction*, 7, 76.
17. Jacques Derrida, *Restitutions* 284; Martin Heidegger, *The Origin of the Work of Art,* 148.
18. Jacques Derrida, *Passe-Partout*, in *The Truth in Painting*, trans. Geoff Bennington and Ian McLeod, Chicago and London, The University of Chicago Press, 1987, 10.
19. *Ibid.*, 327.
20. See Chapter 4.
21. Jacques Derrida, *Restitutions*, 272.
22. Martin Heidegger, *The Origin of the Work of Art*, 158.
23. Meyer Schapiro, *The Still Life as a Object – A Note on Heidegger and van Gogh*, 205; Ref. Jacques Derrida, *Restitutions*, 308.
24. Jacques Derrida, *Restitutions*, 276, 364. In his article, *The Still Life as a Personal Object- A Note on Heidegger and van Gogh*, Schapiro strongly blamed Heidegger for not explicitly identifying the one particular picture that he had in mind, even though he knew quite well that van Gogh painted such shoes many times. It is not at all possible for a reader of the essay *The Origin of the Work of Art* to identify Heidegger's description with the original picture of van Gogh, because nobody knows which of the pictures of van Gogh Heidegger had selected. *De la Faille* documented eight paintings of shoes by van Gogh that had been exhibited in Amsterdam at the time Heidegger wrote his essay. Schapiro investigated these eight pictures and observed that of these eight pictures there were only three with the dark opening of the worn insides. Out of these shoes Schapiro identified the picture F. 225 with undone laces as a possible picture for Heidegger's essay on *The Origin of the Work of Art*. Schapiro argued that they are "clearly pictures of the artist's own shoes, not the shoes of a peasant." They were painted in Paris in 1886-1887. Schapiro wrote to Heidegger to inquire about the painting. Heidegger answered in a letter of May 6, 1965 that the picture to which he referred was one he saw in Amsterdam in March of 1930. This is clearly *de la Faille*'s no. 225. After the verification Schapiro pointed out that "these are clearly pictures of the artist's own shoes, not the shoes of a peasant." Jacques Derrida, *Restitutions*, 285, 308-09, 361.
25. Meyer Schapiro, *The Still Life as a Object – A Note on Heidegger and van Gogh* 205; Ref. Jacques Derrida, *Restitutions*, 365.
26. George Pattison, *The later Heidegger*, 81-82.
27. Ref. Jacques Derrida, *Restitutions*, 275, 292-93.
28. Meyer Schapiro, *The Still Life as a Personal Object—A Note on Heidegger and van Gogh*, 206; Ref. Joseph J. Kockelmans, *Heidegger on Art and Art Works*, 128-29.

29. Ref. *Ibid.*, 203-09. Meyer Schapiro's arguments against Heidegger's description of the painting are published in *The Still Life as a Personal Object.* Heidegger's interpretation of the painting reveals his own personal experience and peasant background that he had in his early years in the 1930's first in Messkirch (Baden) and later in Todtnauberg (in Black Forest) in Germany. During this time he experienced the world of peasant life. But when we examine van Gogh's life, especially during his time in Paris (1886-1888) where he painted the picture in question, we can see that the artist had a very little contact with peasant world. During his stay of two years in Paris, van Gogh painted a few pictures of shoes, self-portraits, scenes of Paris-rooftops, scenes of city-life, windmills, portraits of Parisian women, etc. As far as the paintings of shoes are concerned, *Le Caldano* reported that the artist had painted 5 shoes during the period of 1886-1888. (Derrida, *The Truth in Painting*, 258, 289, 310, and 375). During his stay in Paris, van Gogh was discovering a whole new world of light and colour that had been hidden from him during his earlier years in Holland. The paintings with darkening colour and background show his early-life experiences in Holland. He used to return to his background throughout his life. Up until 1887 he made use of darkening colours in grave background and also some quasi-depressing scenes. Schapiro comes to the conclusion that van Gogh's paintings of shoes reflect the earlier style that marked his work in Holland, and the paintings with bright colours may have been influenced by some of the impressionist painters in Paris. The shoes "The Old Shoes with Laces" (1886) that Heidegger refers to in *The Origin of the Work of Art* is dark and grave and they represent the early style of his work. When Schapiro asked about the details of the shoes that Heidegger described in the essay, Heidegger replied that he had seen them in Amsterdam in March 1930. In this exhibition some of the paintings of van Gogh's earlier period (1882-1886) were also presented. It is also true that some of these paintings of his earlier period represent scenes from the peasant world, for example "Peasants in the Fields" (1883), "Work in the Fields" (1885), "Potato-Eaters" (1885), "Still Life with Wooden Shoes" from Spring-Summer 1885. From this research in the paintings of van Gogh, Schapiro draws the conclusion that Heidegger might have associated "The Old Shoes with Laces" with paintings of the earlier years that are more or less related to the peasant's world. But "The Old Shoes with Laces," was painted in Paris where the artist had a very little contact with the peasant world and therefore, it can neither represent the peasant shoes nor a peasant world. Ref. Hugh J. Silverman, *Textualities*, New York and London, Routledge, 1994, 137. Jacques Derrida, *Restitutions*, 259-60, 329-30, 362-65.

30. Jacques Derrida, *Restitutions*, 320, 369. Schapiro's inquiry into the relationship between van Gogh's life Paris and his paintings in that time indicates that the concerned painting "The Old Shoes with Laces" which Heidegger selected in *The Origin of the Work of Art* is not likely to be peasant shoes. When van Gogh came to Paris, he was very poor; he had just arrived from Anvers. He did not have enough money to purchase materials for painting. Therefore, he used to write to his brother Theo for money to help him pay for his paints and supplies. Because he had little money, he certainly would not have been able to pay models to sit before him. His poor financial situation inspired him to paint landscapes, cityscapes, and other objects that were readily available. Some of his self-portraits may owe their existence to his being short of money. Painters like Fillipo Lippi, Leonardo, Rembrandt, and Dürer painted the most available subject—the painter's own body. For that they only required a mirror. Early in 1886 after arriving in Paris, van Gogh painted himself with a pipe. In the summer of 1887, and also in early 1888, he painted similar self-portraits—sometimes wearing a hat, sometimes without one. One of his famous self-portraits with banded ear which he painted immediately after he had cut one of his ears is well known. Schapiro tries to demonstrate that the shoes in question are not peasant's shoes but the artist's own shoes. Meyer Schapiro, *The Still Life as a Personal Object—A Note on Heidegger and van Gogh*, 206. Ref. Hugh J, Silverman, *Textualities*, 138-39.
31. Jacques Derrida, *Restitutions*, 358.
32. *Ibid.*, 294-95, 320-21.
33. *Ibid.*, 365.
34. *Ibid.*, 299-301.
35. *Ibid.*, 358.
36. Meyer Schapiro *The Still Life as a Personal Object—A Note on Heidegger and van Gogh* 203; Ref. Jacques Derrida, *Restitutions*, 294-95.
37. Martin Heidegger, *The Origin of the Work of Art*, 158.
38. *Ibid.*, 158. Jacques Derrida, *Restitutions*, 331-32.
39. Martin Heidegger, *The Origin of the Work of Art*, 160-61. Jacques Derrida, *Restitutions*, 295.
40. Martin Heidegger, *The Origin of the Work of Art*, 158-59.
41. Jacques Derrida, *Restitutions*, 328.
42. *Ibid.*, 331-32. Derrida provides a detailed account of "wooden-shoes" painted by van Gogh to show the peasant's world. But the particular picture that he selects in the essay on the work of art is not at all wooden-shoes that represent the peasant's world, but

rather the worn-out leather-shoes. He leaves the wooden-shoes and selects some other sort of shoes to describe the peasant's world. It shows that Heidegger is not describing the picture in terms of peasanthood, but the being-product of the product depending upon its usefulness, Ref. Jacques Derrida, *Restitutions*, 329.

43. Martin Heidegger, *The Origin of the Work of Art*, 158. Ref. Jacques Derrida, *Restitutions*, 309, 319-21.
44. Jacques Derrida, *Restitutions*, 295.
45. George Pattison, *The later Heidegger*, 94-95, 98.
46. Jacques Derrida, *Restitutions*, 311, 320.
47. George Pattison, *The later Heidegger*, 95, 98.
48. Jacques Derrida, *Restitutions*, 313-14, 318.
49. *Ibid.*, 312.
50. Meyer Schapiro, *The Still Life as a Personal Object—A Note on Heidegger and van Gogh*. Ref. Jacques Derrida, *Restitutions*, 316-18.
51. George Pattison, *The later Heidegger*, 96-97.
52. Jacques Derrida, *Restitutions*, 313.
53. *Ibid.*, 362, 364-65.
54. *Ibid.*, 260, 367.
55. Jonathan Loesberg, *Aestheticism and Deconstruction*, 79, 261.
56. Jacques Derrida, *Restitutions*, 265.
57. George Pattison, *The later Heidegger*, 88-89.
58. Jacques Derrida, *Restitutions*, 263.
59. Jonathan Loesberg, *Aestheticism and Deconstruction*, 79.
60. Jacques Derrida, *Restitutions*, 311.
61. *Ibid.*, 296, 346.
62. Martin Heidegger, *The Origin of the Work of Art*, 148-56. The three basic preconceptions of thing (as a bearer of traits, as the unity of a manifold of sensation and as formed matter) are the long-familiar modes of thought that preconceive all immediate experience of beings, Ref. *Ibid.*, 156. Ref. Jacques Derrida, *Restitutions*, 296.
63. Martin Heidegger, *The Origin of the Work of Art*, 156-58.
64. *Ibid.*, 159-60.
65. George Pattison, *The later Heidegger*, 85.
66. Jacques Derrida, *Restitutions*, 318.
67. Martin Heidegger, *The Origin of the Works of Art*, 159.
68. *Ibid.*, 160.

69. Annemarie Gethmann-Siefert, *Martin Heidegger und die Kunstwissenschaft*, 263.
70. Jacques Derrida, *Restitutions*, 319.
71. *Ibid.*, 313, 346.
72. *Ibid.*, 311-12, 347.
73. George Pattison, *The later Heidegger*, 81.
74. *Ibid.*, 35, 40. In contrast to Hegel, who considers the progressive nature of teleological movement, Heidegger holds the view that the historical process is no longer progressive. Heidegger is uncertain about the truth of technology, i.e. the mode of revealing, *alētheia*, which is discussed in terms of the truth of thing, product and that of work in the essay on *The Origin of the Work of Art*. When he opines that National Socialism is just like one of the products of technology like Americanism or Communism, he means the dangerous unpredictability of technology. For example, Germans voted for Hitler in 1933, but they did not vote for genocide. Even though they knew that the Right-wing party holds the anti-Semitic view, they elected him because they wanted to re-organize and keep territorial integrity of the Germany with military force. *Ibid.*, 26, 53, 70.
75. Martin Heidegger, *The Origin of the Work of Art*, 159.
76. Jacques Derrida, *Restitutions*, 341.
77. Martin Heidegger, *The Origin of the Work of Art*, 160.
78. Jacques Derrida, *Restitutions*, 321, 338-40, 345.
79. Martin Heidegger, *The Origin of the Work of Art*, 160.
80. Jacques Derrida, *Restitutions*, 349, 355-56. Ref. Martin Heidegger, *The Origin of the Work of Art*, 160.
81. Jacques Derrida, *Restitutions*, 355. Ref. Martin Heidegger, *The Origin of the Work of Art*, 160. The word *gewiss* is translated as soldered in the French translation. (*ist sie ihrer Welt gewiss* = she is soldered to her world) Derrida uses the French translation of solder or solidity to denote the reliability of the product. The solidity of the product provides a stable *world* in opposition to the changing *earth*.
82. Jacques Derrida, *Restitutions*, 353-56.
83. *Ibid.*, 349-51.
84. *Ibid.*, 298-99.
85. Derrida's criticism is examined in Chapter 4.
86. Martin Heidegger, *The Origin of the Work of Art*, 145-46. Ref. George Pattison, *The later Heidegger*, 85-86. Joseph J. Kockelmans, *Heidegger on Art and Art Works*, 110-11, 125-30.
87. George Pattison, *The later Heidegger*, 86.

88. Jacques Derrida, *Restitutions*, 299, 302-03.
89. Martin Heidegger, *The Origin of the Work of Art*, 152. Jacques Derrida, *Restitutions*, 284, 334.
90. Jacques·Derrida, *Restitutions*, 319, 322.
91. *Ibid.*, 342.
92. *Parergon* denotes the problems of the aesthetic representation of truth. Jacques Derrida, *Restitutions*, 15-119.
93. *Ibid.*, 300-02.
94. *Ibid.*, 9.
95. George Pattison, *The later Heidegger*, 98-99.
96. Jacques Derrida, *Restitutions*, 339, 342. Derrida's concept of re-mark is given in Chapter 4.
97. Jacques Derrida, *Force and Signification*, 8.
98. Jacques Derrida, *Restituitions*, 340-42.
99. *Ibid.*, 343.
100. *Ibid.*, 344.
101. Timothy Clark, *Derrida, Heidegger, Blanchot*, 108-10. Ref. Jacques Derrida, *Force and Signification*, 8, 11, 13.
102. Martin Heidegger, *The Origin of the Work of Art*, 161.
103. Jacques Derrida, *Restituitions,* 365.
104. Jacques Derrida, *Dissemination*, 197-316.
105. Jacques Derrida, *Restituitions,* 365.
106. *Ibid.*, 358.
107. *Ibid.*
108. Martin Heidegger, *Introduction to Metaphysics,* 135. William J. Richardson, S.J., *Heidegger Through Phenomenology to Thought*, 261-62.
109. Hugh J. Silverman, *Textualities,* 140.
110. Jacques Derrida, *Restituitions*, 358-59.
111. *Ibid.*, 359.
112. *Ibid.*, 357.
113. Timothy Clark, *Derrida, Heidegger, Blanchot*, 108-09.
114. Martin Heidegger, *The Origin of the Work of Art*, 161.
115. *Ibid.*, 161. Ref. Jacques Derrida, *Restituitions*, 323-24.
116. Martin Heidegger, *The Origin of the Work of Art*, 161. Ref. Jacques Derrida, *Restituitions*, 324.
117. Jacques Derrida, *Restituitions*, 296-99, 319, 324. The shoes, as informed matter, are example of a product. Van Gogh's picture, that

he selected to show the product-being of product, is an example of example. From picture Heidegger passes to being-product. The equimentality of equipment is not concerned with a particular object, but the truth of object in general which cannot be reduced to a truth of particular being.

118. *Ibid.*, 325.
119. Martin Heidegger, *The Origin of the Work of art*, 158.
120. *Ibid.*, 161.
121. Jacques Derrida, *Restituitions*, 324.
122. *Ibid.*, 325.
123. *Ibid.*, 368.
124. *Ibid.*, 255.
125. *Ibid.*, 368.
126. *Ibid.*, 369-70.
127. *Ibid.*, 378.
128. *Ibid.*, 342.
129. George Pattison, *The later Heidegger*, 99-101.
130. Paul Cezanne (1839-1906) is a French Impressionist.
131. Jacques Derrida, *Restituitions*, 255.
132. Julian Nida-Rümelin und Monika Bretzler, eds. *Ästhetik und Kunstphilosophie, Stuttgart*, Betzler, 1998, 208.
133. Jacques Derrida, *Restituitions*, 260, 272.
134. *Ibid.*, 332-33.
135. Hugh J. Silverman, *Textualities*, 140.
136. Annemarie Gethmann-Siefert, *Martin Heidegger und die Kunstwissenschaft*, 254.
137. Jacques Derrida, *Restituitions*, 313.
138. Christopher Norris, *Derrida*, 183. Ref. Richard Rorty, *Is Derrida a Transcendental Philosopher?* in *Derrida: A Critical Reader*, ed. David Wood, Oxford Cambridge, Blackwell, 1992, 236-37.

The Non-Originary Origin of Truth: Heidegger and Derrida

4

In Heidegger and Derrida the term origin does not mean original origin, which has the characteristic of presence. Since the origin of truth can appear only in differing from the original origin, they seek some more originary origin, which, as the title suggests, is called the non originary origin. The implications of the non-originary origin denote Heidegger's basic question concerning the truth or ground of Being itself. Origin as emergence is unpresentable since it is the *site* caught up by the confluence of revealing and concealing, which Derrida works out as the movement of play. During his supervision of this work, Prof. Dr. Früchtl has pointed out that the meaning of 'play' can be better attributed to Derrida's concept of origin than to Heidegger's concept of origin in his essay on work of art. There is no-*thing* at the origin besides the play of presence and absence, by virtue of which, as Küchler concludes, the search for the origin in post-modern era remains beyond any conclusion. The question concerning the origin and its closure is possible within metaphysics. The origin of truth has the significance of movement or openness towards alterity, which does not allow any conceptualization or closure.[1] In the appearance of a thing there is a confluence or an indissociability of what comes to the fore along with it. Heidegger's thought marks the more originary way of thinking which cannot be understood in traditional metaphysical terminology. "The thinking that is to come is no longer philosophy, because it thinks more originally than metaphysics—a name identical to philosophy."[2] The origin of truth of an entity is what it is not. This radical alterity in truth proclaims the irreducibility of the origin of truth in Heidegger and Derrida, the non-originary originary, which causes the essence of truth or the value of presence to be belated. They substitute the meaning of Being as being or something that is with the irreducible difference, which makes the reduction of meaning of beings impossible. Heidegger's destruction and Derrida's deconstruction mean the openness towards the *other*, which resists the idealistic concept of truth. In them difference precedes presence, which results in the removal of the transcendental truth of the traditional philosophy. The destruction and the deconstruction advocate the undecidability and the relativity of the meaning of Being.

Even though they advocate the philosophy of alterity and truth as difference, the confluence of truth and untruth at the origin of truth, there are differences between Heidegger's ontological difference and Derrida's deconstructive thought. Dorothea Frede argues that Heidegger's destruction cannot be taken as deconstruction.[3] Since truth is given in untruth, destruction aims at the uncovering, the dismantling or removal of concealments of the meaning of beings. Since any question on the meaning of Being leads philosophical investigation within the orbit of metaphysics, Derrida begins his philosophizing, unlike Heidegger, without positing question. Philosophy for Derrida is a 'writing' or 'play' without a beginning and an end. His deconstructive thought deepens the Heideggerian notion of the origin of Being, the irreducible difference between Being and beings. This chapter explores the relationship and difference in Heidegger and Derrida with regard to their concepts of origin. Derrida's deconstructive thought does not remove Heidegger's concept of ontological difference, but deepens the meaning of the same. Derrida's deconstruction (*Abbau*) gives us the same message as Heidegger's destruction (*Destruktion*) of metaphysics, i.e. the removal of the centre of truth, the metaphysics of presence, since they argue that philosophy from its inception with Plato adheres to the value of presence, which culminated in Hegel and is also a characteristic feature in contemporary philosophy. Both Heidegger and Derrida give importance to the meaning of 'structure;' both destruction and deconstruction destroy the meaning of the structurality of structure, the fixed origin. These terms signify the meaning of non-totalization, play without end.[4]

Derrida, however, ascribing the value of presence to Heidegger's essay on the work of art, claims that Heidegger too is involved in the pervasive nature of metaphysics, which Heidegger wants to overcome. As a deconstructionist Derrida enters into the Heideggerian text through Heidegger's pitfalls in his essay, i.e. the determination of van Gogh's painting. By questioning Heidegger's determination of the painting and its description, Derrida comes up with his deconstructive concepts, the philosophy of alterity, which according to him is older than Heidegger's ontological difference. Even though I do not think that Derrida succeeded in deconstructing Heidegger's destruction of metaphysics by digging out the subjective determination of truth in the essay on the work of art, I consider his deconstructive thought superb since it deepens and widens the meaning of ontological difference. My goal here is twofold: to point out the meaning of origin in Derrida's deconstructive thought as well as the distinctive characteristics of the meaning of origin as difference in Heidegger and as play in Derrida, and, as a general conclusion to this thesis, to critically evaluate Derrida's critique of Heidegger's truth of origin.

The meaning of origin in Derrida

As Heidegger's destruction signifies, Derrida's deconstruction too stands for the irreducibility of dissimilar elements, which creates a cleft in the origin of the truth of Being. As a Heideggerian, Derrida too criticizes the truth of traditional philosophy holding the view that difference precedes presence. In their thought, difference, which is prior to any determinations of the meaning of Being, is regarded as the common matrix, which is indeterminable and undecidable. However, Derrida's philosophical endeavour testifies that he does not want to remain a true Heideggerian, but rather go beyond him by deconstructing his ontological difference. In order to deconstruct the metaphysics of presence in various texts, including Heidegger's ontological difference, Derrida expounds a system or chain beyond Being of various undecidables that have the implications of the non-originary origin: *difference,* trace, textuality, supplement and re-mark, etc. These terms denote the meaning of appearance as disappearance, which has already been described by Heidegger: truth involves both concealment and unconcealment.[5] At the very outset, I would like to mention that these undecidables do not alter the validity of ontological difference, but strengthen it by proclaiming the origin of truth of referential structure as the play of difference.

Différance prior to ontological difference

Arguing that the Heideggerian difference remains within the milieu of traditional metaphysics with the question of Being, Derrida comes up with his own notion of difference, *différance*, which goes beyond the ontological difference by virtue of its endless 'differing-defering.' The *a* of *différance* means that his concept of *différance* is not identical with that of the Heideggerian ontological difference.[6] He considers the "*différance*, in a certain and very strange way, (is) 'older' than the ontological difference or than truth of Being. When it has this age it can be called the play of the trace. The play of a trace which no longer belongs to the horizon of Being, but whose play transports and encloses the meaning of Being: the play of trace, or the *différance*, which has no meaning and is not. Which does not belong. There is no maintaining, and no depth to, this bottomless chessboard on which Being is put into play."[7] Derrida ascribes the value of presence to ontological difference by saying that it is determined within the field of Being, and advocates the 'play' of difference, which does not belong to the field of Being, but encloses its meaning as undecidable in the groundlessness of its infrastructure. The removal of the centre of thought is the purpose of his thought, as already undertaken by Heidegger. For the latter, truth is the difference between presencing and presence, between Being and the thing that is. Truth as difference is older than Being itself. However, it (Heidegger's difference) is thought, says Derrida, within the horizon of the question of the meaning of Being.[8] Derrida begins to think of a difference which is anterior to ontological difference, beyond the value of Being: "There may be a difference still more unthought than the difference between Being and beings."[9] The difference that is still unthought is, according to Derrida, not ontological difference, but *différance,* which is not thought of as something between Being and beings, but as beyond any determination of Being. It is the un-exhaustible pre-opening of infrastructure. *Différance* prevents any determination of truth because of the play of the 'trace,' the inscription of the *other* in self, which is older than selfhood. He considers ontological difference within the periphery of logocentrism since it determines truth as difference. Deconstruction is turned against the value of presence. *Différance,* which is the prior principle of differentiation, before presence or absence is also called *writing,* (*Grammatological writing*).[10] Derrida's deconstructive terms imply the endless play of difference in bottomless infrastructure.

Différance, which *underlies* and is prior to all metaphysical concepts, denotes three basic meanings of infrastructure: the pre-ontological, the pre-logical and the synthetic truth of Being as an altering difference.[11] First of all, the pre-ontological truth of Being of infrastructure implies the common matrix, in which oppositions are engendered.[12] Infrastructure here means that which accounts for differences. *Différance* is the infrastructure, the common ground for all binary oppositions or any determination of meaning, such as the determination of presence and absence, being and nothingness. Secondly, the infrastructure of the truth of Being accounts for radical exteriority, the *other*, which implies the meaning of the pre-logical truth of Being. And thirdly, the synthetic character of infrastructure resists the sublation of contradictories into a higher unity.[13] He writes the term difference in a new way to mean the implications of weaving and interlacing, in which different threads and lines join together and at the same time differ to form a 'text.'[14] It risks the disappearance of the meaning of a 'text' as a whole, because the infrastructure is the opening up of endless prior-structures.

a. *Différance as the elusive origin of truth*

Having reduced the meaning of things to the significance of textual difference, Derrida does not search for an origin;

différance is not a concept that something *is*. Its signification crosses out the *is,* the meaning of Being, since nothing can appear *as such* in an infrastructure, in which things come to be. Since it is older than Being itself, it does not have the significance of something that being-present, and therefore it has no name in our language.[15] Like Heidegger, Derrida too maintains that philosophy cannot find an ultimate answer to the metaphysical question what is..? since *différance* precedes presence. The notions of 'differing' (to be different) and 'deferring' (to postpone) constitute the basic thrust of *différance.* Presence as essence, as origin, can never be a fulfilled idea; it is constituted as effect within a differential system. Presence as effect means that it is produced by different elements, by the play of differences. *Différance* signifies the differed and the deferred presence, a presence that is different and set aside.[16]

The neologism *différance* is 'neither a word nor a concept.' Derrida makes use of this word because he is unable to expose conceptually what it *is.* The graphic difference between the *e* and the *a* of *différance* cannot be heard or seen. It simply implies nothing, i.e. it is beyond conceptualization.[17] The graphic difference in his neologism signifies that *writing* or difference is prior to speech or meaning. Here the spelling *a* in the neologism indicates the *writing*, the prior structure of difference in an infrastructure. The movement of difference-*différance* (from *e* to *a*)[18] denotes that this neologism does not belong to any kind of system of thought in the usual sense. It is a play on the French verb *différer*, which is derived from the Latin verb *differre*, meaning both to differ[19] and to defer.[20] Since *Différance* is beyond any determinations, it "is to be conceived prior to the separation between deferring as delay and differing as the active work of difference."[21] He coins the term *différance* to denote the dual functions of difference as both a differing (where each sign is differing from the other, which is deferred) and a deferring (the endless chain of signs postpones any termination of the chain in some original signified), but it is more primordial than deferring and differing taken separately. The *a* of *différance* denotes the indecision of the meaning of a term by the functions of differing-deferring, beyond which there is no term or concept.[22] He writes this word with *a* instead of *e* to point to difference in never ending movement: the play of difference.

b. *Différance as prior to Being*

With the introduction of the philosophy of *différance*, Derrida, like Heidegger, tries to eliminate the meaning of Being by putting an end to any desire we might have for a world which is centred in presence. There is no possibility for a substratum or subject, but only *différance*, which is prior to presence - be it either subjectivity or objectivity. He inscribes the meaning of subjectivity and objectivity, i.e. anything under the name of self-presence, within the system of *différance*; in this differential system everything is considered as an effect that is caught up by the detour and postponement of meaning because of 'temporalization' and 'spacing' within a given system.[23] To temporalize is to delay a presence and it is the infinite temporalization in the sense that in a referential structure a 'trace' refers back only to another trace. Spacing is the irreducible outside, the presence of alterity.[24] The pure presence that Western metaphysics sets out to achieve - a theorized account of pure consciousness - is only the effect of *différance*. There is no transcendental signified or logocentric truth beyond the operation of deferring: spacing and tempralization. The neologism *différance* is defined as "what makes possible the presentation of being-present" and at the same time what is never presented. It can be thinkable only as what disappears in any appearance, which is the basic thought of Heidegger too.[25] This neologism shows the impossibility of any transcendental truth since there is no full presence or ontological signified that can be present before the play of differences.

Trace as the non-originary originary

Trace is the strange unity of self and *other* in a referential structure, which denotes the value of self as its own effacement or erasure.[26] The thing that comes to be or the value of presence in general structure is its own effacement by being effaced by the effects of trace. The erasure of selfhood is explained in terms of temporal differentiation; trace is the temporal differentiation—past, present and future,[27] which makes the origin of the truth a non-originary one, erasing the origin or the transcendental truth. David Farrel Krell holds the view that Derrida's concept of origin modelled on the Heideggerian analysis of *Dasein*'s temporalization.[28] For Heidegger and Derrida the inherence of temporal difference in the present—*now* is a problem. Derrida's concept of origin is related to the temporal differentiations. The origin cannot be constituted except by a non-origin, the trace. Trace, which denotes the erasure of origin, also implies that the origin cannot even be constituted except reciprocally by a non-origin. Derrida calls trace the origin of origin or the 'arche-trace,' which implies the meaning of the becoming present of the *other*. For him, the play of difference is a synonym for the non-originary difference. The origin as play presents the dissimulation of itself, i.e., as Gasché explains, the so-called *present* that retains it as *other* at the same time and refers to it as an *absence*.[29] It undermines all the value of the origin upheld by traditional philosophy. Being 'marked' by *other*, or alterity, arche-trace is the erasure of its own self, a self-diverting difference in itself in the referential structure. It designates the notion of *différance* that the so-called presence exists in relation to its alterity. Self-effacement is the basic structure and character of arche-trace, which can exist only through its own effacement.[30] The effect of trace suspends the so-called (first) origin, which has the character of presence in idealistic or materialistic thought. The self-erasure of trace implies its very existence in reference to the *other*, which is inscribed within it. Trace comes to be only in relation to another trace, and its presence in conflating oppositions stands in necessary relation to the energy of its own erasure. Trace prevents the possibility for the reconstitution of any centre or the origin since it has no intrinsic existence in itself. The concept of trace 're-marks'[31] all forms of logocentrism by suspending any form of the first-origin. Trace is the origin by relating to the *other*, by which it *is* what it is, thus being marked and effaced by the *other*. Trace cannot present itself; in presenting itself it gets effaced.[32]

In the essay on *Structure, Sign and Play* Derrida reduces philosophical concepts, which deal with a centre (a point of reference or a fixed origin), to the play of structure, which removes the centre by making it 'within the structure and outside it,' something unthinkable one. "Henceforth, it was necessary to begin thinking that there is no centre, that the centre could not be thought in the form of a present-being, that the centre had no natural site, that it was not a fixed locus but a function, a sort of nonlocus in which an infinite number of sign-substitutions came into play."[33] No concept can be thought without the trace of its difference, the *other*, which is found within its (concept's) very core. The so-called concepts are always already inscribed with the *other* within a system or conceptual chains, in which they are related to the plurality of other concepts, from which they receive their meaning. Arche-trace denotes the truth of referential structure, or structure of reference. The central signified of metaphysics is subjected endless play in the general structure of reference, which makes a moment or locus of presence impossible.[34] The absence of centre or transcendental signified in the system of differences causes play of signification infinitely. A search for the end or origin is an endless journey, for there is no such ground.

Temporality and the concept of spacing

After Heidegger, Derrida too argues that the so-called presence is constituted by temporal differentiation, by which Heidegger deconstructs Husserl's metaphysical privileging of presence.[35] Temporal differentiation does not allow this privilege to the present 'now,' because of the non-present admitted to the originary presence disrupting its presence. In Derrida, as John Sallis concludes, the self-identity of the present does not have the character of simple origin, since it is produced through the compounding of presence and non-presence, in other words, the past-future traces are the essential ingredients of the so-called simple origin.[36] The present now can come to exist only in reference to its alterity and its reference to alterity is called 'spacing,' the 'becoming-time of space.' The dialectics of traces in the present deconstruct what is already there. What is already *there* intrinsically bound up with the temporality and the dialectics of protention and retention in presence are the opposing dynamics that constitute rift in the concept of truth.[37] Derrida's concern is to overthrow the privilege granted to the present now, by relegating the meaning of presence to temporal differentiation. The temporal differences, which constitute the essential factor in the constitution of meaning, do not allow full-presence. According to Kant time is the condition for the possibility of perception; temporal things (*a posteriori*) can only be realized in the *a priori* form of time. Früchtl holds the view that the meaning of a thing inevitably includes the inner and outer dimentions of time. Temporal differentiation is the basic characteristic of truth.[38] In this respect the irreducible alterity in the meaning of a thing is to be understood as the temporal differentiation or the becoming-time of space. Derrida argues for a system which is no longer of presence, but of *différance*, in which difference precedes presence in the sense that transcendental truth is negated on the ground of temporal differentiation.[39]

The precedence of temporal differentiation over the meaning shows that everything is at the lost of the present.[40] *Différance* stands for the elusiveness of meaning in language. In language it functions as a play of interval, which causes the perpetual slippage of meaning from signs in linguistic chains. He calls it *spacing*, the becoming-space of time.[41] It does not imply temporal present, but the ambivalence of appearing and signification, in which presence that is not present as such, but disappears in the act of allowing to appear.[42] In language, it is the action of putting off meaning until later. Since meaning in language functions as a network of differential signs, i.e. in a differential infrastructure a sign or word is related to its *other*, to meaning or Being, there is no possibility for direct or immediate presence. The so-called presence or *now* is a delay or an interval caused by originary division. It is what he calls the becoming-space of time and 'the becoming-time of space.' "Space becomes time and structure history when the spacing which produced determinated being is reproduced in time, when divisions recur Time becomes spatial when reproductions are separated by an interval, when recurrence is spaced out."[43] Here Bannet explains how truth or the so-called now comes to be in the spatio-temporal differences. Temporalization and spacing are mutually related and at the same time they are mutually different from each other: becoming-time of space is the prerequisite for spacing. The inscription or the insinuation of alterity within presence, the falling into space, means that interiority is already inhabited by outside: spacialization.[44] Even though spacing is related to temporalization, it is neither time nor material space; rather it is the split in the present by way of its reference to alterity, the presence of the *other*. It is the opening or the interval in presence. Spacing refers to absolute alterity, which is necessary for the constitution of the present now; spacialization of entity means that it (entity) is befallen by space in order that it can be an entity. Spacing has both passive and active functionality in signification: being an interval, spacing allows for concepts as marked by their relation to other concepts in their primal sense of signification.[45] In the constitution of concepts, spacing relates different elements and refers to something that exists outside of it. Spacing as *writing* means the becoming-absent of subject. Signification of a sign is possible only within the abyss of *différance* without imparting a meaning.[46]

Derrida substituted presence with sptio-temporal difference and, therefore, everything that is 'in the present,' 'in now,' or 'self-evident' is only repetition or representation of the past-present. In the absence of transcendental signified, meaning and presence in infrastructure or in general structure of referral presence are subjected to the economy of endless traces. In general structure, the meaning of a thing is related to alterity; the so-called presence or self *is* what it is only in so far as the interval that constitutes it and simultaneously divides it. This double movement, i.e. the constitution of self-identity and its self-effacement or self-deportation, causes the infinite repetitions of origins. Trace is difference; arche-trace is the self-effacement, which cannot *as such* appear.[47]

Différance implies postponement of self-identity and meaning, which is to be understood in terms of spatio-temporal difference within the present-*now*. In *Positions* Derrida states that each element in a text is constituted on the basis of trace within it of the other elements of the text, so that no element is present in and of itself.[48] He then says that *différance* is the play of traces, of spacing by means of which each of these elements is open to its alterity. Since each element of a text also functions and signifies, takes on or conveys meaning, only by referring to another past or future element in an economy of traces, the spacing to which he refers is also temporalization, "the detour and postponement by means of which intuition, perception, consummation—in a word, the relationship to the present, the reference to a present reality, to a *being*—are always."[49] The temporal differing and the spatial deferral undermine the so-called presence by making it a construct rather than a given. Truth is not something that *is*, but something that is constituted as a fabric of differences in any system of references, e.g. in language "we shall designate *différance* as the movement according to which language, or any code, any system of referral in general, is constituted 'historically' as a weave of differences."[50] Temporal existence is prior to transcendental truth. Truth in traditional philosophy is essentially historical, which, according to Derrida, cannot claim total meaning. What is given 'historically,' 'is produced,' or 'is constituted,' etc. is to be understood as *différance* since in referential structure the so-called self is marked and determined by *other*; in short, difference plays at its origin. The origin is the movement of difference, the effacement of the self through its irreducible duplicity.

In relation to temporalization or trace, the notion of space "is the opening of the first exteriority in general, the enigmatic relation of the living to its other and of an inside to an outside: spacing."[51] Self-identity and self-deportation belong to the truth of referential structure, and doubling is necessary for referrentiality. Spacing or espacement is the interval in the present now or the distance occurring in each element of referential structure.[52] The precedence of spatio-temporal differences over transcendental Idea turns the traditional concept of truth upside down; however, this reversal of the elements of truth does not lead to the elimination of transcendental truth.

The philosophy of textuality

In both the literary and philosophical realms, the term 'text' has long been assumed as a single entity and its meaning derives from a basic unity that is inherent throughout it. But, according to Derrida, a text does not have a simple origin. Clark indicates that like Heidegger's concept of poetry, the meaning of literary language in Derrida too is the question of ontological difference.[53] As the meaning of Being suggests, both the meaning of poetry and that of literary language open to the other constituting an irreducible structure. Etymologically, the term text derives from the Greek word *tek* (τεκ) which means to make, and from the corresponding Latin word *texere* which means to weave.[54] Text is a created fabric woven with interlacing threads, a woven fabric, in which different elements are interrelated. Like the Heideggerian meaning of poetry, Derrida too argues that the meaning of literary is further referred back to the *other*, which is the excess of any entity. Without this excess nothing can come to be as what it is.[55] In the absence of transcendental signified, the meaning of a text is concealed throughout different contexts, which deconstructs the priority of presence. He applies division or difference to entities that are thought to have a being, a presence, identity, an essence, a truth, an inherent coherence. In the absence of a fixed centre, a text is a combination of an infinite number of signs that emerge from a groundless abyss. In the Derridean thought, there is no ultimate ground that has self-validity. The textual functioning of *différance* cannot be comprehended on the basis of logic of identity.[56] A rigorous and scientific concept of context is impossible. An analogous concept for that is his concept of *writing*, which postulates that difference precedes presence.[57] The contextual incompleteness results in relativity of meaning. Since meaning is disseminated throughout many contexts, the meaning of a text is on the move; it gets beyond and beyond without an end in full saturation.

The traditional transcendental Being is caught up in the play of textual interrelationships, in which it is considered as one of the undecidable signifiers. There is no transcendental principle outside the text to control its meaning and signification: 'There can be nothing outside of text.'[58] From the structure of textuality follows that there is no transcendental signified outside the text or outside the play of differences. In the play of difference, everything is found interrelated, without constituting further a centre. Nothing is given as simple or pure present since *différance* precedes all determinations. In *The Truth in Painting*, Derrida explains how the origin or the simple presence is caught up in textual play in the determination of one of van Gogh's paintings done by Heidegger and Schapiro. A text is a web of differential relationships in which one element is related to the *other* without imparting fixed meaning. The origin of truth in general structure of reference is to be thought of as the endless play of difference. "*Différance* is the systematic play of differences, of the traces of differences, of the *spacing* by means of which elements are related to each other."[59] Spacing is the opening of intervals without which nothing can signify. Derrida's deconstructive terms have the meaning of the play of differences and in such a system nothing can be intrinsically true. Nothing can exist in the differential system without referring to *other* elements.[60] Derrida reduces the meaning of Being to the play of structures, through which the centre or origin of truth is found *neither* inside *nor* outside the structure. In traditional philosophy it is found either inside or outside the structure.[61] All of Derrida's deconstructive terms are deprived of permanent content; they have no proper content or essence. The meaning of these terms is spread in non-located grounds of a text. His deconstructive thought opens up to the undecidable resource that sets the text into motion.[62] In order to grasp the philosophy of difference we have to avoid the accepted norm of logic and epistemology and to relay on anti-epistemology. However, it should be noted that we can grasp nothing beyond the milieu of transcendental truth. Transcendental signified is the possibility and pre-requisite for human understanding. Therefore, even the deconstruction of Being can only be understood within the periphery of Being itself. The claim, 'there is nothing outside of text,' implies the saying: there is nothing outside of Being, i.e. outside the differential structure of truth.

The structure of a text shows the impossibility of pure presence since the so-called presence is intrinsically infected with 'what it is not.' The *other* is the essential part in the making of the present. In opposition to logo-philosophy, which excludes one of the aspects of truth by affirming another part, in the philosophy of textuality there is no absolute privilege, which would allow us absolutely to master its textual system. Text is not hierarchical in nature with a definite border. Border between opposition comes to be in the definition of truth; the truth of textuality is indefinable.

Textuality and the meaning of signification in language

The philosophy of textuality is Derrida's deconstructive theory of linguistic signification, which he applies to many philosophical texts in order to reduce them to the play of difference. Derrida deconstructs the transcendental signified by reducing it to the structure of language. "There is nothing outside of the text."[63] In an interview with Richard Kearney, Derrida explains that the expression, 'nothing beyond text, or nothing beyond language' does not have the meaning of nihilism, even though it proclaims the absence of transcendental truth, but, it means the referential dimension of language, i.e. a text or language means that everything is determined in contexts.[64] He questions the transcendental truth in language, which is not linguistics. The meaning of Being is dependent on the contextual references. He argues that there is no transcendental signified outside language that it can refer to, since there are only signifiers and differences in it. The absence of transcendental truth in language makes any object of representation impossible. It makes the structure of appearance as withdrawal, a signifier without signified, which constitutes the characteristics of the Derridean structuralism.[65] In a text, there are only signifiers, the so-called signified or meaning is also a sign or a signifier or language, in which meaning occurs only in the operation of a wide context. The suggestion 'behind' a signifier is always already a *différance*, a text *written* in Derrida's sense. Language, which is devoid of intrinsic truth, is a system of differences. There is nothing 'pure,' unrelated and undifferentiated. What is real is text. Text can impart only relative meaning since it is essentially related to other elements and structures. Relativity is the 'reality' of textuality. The so-called real or transcendental signified is conceived as one of the signifiers in the structure of a text. Everything has got interpretative meaning, in which meaning is caught up in a movement of differential referring.[66]

The meaning of language is a signification within temporal processes, in which the presence of a thing does not have the validity of truth, since it is caught up by the play of differences. "Here the appearing and functioning of difference presuppose an originary synthesis not receded by any absolute simplicity. Such would be the originary trace. Without a retention in the minimal unit of temporal experience, without a trace retaining the other as other in the same, no difference would do its work and no meaning would appear. It is not the question of a constituted difference here, but rather, before all determination of the content, of the *pure* movement which produces difference. *The (pure) trace is difference.*"[67] Temporal differentiation is the essence of originary synthesis and therefore, it cannot have the nature of the absolute simplicity of being-present. It is striking that Derrida's key term *différance*, which for him constitutes the essence of language, is described in terms of the coincidence of meanings in the verb *differer*: to differ (in space) and to defer (to put off in time). Thus *différance* ascribes both spatial and temporal differences to the meaning of language.[68] Linguistic signification is essentially interplay of signifiers, in which meaning is derived, in other words, the meaning of a word is related to other signifiers in differing and deferring dimensions. He speaks of endless differing of presence as the characteristic of a text. He substitutes the transcendental absolute with the temporal differentiations. There is nothing beyond the becoming temporal of presence, the meaning of language is at all levels pregnant with a force toward separation of difference. Given this operation of *différance*, he contends that logocentric concepts such as *eidos, telos, energeia, ousia*, essence, existence, substance, subject, *alētheia*, transcendentality, consciousness or conscious, God, man, and so forth, are all caught up in an infinite circularity of signifiers and will never be able to be present.[69] Any truth-claim, philosophical, ethical, political or theological, will always be dissolved into the 'reality of textuality,' in which it inheres. The textual force brings nothing to be. Timothy Clark, indicating the ontological function of language in Heidegger, argues that there is a difference between the Heideggerian poetical function and the Derridean notion of self-concealment. Out of *phenomenal* force, poetry in Heidegger functions as a work of art by bringing *something* to the fore out of concealment, whereas in Derrida, out of the textual force nothing can be there in truth: "No present in truth presents itself there, not even in the form of its self-concealment."[70] Since there is no absolute origin, the text always depends on numerous contexts that are boundless and indeterminate. There is always something more to be added. There is no fullness because meaning is derived from multi-contextual interrelationships. In short, truth is relative, since it depends upon contexts. It is the effect of sense in any given context because a word consists of the traces of different contexts (semantic) and of the traces of its differential relations to other words (syntactic). Under the name 'The Hinge' in *Of Grammatology*, he describes that a word functions by conjoining different meanings (texts, contexts) to the phonetically differentiated word.[71] In his critique of philosophy and of absolute truth, Derrida emphases that meaning is historical and contextual through and through, which questions the validity of the ground for truth.

The concept of supplement

Similar to the meaning of textuality, Derrida's concept of supplement, by which he deconstructs Rousseau's *Essay on the Origin of Languages*, suggests that there is no self-sufficient concept, because something external or the *other* is inevitably added to it. The concept of supplement "harbours within it two significations whose cohabitation is as strange as it is necessary."[72] The supplement is the essential extra, added to something complete in it, but it is added in order to complete, to compensate for a lack in what was supposed to be complete in itself. These two different meanings of supplement are linked in a powerful logic, and in both meanings the supplement is presented as exterior, foreign to the 'essential' nature to which it is added. Both signifier and signified supplement each other; they are a complement to each other. In the supplementary relationship, meaning or presence is seen as differed-deferred by the structure of complementarity. Everything needs its *other* for its completion. His famous proposition that 'there is nothing outside of text' must be understood as referring to this dynamic, jointly described by his network of structures, rather than to any narrow, conventional concept of text, oral or written.[73] What is real is text, which can impart only relative meaning at a given moment since it is essentially related to and complemented by other elements and structures. Everything is constituted and, therefore, not pure in itself.

The logic of supplementarity shows that the plenitude of Being in fact is built upon its opposite, the notion of non-fullness of Being, that Being requires the moment of non-Being for its articulation and intelligibility. Thus one can see that what traditionally has been conceived as the outside actually inhabits the core of the inside, and the contamination of the purity of Being by the lack of Being is what makes Being seem pure to begin with. The usual logic emerges out of the inter-connections of opposites eradicates the possibility of presence. Therefore, Derrida puts the meaning of Being under erasure. This is to write a word, cross it out, and then print both word and deletion. This special writing shows the inner split in meaning. Words do not carry any proper meaning as we are told by the traditional systems of thoughts. Since the word is inaccurate to denote what it means, it is crossed out. Since *différance* precedes presence, nothing can define the question of the meaning of Being.[74] Nothing and Being cohabit in one and the same event of presence, each inhabiting or entrapping the *other* as its essential constitutive moment; neither is earlier or later, they appear eqi-primordially. Therefore, the concept of *différance* remains forever as an unsettling force, without constituting an origin anywhere. There is no absolute point zero, there is no pure point of genesis. A situation of *both... and*, an event of *neither... nor*, is the characteristic feature of *différance*.[75] Textual equivocity is the result of Derrida's writings.

His concepts of textuality and supplement denote that there is nothing that exists as something that it is because of the re-mark of the *other*, the presence of the *other* in the present *now*.

Remark and retrait: the meaning of withdrawal

The whole deconstructive thought of Derrida can be summarized as the meaning of anterior structures, which can be explained by Heidegger's concept of the withdrawal of Being. For Heidegger, the question of Being not only deals with the transcendental constitution of the meaning of beings, but also with the withdrawal of Being, its concealment. Transcendental truth as the essence and the meaning of beings retreats. Jean-Luc Nancy describes the withdrawing presencing of transcendental and ontological truth: "neither the withdrawal of Being nor its given presence; but this presence itself, Being itself, and as Being, exposed in a trace or as a tracing: withdrawing the presence, but presenting the withdrawing, in its property of being non-presentable—which is *the* absolute property or the property of the absolute."[76] The meaning of a thing is possible only in and through the traces of prior-marking, or prior-text. A mark, i.e. a thing that is understood *as* something in its *other* in the referential totality, is a remark, i.e. that which is already marked in advance before its emergence.[77] J. Hillis Miller argues that Derrida's concept of mark or re-mark attains the significance of Husserlian meaning of *alter ego*, i.e. the ego or the self-consciousness of the *other*. It means the *constituted* nature of the subjective form of transcendental experience. The *alter ego* or what we call the subjectivity or self-presence can only be presented indirectly, it can be something that is radically *other* to itself. The peculiarity of *alter ego* is that it does not present to it as such. Thereby everything that the ego constitutes by thinking of it is broken by a non-presence that constitutes the ego. *Alter ego* implies the meaning of something unpresentable, unknowable, etc.[78]

For Clark, re-mark is the duplicity or doubling of the presence of the present, the interplay between that which appears and its appearing, in which the meaning (disclosure or the coming-into-the-open) of that which is apparent disappears. He concludes that the Derridean difference explores mainly the Heideggerian nuances in linguistic function which explains how things are revealed in their Being.[79] For Heidegger, withdrawal or holding back is the nature of language; in the very act of bringing entities to presence, it *withholds* itself.[80] The withdrawal of the meaning of Being has the structural pattern of a text, which exists in and through its pre-texts or anterior structures. A text, which is opened toward different contexts, has no intrinsic truth in itself. In *The Double Session* Derrida describes the ontic-ontological structure, which has the character of withdrawal, folding-back.[81] Spatio-temporal difference always remarks a particular text.[82] The remarked site of the mark, the mark's spaced-out opening, is necessary for referentiality.[83] Remark produces a blank meaning in so far as it "refers to the non-sense of spacing, the place where nothing takes place but the place."[84] The remarking of the mark or the remarking of the totality of the marks in a series is not only to be understood as the represented inscription of the spaced-out semi-opening in the mark but also as the withdrawal of what makes the marks possible from the marks themselves. Remark is the withdrawal or re-coil of mark, remark effaces that which makes signification possible at any given moment. Remark means the effacement of mark itself, without giving any meaning of signification. The textual mark, which does not represent anything, is a remark. Philosophy, for Derrida, is a text which does not have the meaning of presence.

Gasché and Clark hold the view that Derrida's notion of remark is essentially Heidegger's concept of Being as withdrawal. The concept of remark implies the meaning of Derrida's retrait, which is the development of Heidegger's concept of trait, the meaning of Being as withdrawal: the meaning of Being as revealing-concealing and *as*-structure.[85] It denotes the Heideggerian notion of the understanding of truth as *as*-structure, the pre-predication of fore-knowledge, fore-sight.[86] The *Da* of *Sein* means that the very opening or revealing of beings is also their concealing. Since truth is given in untruth, the *there* or the *Da* of *Dasein* is the rift in-between Being and beings. Trait denotes the withdrawal of Being, Being *as* Being or difference between Being and being. *Dasein* is the gap or the rift in the meaning of Being.[87] Derrida, however, after ascribing the value of presence to the truth of *Dasein*, reforms and deconstructs the implication of withdrawal. In his article *The Retrait of Metaphor*, he elucidates the notion of trait: "the trait is, *a priori*, retreat, i.e. unappearance, and effacement of its mark in its incision."[88] Trait means retrait, and the *re* of retrait implies that trait can exist only by being its obliteration. It is trait's withdrawal; trait is obliterated forever from itself. He calls retrait 'the *withdrawal of withdrawal*,' which means the non-occurrence of presence in the difference.[89] Derrida deconstructs the value of presence in Hedegger's difference by means of the *re* in retrait, which denotes the *withdrawal* of the difference between Being and beings. Remark deconstructs the occurrence of difference in a given text by its self-effacement. The concept of re-mark interrupts the possibility of totalization or full-presence.

Difference as the origin in Heidegger and Derrida

This part is the critical evaluation of the origin of truth as it is expounded by Heidegger and Derrida. For Heidegger the question of Being is the search for the ground, which does not have the meaning of substructure, but it is understood as bottomlessness or abyss. Derrida too accepts this concept and defines trace as neither a ground nor an origin. Both of them consider the origin of truth as non-originary, which suggests that difference precedes presence. In their ambition to remove transcendental truth from the realm of thought, Heidegger searches for a more originary origin and Derrida too is determined to revolutionize the traditional thinking. Derrida calls his philosophy 'a new transcendental aesthetic,'[90] which is entirely different from his predecessors, especially from that of Husserl, who discovers a transcendental content as the ultimate truth. For Derrida, the origin can only be origin if it is lost or alienated into what springs forth from it. Origin for him is the condition for the possibility of that. The infrastructural possibilities represent irreducible plurality in contrast with the uniqueness of origin. Both in Heidegger and Derrida, origin does not dominate the system. With the ambition to ground all forms of thinking on his thought, he says that it a new system.

Difference is at the origin. It is, according to Heidegger, the *origin* that is more originary than anything that is. Difference and *différance* are inseparable; there is no Derrida without Heidegger. Derrida's *différance* cannot stay alone without the support of Heidegger's difference. Given Derrida's two important claims that he has deconstructed the metaphysics of presence in Heidegger's essay on the work of art and that his deconstructive thought is older than Heidegger's ontological difference, it is necessary to evaluate critically, first of all, Heidegger's concept of origin. It is to be critically evaluated in relation to the following two questions: is the Derridean deconstructive thought older than the ontological difference in the sense that ontological difference contains the centre or the value of presence? Can Derrida's critique of Heidegger's essay on the work of art be justified? The answer to these questions is that Derrida does not do away with the Heideggerian difference, but he deepens the meaning of origin given by Heidegger.

The origin as difference in Heidegger

The difference between Being and beings does not exist *as such*. The very moment a thing is determined as something, there occurs truth as withdrawal. Since the metaphysical meaning of presence (*Anwesendes*) is oblivious to the essence of presencing (*Wesen des Anwesens*), Heidegger explores the meaning of presencing in terms of the truth of *Dasein* and that of the work of art, in which he explains the essence of presencing as the confluence of the movements of the presence and the absence. According to him, the truth of *Dasein* and that of the work of art denote the notion of difference as the origin of the transcendental presence of Being. For example, *Dasein*'s existential structure as Being-in-the-world makes its ground a differential structure, an intermittent happening of presence and absence, which constitutes its essence (*Wesen*) as *Da-sein*. After the *Kehre*, he abandons the inquiry into the question of Being in terms of the existential analysis of *Dasein*, its transcendence and engages directly in expounding Being as being caught up in a strife that is the characteristic of origin in the essay on *The Origin of the Work of Art.* Originary strife opens the space of the *there* (*Da*), where the truth of Being happens: the origin of the work of the art. The space opened up in the differential structure in terms of the truth of *Dasein* and that of the work of art is to be considered as abyss or non-ground of the openness of the *There* (*Da*), which, according to Derrida, is the originary play of presencing; accordingly, a thing that *is* is at the same time *is not.*

Heidegger's interpretation of truth as unconcealment results in the decentring of the subject, which is the centre and ground of beings in the world. In this respect he fulfils the task of the destruction of the centre of philosophy. In the disclosedness of the world, meaning is not at all the property of beings. He refers to a still more originary realm of truth that precedes propositional truth. What is at stake in the decentring and ungrounding of the subject, is the principle of truth as *agreement.* The relationship that links entities to thought does not build an agreement, but rather a difference.[91] He substitutes the truth of agreement with the unsettling force of the truth of *Dasein* as Being-in-the-world. Truth as revealment in Heidegger substitutes the grounded presence of metaphysics with the ungrounded differential structure of presencing. Truth implies not only unconcealment, but also concealment. It denotes the difference at the origin, the unsettling force in truth in Heidegger's essay too. In his search for truth, he may have received impulses from pre-Socratic philosophers, particularly from Heraclitus, who used the term *physis* to mean the play of truth of Being; *physis* as emerging-on-its-own has the characteristic of concealment.[92]

Heidegger perceives the originary difference at the core of the presence of the unified notion of Being to mean that difference precedes all metaphysical, transcendental presence of ground or reason. In *The Principles of Reason*, he announces the ungrounded origin of Being by thinking of Being as abyss, which means that the truth of Being escapes the metaphysical notions of reason and ground.[93] In order to displace the metaphysical centre, Heidegger subjugates and relates Being to difference rather than to reason, and it becomes the hallmark of post-modern thinking, since it takes into account the play of difference in the notions of Being and reason, particularly in the writings of Derrida. The differential structure of the truth of *Dasein* and that of the work of art does not have the quality of what-ness, but designates the originary movement of bringing-forth, which cannot be controlled by a set of rules; it is a play without *why*,[94] an ungrounded play without a sufficient reason, which is unthinkable within the systems of metaphysical thinking. Heidegger's overcoming of metaphysics has two sides: the overcoming deals with the problems of metaphysical positions and at the same time deepens and exposes their non-metaphysical essence.[95] His analysis of truth rejects the notion of truth as correspondence. Having explained the truth of *Dasein* and that of the work of art, he tries to transcend the metaphysical ground and the central position of the human subject by inscribing it into larger, prior structures; it simultaneously results in the dissolution of the ground of truth. His dissolution of metaphysical structures leads to a play which is intermittent in its happening, i.e. truth as bringing-forth always has two contradictory moments: concealment and unconcealment, or presence and absence. His concept of play in terms of the truth of *Dasein* cannot be regarded as a metaphysically grounded concept.

Lafont criticizes *Dasein*'s quasi-transcendental structure in relation to world, which provides the *a priori* constitution of its Being. She argues that the ontological difference in *Being and Time* substitutes empirical-transcendental duality.[96] Here I would like to mention that one cannot ascribe any normative value to *Dasein*'s relational structure, to the world. The whole structure of *Dasein* is aimed at the destruction of any objectification. The world opened up is not something that has objective, metaphysical value, but it (world) implies *Dasein*'s mode of existence, its (*Dasein*'s) relational structure as such.[97] The relation between *Dasein* and the world is relational in the sense that the world, which is the projection of *Dasein,* is the very condition for the possibility of its own self.[98] The world, which is *Dasein*'s relation to the beings as whole, is not taken as a being, but the world as a whole denotes that its projection of the world is at the same time its thrownness, its absorption in and by beings or withdrawal. Lafont argues that the understanding of entities is always pre-given to human beings, and we share the language and heritage of culture, truth as disclosedness, which is given in terms of *Dasein,* radicalizes Husserl's phenomenology.[99] Here I want to explore the truth of equiprimordiality in *Being and Time*. The world and *Dasein* are equiprimordial in the sense that both the world and *Dasein* exist in a reciprocal play of transcendental grounding.[100] *Dasein*'s Being-in-the-world can be called transcendental. However, it has no intrinsic value in itself, but it denotes the value of belonging-togetherness, which creates problem of transcendence itself.[101] "Transcendence constitutes selfhood. Yet once again, it never in the first instance constitutes only selfhood; rather, the surpassing in each case intrinsically concerns also beings that Dasein 'itself' is *not.*"[102] *Dasein*'s transcendence, the relationship between *Dasein* and the world is to be grasped as a play, which explains the originary happening of truth of Being beyond metaphysical truth. He regards the transcendence of *Dasein* as the *origin* of grounding, *freedom*,[103] which denotes the meaning of the movement of play beyond any determinations. With Heidegger, freedom implies the grounding function of metaphysical truth, but it cannot be explained in terms of traditional philosophy. Difference is the origin of ground in general. Derrida's deconstructive terms deepen the implications of the Heideggerian difference as the origin.

The transcendence that is *Dasein*'s projection of the world itself is the ground of truth. The reciprocity between world and *Dasein* that constitutes the origin of ground does not have any objective values. The ground is projected and it becomes the very condition for the possibility of *Dasein*'s existence. Here the term ground does not have the meaning of presence, but it designates an *abyss of ground*, or *non-ground*, in which the truth of *Dasein* happens in relation to the projection of the world. In projecting, *Dasein* exceeds itself, and its potentiality for being-in-the-world is a withdrawal. He describes the characteristic of *Dasein*'s transcendence as that which exceeds and withdraws. The truth of entities unveiled in transcendence remains concealed *as such*. The truth of entities is grounded in

Being and this transcendental dimension provides the space for the ground of truth. The origin of the grounding of the truth of entities is essentially transcendental, which is the possibility, basis and account of metaphysical truth. The equi-originary transcendental springing forth of grounding is strewn into the projection of world, absorption within beings, and ontological grounding of beings. Transcendence, *Dasein's* projection of the world, explains the possibility, basis and account of the meaning if its existence is considered as a playing place because it entails *Dasein*'s coming-to-be (exceed) and withdrawal as well. He explains the play of transcendence as a movement of oscillation in order to denote the intermittent happening of presence and absence, which replaces the subjective value of truth.[104] Kühler explains the transcendence as *Dasein*'s oscillating movement between the projection of a world and its simultaneous control by this world.[105]

The transcendence as ground has non-essence because it springs from finite freedom. "The ground that springs forth in transcending folds back upon freedom itself, and freedom *as origin* itself becomes 'ground.' *Freedom is the ground of ground*... As *this* ground, however, freedom is the *abyss of ground* (Ab-grund) in Dasein. Not that our individual, free comportment is groundless; rather, in its essence as transcendence, freedom places Dasein, as potentiality for being, in possibilities that gape open before its finite choice, i.e. within its destiny."[106] Transcendence denotes the coming-into-being of *Dasein*'s worldly context, the basic mode of its existence, which is to be seen as an originary difference without constituting the presence of ground. Its 'destiny' is exsistence, or thrownness into the world, by which it is deprived of being a Self. With regard to *Dasein*'s transcendence, Küchler concludes that *Dasein*'s existence is "*suspended* in the midst of beings, or exposed to the groundless abyss (*Ab-grund*) of the transcendental playing space. The playing movement of *Dasein*'s transcendence thus marks an ontological situation where a stable, unchanging ground has indeed become unavailable, or where the metaphysical ground has disappeared in the *grounding* movement of transcendence, which, according to Heidegger, is a movement of play."[107] Suspended over abyss, *Dasein* is exposed to the ungrounded condition of Being's originary play. It is held out into nothing: "Da-sein: als Hineingehaltenheit in das Nichts von Seyn, als Verhältnis gehalten."[108] Heidegger thinks the origin of the truth of Being in terms of abyss, which, however, does not mean pure Nothingness, but rather the more abysmal source of Being. Thinking of Being as abyss denotes the non-ground of the openness of the *Da* of *Sein*.

Dasein's thrownness implies the unmasterable condition of its Being, the historicity of *Dasein*. It denotes the historical character of human Being-in-the-world. The essence of man is ek-sistence: "Man stands ek-sistingly in the destiny of Being. The ek-sistence of man is historical as such,"[109] which is never present itself. Heidegger calls it the destiny of Being: "Being comes to destiny in that It, Being, gives itself. But thought in terms of such destiny this says: it gives itself and refuses itself simultaneously."[110] The essence of Being is characterised as giving itself and refusing itself simultaneously denotes the intermittent happening of the opening and the withdrawal of Being.[111] It can be explained as the fate or destiny of Being, the *is there* of Being. The *is* is Being itself, which gives. *Es gibt* or it gives substitutes 'Being is.'[112] "The 'gives' names the essence of Being that is giving, granting its truth. The self-giving into the open, along with the open region itself, is Being itself."[113] By giving its truth, Being can never be present. By giving it withdraws. The play originates in the simultaneous happening of presence and absence, of sending and withholding, which replaces metaphysical ground. The meaning of Being comes from itself, from the movement of presencing in and out of a play. The essence of Being as presence is substituted with the truth of *Dasein* as the intermittent happening of presence and absence, opening and withdrawal.[114]

In the essay on *The Origin of the Work of Art* Heidegger explores the meaning of art as origin; art as 'putting-into-work' of truth implies the strife between the world and the earth. In the work of art the essence of presencing is polemical in the sense that there is a disagreement between the opening up of the world, i.e. the unconcealment and the withdrawal or concealment, i.e. the meaning of the earth. The origin of the work of art is the strife since the world opens itself in that the earth comes to rise up. By instigating strife, the work of art has the very essence of Being, i.e. it lets the place of openness happen: "...then Being, by way of its own essence, lets the free space of openness (the clearing of the There) happen, and introduces it as a place *of the sort* in which each being emerges in its own way."[115] The work of art puts truth into work means that it opens up the space, the *Da*, the originary strife of concealment and unconcealment, in which beings emerge or come into their truth. Here the space opened is the *rift*, which, however, cannot be regarded as separation, but that which holds difference elements (concealment and unconcealment) together. "Truth happens only by establishing itself in the strife and the free space opened up by truth itself."[116] Art is the origin of truth means that in and through the play of opening and withdrawal, truth comes into being. Truth happens in the work of art in and through the opening, in which the work of art becomes a *being*. In other words, a being comes to be *as* something only in and through the opening of the work of art. Heidegger explains the dialectic nature of truth through the example of peasant shoes; equipment can be what it is only in its truth, and at the same time here the truth of the equipment disappears in the world of a peasant woman opened up by it. The setting up of the world means the epoch within the history of Being, here the meaning of the peasant world; the setting forth of the earth is the disappearance of the truth of equipment by the new happening of truth. The truth as conflict sets aside the pre-predicative aspect of the origin. The *There* (*Da*) of *Da-sein* cannot be determined as something that *is*, but rather as the play of difference in which the clearing or truth happens in an originary sense. The space opened in the clearing of a thing is not a place in space with objective content, rather it is the way in which Being is thought of as giving and withdrawing, which lets the entities appear. Play as giving and withdrawing is explained in the essay on the work of art in terms of strife. In *The Principle of Reason* Heidegger develops the notion of play that brings entities to be: "The history of Being is the

'Geschick' of Being that proffers itself to us in withdrawing its essence."[117] The *Geschick* of Being is its destiny, i.e. that which brings entities into the open while itself withdraws in that very act.

By introducing the truth of *Dasein* and the origin of the work of art, which proclaim the differential structure as origin, Heidegger deconstructs the essence of Being as presence, the centre of philosophy. Gasché maintains that the Derridean deconstructive thought, which removes the transcendental signified, is essentially based on Heideggerean notion of Being as revealing-concealing.[118] However, Derrida claims that the undecidability of his deconstructive terms is not similar to that of equivocality, the inexhaustible ambivalence of a word in a language.[119] His notion of undecidability does not have a semantic significance since it springs from the irreducible excess of the alterity.

Origin as the play of presence in Derrida

After Heidegger's notion of origin as emergence, the truth of which consists of different elements, Derrida too develops the truth of infrastructure, i.e. the essence of origin as play. The meaning of infrastructure cannot be understood in terms of unity, synthesis or totality since it denotes the meaning of endless play without a presence in either side: absence and presence. For Derrida origin is preceded by play, which disrupts presence. Regarding the significance of play he says that his concept of origin implies the irreducible tension in the present now. However, he adds that in the system of difference, play not only implies that the origin is the movement of presence and absence, but also, as it is thought radically, must be considered 'before the alternative of presence and absence.'[120] The presence of alterity in the truth of a given moment is what constitutes the Derridean concept of play. His deconstructive thought exposes the ambiguous truth of infrastructure, which combines heterogeneous predicates. Gasché maintains that the Derridean concept of origin is not similar to Heidegger's concept of truth as equi-primordial, because *Dasein*'s pre-reflexive understanding still remains part of subject-centred metaphysics.[121]

Referring truth to the implications of infrastructural chains that call off any assertion, Derrida's thought carves out the essence of origin. The force of infrastructure is the condition for the possibility, in which the spontaneous present-now can emerge as the 'pure initiality of the event only on the condition that it does not itself *present itself*.'[122] There is nothing present in the presencing. The origin is only an effect in the originary movement of presencing, which marks the departure from the metaphysical understanding of Being as ground and presence. The philosophy of deconstruction shakes the totality of philosophy, the common field of traditional philosophy. Derrida substitutes it with a field of infinite substitutions of finite and contingent elements.[123] The pluralization of the origin is a first step toward the deconstruction of the value of origin. He argues a system of infrastructure consisting of infinite chains, *writing*, which undermines the possibility of referring to a point of presence and to an origin to which everything can be deduced.[124] There is no infinite truth in differential structures; its origin disappears as it is opened. What makes visibility possible in classical philosophy remains effaced and invisible in originary doubling as the impure opening.

Différance, which is neither a word nor a concept, implies the origin of differences. Here, the term origin shall not be considered in metaphysical sense. It is an incomplete non-concept of deferred difference. "*Différance* is the non-full, non-simple, structured and differentiating origin of differences. Thus, the name 'origin' no longer suits it."[125] *Différance,* being necessitated by a radical alterity, cannot be mastered by any given text, philosophical or any other. Such an alterity would be neither inside nor outside a text. Rather it is simultaneously both inside and outside a text. With this strange word he suspended the question of Being. He crosses out the 'is.' *Différance* 'is not.'[126] If Being 'is,' *différance* is neither 'is' nor 'is not.' The play means the structural moment of non-totalization,[127] the play without a centre. The play without a centre refers to the endless movement of deferral that never reaches an end. His deconstructive concepts like textuality and *writing* denote the irretrievable disappearance of the meaning of something that is present.

Whereas Heidegger with the question of the meaning of Being tries to reach the thing itself, Derrida does not. However, both of them argue that the thing itself *is* not. Derrida does not ask the question of the meaning of Being, for he would says that we are left only with traces, the disappearance of origin, which, according to him, is the trace or the non-origin, the origin of the origin.[128] Because of the trace, the property of the signified is to be itself and *other* simultaneously. We have only signs, the threads of too many lines of traces, and never meaning in its full sense. Thus he shows that there is a *play*; the absence of the transcendental signified calls for limitless play, which is the result of the deconstruction of metaphysics of presence. "...no element can function as a sign without referring to another element which itself is not simply present. This interweaving results in each 'element'—phoneme or grapheme—being constituted on the basis of the trace within it of the other elements of the chain or system."[129] Meaning transpires in the network of traces. Meaning is constituted by the process of weaving: language. Since everything transpires within language constituted by the network or system of signifiers and is locked within that system, there is no escape from the system of signifiers and traces. For Derrida philosophy is literary.[130] In order to understand the fatal implication of this statement, one has to ask what his understanding of literature is. According to him, Literature has no essence, no origin. Literature proclaims that there is no literature.[131] It is indefinable since it is beyond a definite structure. Even though Clark acknowledges the phenomenal force in Heidegger's poetry, which brings *something* to the fore, he opines that Heidegger's question of Being is basically synonymous to Derrida's concept of literature, which does not present something in truth nor in the form of negation, i.e. self-concealment.[132] Derrida's notion of literature and Heidegger's concept of language are open towards the *other* and the meaning of beings consists in the doubling of present and non-present. The non-originary origin of literature resists the ontological question that starts with *what is...?*[133] In order to transcend the field of essence, Derrida shifts the focus from philosophy to language, to the multiply structured arrangements of signifiers. The supplementary character of text decentralizes the notion of the self-presence of a reality.[134] Like the meaning of a text, meaning of literature too depends upon its prior-structures.[135] He calls the anterior meaning of a text *arche-trace* or *arche-writing*, which implies the meaning of self-erasure of the present. He reduces philosophy or transcendental truth to the level of literary in order to denote the necessity of presence and at the same time its effacement or displacement. In so far as Derrida and Lafont attribute quasi-transcendental truth to the Heideggerian origin, Derrida's deconstructive terms are also liable to the same criticism.

To liberate philosophy from the grip of metaphysics of presence, Derrida's *différance* reduces the transcendental truth to a linguistic signifier. Being, which institutes itself as the highest transcendental signified, is a matter of referent in metaphysics; but it is, for him, only one of the signifiers or effects in the philosophy of *différance*. There is no first-origin that can be conceived as the underlying principle, the ultimate cause of all. If one can speak of origin, there can be only *différance,* but in the classical sense it can never be an origin at all because it carves out any single origin in infrastructural chain. Originary *différance,* according to Derrida, is neither presence nor absence; it is neither positive nor negative. It denotes a structure of irreducible complexity, within which the play of presence or absence takes place.[136] "The play of difference supposes, in effect, synthesis and referrals which forbid at any moment, or in any sense, that a simple element be *present* in and of itself, referring only to itself. ... This interweaving, this textile, is the *text* produced only in the transformation of another text. Nothing, neither among the elements nor within the system, is anywhere ever simply present nor absent. There are only, everywhere, differences and traces."[137] Nothing has intrinsic validity in itself because everything is interrelated in the interweaving system of difference. The so-called presence is only the effect of *différance,* and the self-presence of traditional metaphysics is substituted with traces and differences of non-present. Derrida's linguistic concept rejects the view that the words we utter have a determinative meaning. The words we use can neither reach to anything non-linguistic, which would determine their meaning. This argument refuses to accept the fundamental position of traditional linguistic philosophy, e.g. that of Fregean senses, which speaks of the relationship between the abstract object and the words we utter.[138] Derrida's dictum, 'There is nothing outside the text,' rejects the foundation of traditional linguistic philosophy, which holds the view that the intentions that we have when we utter something give our words a determinative sense. By the term presence Derrida means anything non-linguistic that might serve to give utterances any determinative meaning.

The multi-contextual relations of signifiers produce relativity of meaning. According to Derrida, meaning can be determined out of context ('there is nothing outside the text'), but no context is determinable.[139] Therefore, all texts are undecidably relative because of the impossibility of completely determining textual contexts. The impossibility of exhausting contextual possibilities leads to the impossibility of controlling effects of signification. Meaning is context-bound, but context is boundless, which means that signification within a text is unmasterable. Since meaning is context-bound, intentions alone do not suffice to determine meaning, context must be mobilised. Since context is boundless, any account of the context can yield full determination of meaning. Against any set of formulations, one can imagine further possibilities of context. The unmasterable context is "Something promises itself as it escapes, gives itself, as it moves away, and strictly speaking it cannot even be called presence. Such is the constraint of the supplement, such, exceeding all the language of metaphysics, is this structure 'almost inconceivable to reason.'"[140] The supplementary force in the meaning of entity makes it at the same time non-present. In such condition, nothing can be definable and no concept is fully exhaustible. In Derrida's view there is no possibility of arriving at absolute knowledge with absolute certainty.

As Christoph Menke concludes, Derrida's deconstructive thought imples aesthetic experience that involves the confluence of aesthetic as well as non-aesthetic validity. Since the aesthetic experience is possible only through a processual negativity, i.e. it (aesthetic experience) involves the confluence of both truth and non-truth, it questions the sovereignty of aesthetic experience itself.[141] By the very fact that the meaning of Being is built upon its alterity, it requires the moment of non-Being for its intelligibility. Roughly, the point is to show what is traditionally and initially regarded as the outside actually inhabits the core of the inside, and causes the contamination of the purity of Being. Nothing and Being cohabit in one and the same event of presence, each inhabiting or entrapping the *other* as its essential constitutive moment; neither is earlier or later, they are in play in simultaneous and ambivalent way. In what is named text, the border between opposites is blurred, and what seems to be an *either...or* situation turns out to be a *both...and* situation; *both...and* is typical textual character with the logic of *neither...nor*.[142]

Derrida on Heidegger: a critical appraisal

In our time there are critics, who argue that Heidegger's ontological difference remains with in the milieu of presence. Ascribing the value of presence to ontological difference, Derrida begins to think that there is a possibility of more originary origin, which is older than the origin of Heidegger.[143] Does Heidegger's concept of difference still belong to the horizon of metaphysics? This thesis explains deconstruction after the meaning of destruction without eliminating the value of the latter.

Derrida's criticism that the very notion of Heidegger's difference reconstitutes the value of presence is to be regarded as a distortion of the meaning of the Heideggerian difference since Heidegger explicitly says that the difference between Being and beings cannot have the value of presence and appear *as such*.[144] The truth of *Dasein* and that of the work of art implies the notion of difference, which is to be regarded as a play of presence and absence. According to Heidegger, determination of the truth of entities is impossible. In this context, Lafont's argument that the ontological difference substitutes the empirical-transcendental difference by determining the meaning of ontic on the basis of *a priori* knowledge revealed in language is to be rejected.[145] Unlike transcendental philosophy, which defines the truth of entities, Heidegger's *Dasein* and the truth of the work of art bring the strange relationship between entities and their meaning to light. For him the centre of truth is this relationship, which cannot be regarded as a further determination of the meaning of Being. Rather this relationship (between Being and beings) is devoid of the quality of presence, since it makes the value of the presence an issue.

In opposition to the philosophy of identity, the Heideggerian and the Derridean philosophy can be called the philosophy of difference because it eliminates the possibility of the single origin of truth. The truth of the referential structure in Heidegger and the meaning of the arche-trace or *différance* in Derrida indicate the strange unity or synthesis of so-called presence or self and its *other* before all conceptual truth. The truth of an entity, being inscribed by what it is not, constitutes non-presence, which is more primordial than any possible determination. Destruction and deconstruction question the truth of Being since its infrastructures do not allow reflection (i.e. different systems of thought) to reach out for a solid and present ground. Infrastructure limits truth as revealment and rules out the possibility of presence. Destruction and deconstruction show how metaphysical concepts draw their possibility from that which ultimately makes them impossible. In search of the truth of Being Heidegger and Derrida pursue the *other*, which is discarded by metaphysics. They find the *other* at the very origin of truth.

However, as Hills Miller indicates, Derrida does not concede that Heidegger's thought is free from the subject-centred metaphysics.[146] In Derrida's scrutiny of Heidegger's essay on the work of art, Derrida claims that he detects Heidegger's failure, his falling back to the traditional metaphysical determination of truth.[147] Does Heidegger's description of the painting reveal the notion of origin in the traditional sense?

"Truth is the openness of beings. To know is accordingly to be able to stand in the openness of beings, to stand up to it."[148] We have to investigate whether in his essay on the work of art there occurs an openness of being, in which the meaning of van Gogh's painting comes to be in truth. In other words, does the painting provide the knowledge of a pair of shoes of a peasant woman?

Derrida holds the view that Heidegger, in attributing subject to van Gogh's picture (the shoes), continue to stick to traditional metaphysics, because he determines the shoe-equipment as something that it is by means of alterity (i.e. by means of usefulness and reliability). Derrida points out that the whole thrust of the essay on the work of art is the exposition of the concept of ontological difference, the *fort-da*,[149] which implies the meaning of withdrawal. The determination of the painting by Heidegger as peasant shoes results in tying the *fort* with *da*; the *da* of the thing is determined by its anterior truth, by *Sein* or Being. Thereby the irreducible *fort/da* is reduced to a system of truth. Derrida argues that the description of van Gogh's painting blurs the distinction between ontic and ontological. Derrida develops the logic of the laces to show how the determination of shoes eliminates the boundaries between being and Being in the essay on the work of art. The concept of the origin is not free from Heidegger's consciousness.[150] In Heidegger's determination of the painting his consciousness plays a vital role because, Derrida writes, "the whole path of thought, for Heidegger, leads back, by a dis-stancing , to a *Da* (thus the *Da* of *Sein*) which is not merely close, but whose proximity lets the distance of the *fort* play within it."[151] In the determination of mere thing on the basis of its truth, there come to meet two contradictory factors: being and Being. This argument, i.e. the gathering together or the truth of *fort-da* in one single moment, thwarts Heidegger's endeavour in his essay on the work of art, since he too considers the pre-given origin as the trap of all traps.

The inevitable outcome of the determination of van Gogh's shoes deprives the text of its own textuality, of its characteristic, the plurality of potentials. Since the truth of textuality keeps the ambivalence of *neither...nor*, both Heidegger and Schapiro commit the error of choosing one position and eliminating the other. The essay *Restitutions* shows how Heidegger and Schapiro continue to be the representatives of traditional philosophy by affirming one of the many aspects of textual differences. In dealing with Heidegger's essay Derrida develops the probleme of restitutions in order to achieve his aim: to show textual play within it (i.e. the subject of the shoes is *neither* the peasant woman *nor* the artist). He finds a suitable opportunity to carry out his task of deconstruction in the correspondence between Heidegger and Schapiro, but fails to grasp the integrity of Heidegger's essay. The Derridean style of reasoning is motivated with a single purpose, which is to deconstruct the text; such kind of approach is typical of his critique of various philosophical texts too.

Derrida strongly criticizes Heidegger's description of the shoes, particularly, the last sentence of his description: "From out of this protected belonging the equipment itself rises to its resting-with-itself,"[152] which undermines Heidegger's own argument in the essay. Here the truth is revealed in the traditional sense of *a-lētheia*, which contradicts the Heideggerian exposition of origin as conflict or fissure. The shoe-equipment, out of being protected in the world of the peasant woman, manifests its subject; the subject of the shoes originates (rests) from the shoes themselves. Derrida maintains that in exploring the traditional sense of truth based on the usefulness and reliability of the equipment Heidegger's subjectivity plays an important role in the description, thus returning to the tradition of Western philosophy that he wants to criticize. Derrida criticizes Heidegger's interpretation of the painting by van Gogh: "It is indeed *this* pair in *this* painting which opens to the truth of the being-product."[153] His treatise on the work of art discloses 'what the product is,' its product-being as what the pair of peasant's shoes is, in truth. Can one justify this criticism? Derrida observes that the essence of the equipment, not through considering an actual artefact in use, but by looking at a painting by van Gogh that has spoken and revealed to us what these shoes really are. "What happens here? What is at work in the work of art? Van Gogh's painting is the disclosure of what the equipment, the pair of peasant shoes, *is* in truth. This being emerges into the unconcealment of its Being."[154] What happens here is the revelation, truth. The work of art opens up its truth, what it is in its Being, i.e. the peasant shoes. This opening up or disclosure is the happening of truth. The essence of the work of art is thus the unfolding of truth. In the work of art truth is at work.[155] This theory of art is the revival of the original Greek conceptions of *technē* and *poiēsis*, which denote disclosure. Original *poiēsis* produces, leads forward, brings to light what is hidden and does not immediately show itself (by itself, physis, 'naturally') without this act of production. What is made, wrought, created in art is not a thing but, above all disclosure. The essence of production as disclosure is showing itself or manifestation. In the essay, truth is manifested or revealed as what it is in and through Heidegger's description of the painting.

Here Derrida is to be blamed for the misreading and the misinterpretation of the Heideggerian notion of truth, since Heidegger takes van Gogh's painting as an example of the truth of equipment: "We chose as example a common sort of equipment—a pair of peasant shoes."[156] In order to describe the truth of the painting in terms of traditional philosophy, it is apt to facilitate the visual realization of the shoes. In the essay Heidegger mentions that he selected one of van Gogh's paintings and the Greek temple as examples to describe the truth of traditional metaphysics, but his own notion of truth is an entirely different issue, which he explains as strife between the world and the earth. We cannot attribute the transcendental signified to the Heideggerian philosophy, since he wants to overcome the same position in the essay. According to Kockelmans, Derrida misreads Heidegger's important aim in it that by describing the equipment he intends to show how its truth can be determined on the basis of its usage. Heidegger is well aware of the fact that these shoes are subject-less: "we cannot even tell where these shoes stand."[157] He is also well aware of the consequences of the interpretation of the equipment on the basis of its pre-origin, usefulness and reliability, but here, as Pattison and Kockelmans maintain, he gives us an example of the truth of the Being of the equipment, which cannot be considered as his falling back on traditional metaphysics in order to determine the truth of a thing on the basis of the underlying principle.[158]

In the essay Heidegger does not want to determine the truth of a thing, here by determining the subject of the painting that lies *underneath* the shoe-picture and by going beyond the proper characteristics of the shoes, which he criticizes as the assault of metaphysics upon mere thing. Instead he wants to uphold truth as irreducibility which is the characteristic feature of the truth of *Dasein* and that of work of art. In *Being and Time* Heidegger describes that *Dasein* carries the voice of the public (*They*) within it. The *Da* of *Sein* contains the truth of the *other*. The exteriority remains in *Dasein*, the site opened up in *Dasein*, cannot be attached to its truth. The site of the *other* in *Dasein* is irreducible. His essay on the work of art opens the structure of the bottomless ground that he describes in terms of truth as a unit of strife. Derrida's too makes use of the notion of abyss as bottomless ground without a centre.

Neither Heidegger nor Derrida come up with a fixed centre or origin of the truth of a thing; even though Heidegger's ontological difference constitutes a *structure* of truth, it has the same significance, in relation to the question of the origin of truth, as that of Derrida's *différance,* which does not provide a unit of truth. The sole intention of Derrida's reading of Heidegger is to go beyond the ontological difference by deconstructing it. However, Derrida's deconstruction does not eliminate the meaning of Heidegger's difference, but his *différance* follows the ontological difference. *Différance* is not *older* than difference. But it must be pointed out that Derrida follows and goes beyond Heidegger in the sense that without eliminating ontological difference, his critique and his thought deepen its implications. Derrida's concept of truth as play implies the same concept of truth as that of ontological difference: truth as difference means that at the very time of its realization it differs and defers without proving a meaning. For example, the logic of laces, which Derrida develops in *The Truth in Painting* to attack Heidegger's restitution of the painting, contains the meaning of his deconstructive thought, a position that

Heidegger shares in the essay too.[159] In *Restitutions* Derrida, following in Heidegger's footsteps by employing his thought, describes and deepens the implications of ontological difference.

Moreover, we cannot judge the entire nuances of the Heideggerian truth solely on the basis of naming van Gogh's shoes, namely peasant shoes, without giving attention to the gist and purpose of the entire text. Heidegger is well aware of the fact that by experiencing entities as something that come to presence, one forgets what makes this presence possible, i.e. the presencing of what is present. In this respect Derrida misreads Heidegger's essay by twisting its overall meaning and aim so as to achieve his purpose.

Deconstruction as a practice has some kind relevance too. It does not solve the philosophical problem of the origin of truth through traditional procedures. It infects a text in order to make explicit its inconsistencies, contradictions or aporias, which are inevitable for the discursiveness of philosophy and for the elucidation of meaning. The Derridean deconstruction proceeds by demonstrating the inescapable *différance*, to which the transcendental signified lends itself. In the philosophy of *différance* there is no possibility of transcendental truth; there are only signifiers. In the absence of transcendental truth, signifiers are related to each other in differential relationship. '*Différance* differs-defers;' there is no truth or element outside this movement of *différance*. Given this operation of *différance*, Derrida contends that logocentric concepts are caught up in an infinite circularity of signifiers and that they are not able to present the transcendental absolute.[160] Its consequences are unpredictable to philosophy. It shakes the foundation of Western metaphysics. Beyond that, the deconstruction has another positive side to it. It helps philosophy to get ride of all preconceptions. One of the major complaints against metaphysics is that it is a blind construction of ideas and ideals. It creates the meaning of a utopian world over the real world.

During a colloquium at the faculty of philosophy at the university of Münster, Prof. Dr. Josef Früchtl has expressed the view that the relevance of Derrida's critique consists in the creation a small *opening* in the Heideggerian text, through which one can observe a certain regressive recoil from the other scenes: the work field, peasant woman, her work in the field, the worries and anxieties of her life, etc. His critique creates a small opening that presents an unprecedented effect, a meaningful world in Heidegger's concept of origin that Heidegger never thought of. Derrida's merit consists in unveiling an irreducible heterogeneity in the Heideggerian text that can no longer be reattached to Heidegger. Because Heidegger too wants to overcome Platonism, which thinks of Being of entities as beingness that is understood as the property of entities, which in his view, is the withdrawal of the entities revealed. He knows that by asking, thinking and experiencing entities as what they are, Being remains forgotten, which, according to him, happened at the very beginning of Greek philosophy.[161] He advocates the philosophy of alterity, the irreducible difference between Being and beings. Heidegger's concept of *fort-da* is the trace of the *other* within the present thing. *Fort-da* is the trace of this heterogeneous structure and his affirmation of and resistance to the unpresentable origin or support that gathers and disseminates meaning. The very moment we think of a thing as something, we lose its meaning. A thing that is revealed in truth *as* something has its origin in untruth. The Heideggerian-Derridean truth destructs or deconstructs the known ground of metaphysics.

The epistemological significance of the Heideggerian-Derridean difference shows the strange relation of truth and untruth at the same time at the same stage. This game of double science, as Derrida points out, "attempts an interminable event of vacillating between two poles of the opposition *without ever* constituting a third term."[162] The philosophy of Heidegger and Derrida cannot be confined to any of the determinable positions of truth; it is neither Being nor non-Being, rather it is *both* or *neither...nor*. Transcendentality is reduced to contextuality. By expounding the truth of *Dasein* as Being-in-the-world and that of the work of art as the opening up of another context, Heidegger comes up with a more originary origin of truth, the irreducibility of ontological difference, which does not allow the determination of a thing by means of transcendental truth. In and through Heidegger and Derrida the spirit of Heraclitus is revived and revisits the modern philosophical era; truth for both is the unity of multiple possibilities and, therefore, any determination is the violation of its ambivalence. The determination of truth as something 'is' or 'is not' is the moment this unity or ambivalence breaks.

Even though they attack the centre of metaphysics, the transcendental truth, they differ in the sense that Derrida goes further to complete the task set by Heidegger. Since Heidegger's project of destruction is further addressed by Derrida, argues Gasché, the distinction between the notions of destruction and deconstruction shall not be blurred.[163] Gasché opines that in the context of Greek polemic, truth, for Heidegger, is the simultaneity of equally original instances.[164] His destruction or dismantling of traditional philosophy is the construction of Being. Even though he inaugurated the destruction, it still revolves around the construction of Being.[165] The same criticism is applicable to Derrida too. Their claim that difference precedes the transcendental signified is hard to understand, since every understanding depends upon the precedence of Idea over particulars or difference. It remains an unending task to try to confine the metaphysics of presence to a framework of difference since it transcends everything and determines our reasoning. The Heideggerian notion of destruction is non-reflective (i.e. the reflection does not have any object), because it reaches out to something that is not present in any way whatsoever. The ultimate foundation towards which deconstruction reaches out lies exterior to the milieu of metaphysics.

References

1. Tilman Küchler, *Postmodern Gaming: Heidegger, Duchamp, Derrida*, New York, Peter Lang Publishing, 1994, 127.
2. Martin Heidegger, *Letter on Humanism*, 265.
3. Dorothea Frede, *The Question of Being: Heidegger's Project*, 60.
4. Tilman Küchler, *Postmodern Gaming: Heidegger, Duchamp, Derrida*, 127-28.
5. Luc Ferry and Alain Renault, *French Heideggerianism*, in *Jacques Derrida: Critical Assessments of Leading Philosophers*, Vol. I, eds. Zeynep Direk and Leonard Lawlor, London and New York, Routledge, 2002, 342.

6. *Ibid.*, 340. Jacques Derrida, *Différance*, 26.
7. Jacques Derrida, *Différance*, 22.
8. *Ibid.*, 22-25, 65-66.
9. *Ibid.*, 67.
10. Jacques Derrida, *Of Grammatology*, 14, 51-52.
11. Jacques Derrida, *Qual Quelle: Valéry's Sources*, 290.
12. In the traditional sense structure refers to the constructed system functioning within itself. For example, *eidos*, essence, etc. implicit significations in them. Structure has the meaning of closure, centrality. For Derrida structure is the possibility of what opens up the closed structures, and what closes structures off against any exterior interference. It is irreducible complexity, which guides the decentring and centring of structures. Jacques Derrida, *Of Grammatology*, 167.
13. Sublation is Derrida's translation of Hegel's *Aufhebung* meaning the raising of sensible meaning to a higher spiritual order. Hegel's *Aufhebung* implies the new level of meaning, but Derrida's sublation implies the effacement of meaning in the play of oppositions: nature and spirit, sensible and intelligible, etc. Ref. Paul Ricoeur, *Meta-phor and Meta-physics*, in *Jacques Derrida: Critical Assesments of Leading Philosophers*, Vol. I, eds. Zeynep Direk and Leonard Lawlor, London and New York, Routledge, 2002, 202-03.
14. Jacques Derrida, *Speech and Phenomena*, trans. David B. Allison and Newton Garver, Evanston, Northwestern University Press, 1973, 132.
15. Jacques Derrida, *Différance*, 25-26.
16. Jacques Derrida, *Positions*, 28-29.
17. Jacques Derrida, *Différance,* 3, 5.
18. *Différance* sounds exactly the same as difference, but the ending *ance*, which is used to produce verbal nouns, makes it a new form of meaning: 'difference-differing-deferring.' It designates both a passive difference already in place as the condition of signification and an act of differing which produces differences. Jacques Derrida, *Speech and Phenomena*, 132-33.
19. Jacques Derrida, *Speech and Phenomena*, 136. Referring to the meaning of temporalization, differ means detour which suspends the fulfilment of a desire or will. The significations of the term *différance* are, to a certain extent, correlated to Suassurean concept of linguistic philosophy. In Suassure the notion of difference emphasizes the way in which signs are arbitrary. It does not matter which sounds we choose to mean hot or cold, what matters is that they are used to mark a certain difference, and this structural property is the true

carrier of meaning. The phonetic difference, which is the condition of the possibility for language, is called by Derrida the inner *trace*, prior *writing* or the *arche-writing*, a writing which marks difference before writing. Jacques Derrida, *Of Grammatology*, 36-37, 52.

20. The French term *differer* also means to defer in the sense of to postpone. In reference to temporalization, the act of deferring denotes the present which is constituted by different moments of time- past, present and future-, the modifications of the now. The present *now* is the combination of the three different points. The present cannot come into existence without radical alterity. Jacques Derrida, *Speech and Phenomena*, 142-43. The meaning is always deferred also in referential structure, text; no one word bears a meaning until it relates to the next, which must relate to the next and so on. Ref. Jacques Derrida, *Of Grammatology*, 158.
21. Jacques Derrida, *Speech and Phenomena*, 88.
22. Jacques Derrida, *Positions*, 27.
23. *Ibid.*, 28-29.
24. Dominique Janicaud, *Presence and Appropriation*, 21.
25. Jacques Derrida, *Différance*, 5-6.
26. Jacques Derrida, *Of Grammatology*, 61.
27. The essence of trace is the dialectic of protention and retention, which is installed in the present. Jacques Derrida, *Of Grammatology*, 67.
28. David Farrell Krell, *The Perfect Future: A Note on Heidegger and Derrida*, 117.
29. Jacques Derrida, *Of Grammatology*, 47, 61. Ref. Rodolphe Gasché, *Deconstruction as Criticism*, in *Jacques Derrida: Critical Assessments of Leading Philosophers*, Vol. II., eds. Zeynep Direk and Leonard Lawlor, London and New York, Routledge, 2002, 105.
30. Jacques Derrida, *Of Grammatology*, 61.
31. Re-mark means a prior mark, or a prior text. It is Derrida's deconstructive strategy, which means meaning is relative and related to its prior mark.
32. Jacques Derrida, *Speech and Phenomena*, 154. Jacques Derrida, *Différance*, 23.
33. Jacques Derrida, *Structure, Sign and Play*, 353-54.
34. Jacques Derrida, *Différance*, 24.
35. Jacques Derrida, *Speech and Phenomena*, 70-87. In *Speech and Phenomena*, Derrida refers to Heidegger's *Kant and the Problem of Metaphysics*, in which Heidegger criticizes Husserl's vocal self-affection as the pure undivided hearing-oneself-speak. Heidegger

maintains that temporal production of the vocal self-presence, i.e. the temporal differentiation constitutes or produces the self-affection. 'The originary-point, the originary impression, from which the movement of temporalization is produced, is always pure self-affection. Ref. Jacques Derrida, *Speech and Phenomena*, 83. In *Being and Time* Heidegger explains that the whole doctrine of Being appears to have determined Being in the perspective of one singular mode of time, the mode of the present. He explains the truth of Being in temporal differentiation: past, present and future. Martin Heidegger, *Being and Time*, 41, 374-76.

36. John Sallis, *Doubling*, in *Derrida: A Critical Reader*, ed. John Wood, Oxford and Cambridge, Blackwell, 1992, 130-31.
37. Jacques Derrida, *Of Grammatology*, 67. Protention is the dialectic of the present with the anticipation of the future; retention is the dialectic of the present with memory of the past.
38. Josef Früchtl, *Zeit und Erfahrung: Adornos Revision der Revision Heideggers*, 295.
39. Jacques Derrida, *Différance*, 13.
40. *Ibid.*, 8, 18-21.
41. *Ibid.*, 13.
42. Jacques Derrida, *Dissemination*, 264-65. Ref. Timothy Clark, *Derrida, Heidegger, Blanchot*, 114-15.
43. Eve Tavor Bannet, *Structuralism and the Logic of Dissent*, 189.
44. Jacques Derrida, *Of Grammatology*, 70-71.
45. Jacques Derrida, *Positions*, 27.
46. Jacques Derrida, *Of Grammatology*, 69.
47. *Ibid.*, 112.
48. Jacques Derrida, *Positions*, 26.
49. *Ibid.*, 29.
50. Jacques Derrida, *Différance,* 12.
51. Jacques Derrida, *Of Grammatology*, 70.
52. Jacques Derrida, *Speech and Phenomena*, 136-37.
53. Timothy Clark, *Derrida, Heidegger, Blanchot*, 108.
54. Joachim Ritter and Karlfried Gründer, eds., *Historisches Wörterbuch der Philosophie*, Vol. 10, Basel, Schwabe & Co. AG, 1998, 1038.
55. Timothy Clark, *Derrida, Heidegger, Blanchot*, 108. Ref. Jacques Derrida, *Force and Signification*, 13.
56. The logic of identity suggests that everything is it is, and not something else.

57. Jacques Derrida, *Of Grammatology*, 51-52.
58. *Ibid*., 158.
59. Jacques Derrida, *Positions*, 27.
60. *Ibid*., 26.
61. Jacques Derrida, *Structure, Sign and Play*, 352-53.
62. Jacques Derrida, *Positions*, 3-4.
63. Jacques Derrida, *Of Grammatology*, 158.
64. J. Hillis Miller, *Derrida's Other*, 154-55.
65. Timothy Clark, *Derrida, Heidegger, Blanchot*, 40, 108.
66. Jacques Derrida, *Afterword: Toward an Ethic of Discussion*, 148.
67. Jacques Derrida, *Of Grammatology*, 62.
68. Alan Bass, *Introduction* to, *Writing and Difference*, Jacques Derrida, xvii-xviii.
69. Jacques Derrida, *Différance*, 10.
70. Jacques Derrida, *Dissemination*, 240. Ref. Timothy Clark, *Derrida, Heidegger Blanchot*, 116.
71. Jacques Derrida, *Of Grammatology,* 69.
72. *Ibid*., 144.
73. *Ibid*., 158-59.
74. Jacques Derrida, *Of Grammatology*, 19. Both 'is' and 'thing' are written and then crossed out simultaneously by the external graphic marks. Gayatri Chakravorty Spivak, *Introduction* to *Of Grammatology*, xiv.
75. Briankle G. Chang, *The Eclipse of Being: Heidegger and Derrida*, in *International Philosophical Quarterly*, Vol. XXV, 1985, 130.
76. Jean-Luc Nancy, *Elliptical Sense*, in *Derrida: A Critical Reader*, ed. David Wood, Oxford Cambridge, Blackwell, 1992, 43.
77. Derrida develops the concept of remark in his essay on *The Double Session*, in which it denotes the mark which is added to another mark. The remarking of a mark comes not from outside; no mark can function without referring to that which makes it possible, the mark is in advance remarked. The remark is that which opens up the possibility of referentiality within the play of the application of one mark to another. Since, in such a play, the referent is set aside in infinite reference, the remark renders the function of truth possible by limiting it. Every determination unfolds the meaning of another, which disrupts the meaning of presence. Jacques Derrida, *Dissemination*, 216, 269.
78. J. Hillis Miller, *Derrida's Others*, 158-59.

79. Timothy Clark, *Derrida, Heidegger, Blanchot*, 33.
80. Martin Heidegger, *On the way to Language*, 59, 81.
81. Jacques Derrida, *Dissemination*, 269.
82. Derek Attridge, *Introduction* to *Acts of Literature*, Jacques Derrida, ed. Derek Attridge, New York and London, Routledge 1992, 15-16.
83. Jacques Derrida, *Positions*, 46.
84. Jacques Derrida, *Dissemination*, 264-65.
85. Rodolphe Gasché, *Joining the Text: From Heidegger to Derrida*, 156-60. Ref. Timothy Clark, *Derrida, Heidegger, Blanchot*, 120-23.
86. Martin Heidegger, *Being and Time*, 189, 192-93, 196, 200. See also Chapter 2.
87. Rodolphe Gasché, *Joining the Text: From Heidegger to Derrida*, 158.
88. Jacques Derrida, *The Retreat of Metaphor*, trans. F. Gasdner, in *Enclitic*, 2, no. 2, Fall 1987, 29. Ref. Rodolphe Gasché, *Joining the Text: From Heidegger to Derrida*, 157.
89. Jacques Derrida, *The Retreat of Metaphor*, 31. Ref. Rodolphe Gasché, *Joining the Text: From Heidegger to Derrida*, 157.
90. Jacques Derrida, *Of Grammatology*, 290.
91. Martin Heidegger, *Being and Time*, 261.
92. Martin Heidegger, *The Principle of Reason*, 111-12.
93. *Ibid.*, 111. Ref. Tilman Küchler, *Post-modern Gaming: Heidegger, Duchamp, Derrida*, 26.
94. Martin Heidegger, *The Principle of Reason*, 113. Ref. Martin Heidegger, *On the Essence of Ground*, 130.
95. Tilman Küchler, *Post-modern Gaming: Heidegger, Duchamp, Derrida*, 28.
96. Christina Lafont, *Heidegger, Language, and World-Disclosure*, 21, 83.
97. Martin Heidegger, *On the Essence of Ground*, 121.
98. *Ibid.*
99. Christina Lafont, *Heidegger, Language, and World-disclosure*, 24-25. Phenomenology is a philosophy of consciousness which attempts to avoid the dualistic views such as empiricism and idealism by putting aside all preconceptions about the relationship between mind and world. It begins to think the fundamental distinction between subject and object, and go beyond them to the realm of consciousness to relate the world of phenomena. Consciousness, according to Husserl's phenomenology, is always directed outside

itself to the world, and this relationship is referred to as one of intentionality. His purpose of phenomenological reduction is 'to go to the thing itlself,' by putting aside (or bracketing off, epoche) the contingent and personal and reveal the underlying universal structures, for example, imagination or perception. It deals with phenomena as they are 'intended' by consciousness. Heidegger and Derrida criticize the phenomenological attempt to ground knowledge in experience, evidence and self-presence.

100. Martin Heidegger, *On the Essence of Ground*, 125, 134. Tilman Küchler, *Post-modern Gaming: Heidegger, Duchamp, Derrida*, 29.
101. Martin Heidegger, *On the Essence of Ground*, 110-11.
102. *Ibid.*, 108.
103. Freedom has nothing in common with ground, or cause or substance. *Ibid.*, 135, Footnote b.
104. *Ibid.*, 127-31.
105. Tilman Küchler, *Post-modern Gaming: Heidegger, Duchamp, Derrida*, 31.
106. Martin Heidegger, *On the Essence of Ground*, 134.
107. Tilman Küchler, *Post-modern Gaming: Heidegger, Duchamp, Derrida*, 31.
108. Martin Heidegger, *Zein und Zeit*, Tübingen, Max Niemeyer Verlag, 2001, 439, note 7d.
109. Martin Heidegger, *Letter on Humanism*, 239.
110. *Ibid.*
111. Tilman Küchler, *Post-modern Gaming: Heidegger, Duchamp, Derrida*, 36.
112. Martin Heidegger, *Being and Time*, 255. Martin Heidegger, *Letter on Humanism*, 238-39.
113. Martin Heidegger, *Letter on Humanism*, 238.
114. Tilman Küchler, *Post-modern Gaming: Heidegger, Duchamp, Derrida*, 34-35.
115. Martin Heidegger, *The Origin of the Work of Art*, 186.
116. *Ibid.*, 186.
117. Martin Heidegger, *The Principle of Reason*, 61.
118. Rodolphe Gasché, *Joining the Text: From Heidegger to Derrida*, 161.
119. Jacques Derrida, *Dissemination*, 229.
120. Jacques Derrida, *Structure, Sign and Play*, 369.
121. Rodolphe Gasché, *The Tain of the Mirror*, 240.

122. Jacques Derrida, *Qual Quelle: Valéry's Sources*, 296-97.
123. Jacques Derrida, *Structure, Sign and Play*, 365.
124. Jacques Derrida, *Qual Quelle: Valéry's Sources*, 277.
125. Jacques Derrida, *Différance*, 11.
126. *Ibid.*, 6.
127. Jacques Derrida, *Structure, Sign and Play*, 365. Totalization implies closure or end, which provides a concept or meaning. The play is not a concept that imparts meaning; it can no longer be concluded. For Derrida, every conclusion announces further play. There is no end of play in the differential structure.
128. Jacques Derrida, *Of Grammatology*, 61.
129. Jacques Derrida, *Positions*, 26.
130. Jacques Derrida, *Qual Quelle: Valéry's Sources*, 293.
131. Jacques Derrida, *Dissemination*, 232.
132. Timothy Clark, *Derrida, Heidegger, Blanchot*, 2, 116.
133. Jacques Derrida, *The First Session*, in *Acts of Literature*, ed. Derek Attridge, New York and London, Routledge, 1992, 127. Jacques Derrida, *Dissemination*, 232.
134. Jacques Derrida, *Of Grammatology*, 158.
135. Derek Attridge, *Introduction* to *Acts of Literature*, 10.
136. Jacques Derrida, *Of Grammatology*, 167.
137. Jacques Derrida, *Positions*, 26.
138. Rainer Born, *Frege*, in *Routledge History of Philosophy,* Vol. IX, ed. Stuart Shanker, London and New York, Routledge 1996, 141.
139. Jacques Derrida, *Signature Event Context* in *Margins of Philosophy*, trans. Alan Bass, Chicago, The University of Chicago Press, 1982, 310.
140. Jacques Derrida, *Of Grammatology*, 154.
141. Christoph Menke, *The Sovereignty of Art: Aesthetic Negativity in Adorno and Derrida*, trans. Neil Solomon, Cambridge, Massachusetts, and London, The MIT Press, 1999, 181.
142. Jacques Derrida, *Of Grammatology*, 154-55.
143. Jacques Derrida, *Ousia and Gramme: Note on a Note from Being and Time*, 67.
144. Martin Heidegger, *The Anaximander Fragment*, 51.
145. Christina Lafont, *Heidegger, Language and World-disclosure*, 18.
146. J. Hillis Miller, *Derrida's Others*, 158.
147. See Chapter 3.

148. Martin Heidegger, *Introduction to Metaphysics*, 23.
149. Jacques Derrida, *Restitutions*, 357-58.
150. Ned Lukacher, *Writing on Ashes: Heidegger Fort Derrida,* in *Diacrities*, 19.3-4, 1989, 132. Ref. Jacques Derrida, *Restitutions*, 354-55.
151. *Ibid.*, 357.
152. Martin Heidegger, *The Origin of the Work of Art*, 160.
153. Jacques Derrida, *Restituitions*, 325.
154. Martin Heidegger, *The Origin of the Work of Art*, 161.
155. *Ibid.*, 181.
156. *Ibid.*, 158.
157. *Ibid.*, 159.
158. Joseph J. Kockelmans, *Heidegger on Art and Art Works*, 110-11, 125-30; George Pattison, *The later Heidegger*, 85-86.
159. Jacques Derrida, *Restituitions*, 340.
160. Jacques Derrida, *Structure, Sign and Play*, 353.
161. Martin Heidegger, *Introduction to Metaphysics*, 18.
162. Jacques Derrida, *Positions*, 43.
163. Rodolphe Gasché, *The Tain of the Mirror*, 118.
164. *Ibid.*, 181.
165. Martin Heidegger, *The Basic Problem of Phenomenology*, 22-23.

Zusammenfassung

Metaphysik Heidegger zufolge stellt das Sein als Seiendes vor, indem sie die Unterscheidung zwischen dem Seienden und dem Sein unterlässt. Die Aussage über das Seiende betrifft um seine *Seiendheit* (*essentia*), die Sichtbarkeit des Seienden. Mit der Grundfrage der Metaphysik: "Warum ist überhaupt Seiendes und nicht vielmehr Nichts?," stellt Heidegger den Sinn des Seienden im Ganzen in Frage. Mit der phänomenologischen Untersuchung des Ursprungs des Kunstwerks (in *Der Ursprung des Kunstwerkes*) und des *Daseins* (in *Sein und Zeit*) verdeutlicht er das Problem der kategorialen Bestimmung der Richtigkeit der Aussage über das Seiende. Indem er die Geschichte des Seins als Seinsvergessenheit nachzeichnet, versucht er zu der ursprünglichen Bedeutung des Seins als *physis* and *alētheia* zurückzukehren, ganz im Sinne der Vorsokratiker, insbesondere Heraklits, dem zufolge das Sein des Dinges Verborgenheit ist. Heidegger stellt die Gültigkeit des Begriffs der Metaphysik als Anwesenheit in Frage, der seinen Anfang bei Platon und Aristoteles nimmt und seinen Höhepunkt bei Hegel und dessen Nachfolgern erreicht. Zur Untersuchung des Sinns von Sein, d.h. um zu erkennen, was ein Ding ist, verwendet Heidegger die phänomenologische Methode, die die Struktur des Seins als Verborgenheit enthüllt. Die Phänomenologie stellt ein Verfahren zur wissenschaftlichen Untersuchung der Wahrheit von Dingen dar; sie zeigt das Wesen eines Dinges, wie es ist, bevor es uns erscheint, und ohne welches es nicht erkennbar wäre. Sein geht Seiendem voraus. Die Phänomenologie weist auf die bisher unerforschte Wahrheit der *apriori*schen Unverborgenheit der

Dinge hin, das Sein des Seienden. Anhand der Analyse des *Daseins* (in *Sein und Zeit*) sowie der Idee der Wahrheit als eines Widerstreites zwischen Welt und Erde (in *Der Ursprung des Kunstwerkes*) erklärt Heidegger die transzendentale Struktur des Sinns von Sein, dessen Wesen er als ursprüngliche Differenz begreift. Ein Phänomen zeigt sich nicht wie es ist, sondern als das Ergebnis einer Welterschließung. Somit wird sein Wesen in seiner *Andersheit* als ursprüngliche Differenz begriffen.

In der vorliegenden Arbeit habe ich mich mit dem Begriff des Ursprungs nach Heidegger und Derrida auseinandergesetzt. In *Sein und Zeit* erschließt Heidegger die Wahrheit der Unverborgenheit mit dem Begriff des *Daseins*. Dieses wird als Existenz (Ex-sistenz) begriffen, d.h. als Hinausgehaltensein ins Sein. Die Wahrheit des Seienden in seiner Welterschließung ist ursprünglich Unwahrheit. In seinem Kunstwerk-Essay erläutert er den Ursprung der Wahrheit als einen Widerstreit zwischen der Verborgenheit und der Unverborgenheit, welche keinen Präsenzcharakter zulässt. Heidegger folgend, begreift auch Derrida die Geschichte der Philosophie als Logozentrismus, der ein adäquates Verständnis des Seins unmöglich macht. Dessen ursprüngliche Bedeutung versuchen beide Denker stattdessen in der reinen Struktur der Differenz zu finden: Sein entzieht sich jeglicher Bestimmung, erhält nie Präsenzcharakter. Heidegger wie Derrida lehnen den Gedanken einer eindeutigen Bestimmbarkeit ab und ersetzen ihn durch das Wechselspiel der gegensätzlichen Momente des Seins und des Nichtseins in der ursprünglichen Bedeutung der Wahrheit. Für Derrida jedoch liefert die phänomenologische Methode, anders als bei Heidegger, niemals die Wahrheit eines Textes, denn dieser charakterisiert sich durch ein unendliches Entziehen. Indem Derrida aber das Sein wegstreicht, zeigt sich seine Nähe zu Heidegger, der mit seinem Begriff der Differenz die Wahrheit des Ursprungs in Frage stellt. Trotz Derridas Kritik an Heideggers ontologischer Differenz und dessen Auffassung über den Ursprung des Kunstwerkes, und ungeachtet großer Unterschiede in Stil und Terminologie besteht nach meiner Ansicht zwischen beiden Denkern eine große Übereinstimmung in Bezug auf den Begriff des Seins, der sich einer metaphysischen Bestimmung entzieht.

Während in der bisherigen Geschichte der Philosophie das Subjekt das Zentrum von Wahrheit und Erkenntnis darstellte, geben die beiden Philosophen den Gedanken eines festen Zentrums der Wahrheit überhaupt auf und verkünden damit das Ende der Metaphysik. Derridas Kritik, Heidegger sei an der Überwindung der traditionellen Philosophie gescheitert, sowie seine Behauptung, er habe dessen Aufsatz über das Kunstwerk dekonstruiert, wurden in meiner Dissertation kritisch betrachtet. Dennoch erkenne ich das Potential der Philosophie Derridas an, Heideggers Idee der Differenz weiterzuführen und zu vertiefen.

Die Funktion der Derridàschen dekonstruktivistischen Terminologie ist eine andere als die der ontologischen Differenz Heideggers. Während die ontologische Differenz die transzendentale Wahrheit durch Gleichursprünglichkeit und den Streit bzw. das Wechselspiel von Gegensätzen ersetzt, führt die phänomenologische Reduktion Derridas zu einem unendlichen Regress. Unendliches Entziehen oder Selbstauslöschung sind charakteristisch für Derridas Auffassung von Text: dieser eröffnet die Möglichkeit der Bezugnahme durch sein Sich-Entziehen (*Remark*). Sowohl Heidegger als auch Derrida sind Vertreter der Idee einer sich entziehenden Wahrheit: Derridas Dekonstruktion bedeutet eine Neuauflage und Vertiefung von Heideggers Begriff der Differenz.

Bibliography

Primary sources

Derrida, Jacques. *Afterword: Toward an Ethic of Discussion*, in *Limited INC*, Evanston, Illinois, Northwestern University Press, 1988.

— *Différance*, in *Margins of Philosophy*, trans. Alan Bass, Chicago, The University of Chicago Press, 1982.

— *Dissemination*, trans. Barbara Johnson, London and New York, Continuum, 1981.

— *The First Session*, in *Acts of Literature*, ed. Derek Attridge, New York and London, Routledge, 1992.

— *Force and Signification*, in *Writing and Difference*, trans. Alan Bass, London and New York, Routledge, 1978.

— *Freud and the Scene of Writing*, in *Writing and Difference*, trans. Alan Bass, London and New York, Routledge, 1978.

— *Of Grammatology*, trans. Gayatri Chakravarti Spivak, Baltimore and London, The John Hopkins University Press, 1974.

— *Of Grammatology*, in *A Derrida Reader*, ed. Peggy Kamuf, New York, Columbia University Press, 1991.

— *Ousia and Grammē: Note on a Note from Being and Time*, in *Margins of Philosophy*, trans. Alan Bass, Chicago, University of Chicago Press, 1982.

— *Passe-Partout*, in *The Truth in Painting*, trans. Geoff Bennington and Ian McLeod, Chicago and London, ...rsity of Chicago Press, 1987.

— *Positions,* trans. Alan Bass, Chicago, The University of Chicago Press, 1972.

— *Qual Quelle: Valéry' Sources*, in *Margins of Philosophy*, trans. Alan Bass, Chicago, University of Chicago Press, 1982.

— *Restitutions*, in *The Truth in Painting*, trans. Geoff Bennington and Ian MacLeod, Chicago and London, The University of Chicago Press, 1978.

— *The Retreat of Metaphor*, trans. F. Gasdner, in *Enclitic*, 2, No. 2, Fall, 1987.

— *Signature Event Content*, in *Margins of Philosophy*, trans. Alan Bass, Chicago, University of Chicago Press, 1982.

— *Speech and Phenomena*, trans. David B. Allison and Newton Garver, Evanston, Northwestern University Press, 1973.

— *Structure, Sign and Play*, in *Writing and Difference*, trans. Alan Bass, London and New York, Routledge, 1978.

— *White Mythology*, in *Margins of Philosophy*, trans. Alan Bass, Chicago, The University of Chicago Press, 1982.

— *Writing and Difference*, trans. Alan Bass, London and New York, Routledge, 1978.

Heidegger, Martin. *Addendum* to *The Origin of the Work of Art*, in *Basic Writings*, ed. David Farrell Krell, London and New York, Routledge, 1993.

— *The Anaximander Fragment*, in *Early Greek Thinking*, trans. David Farrell and Frank Capuzzi, New York, Harper and Row, 1975.

— *The Basic Problems of Phenomenology*, trans. Albert Hofstadter, Bloomington & Indianapolis, Indiana University Press, 1982.

— *Being and Time*, trans. John Macquarrie & Edward Robinson, Oxford and Cambridge, Blackwell, 1962.

— *Building Dwelling Thinking*, in *Poetry, Language, and Thought*, trans. Albert Hofstadter, New York, Harper & Row, 1971.

— *The End of Philosophy*, trans. Joan Stambaugh, New York, The University of Chicago Press, 2003.

— *Elucidations of Hölderlin's Poetry*, trans. Keith Hoeller, New York, Humanity Books, 2000.

— *On the Essence and Concept of Φύσις in Aristotle's Physics B,I*, in *Pathmarks*, trans. Thomas Sheehan, ed. William macNeill, New York, Cambridge University Press, 1998.

— *On the Essence of Ground*, in *Pathmarks*, ed. William McNeill, New York, Cambridge University Press, 1998.

— *On the Essence of Truth*, in *Pathmarks*, ed. William McNeill, New York, Cambridge University Press, 1998.

— *The Essence of Truth*, trans. Ted Sadler, London and New York, Continuum, 2002.

— *The Fundamental Concepts of Metaphysics*, trans. William McNeill and Nicholas Walker, Bloomington and Indianapolis, Indiana University Press, 1995.

— and Eugen Fink, *Heraclitus Seminar*, trans. Charles H. Seibert, Evanston, Illinois, Northwestern University Press, 1979.

— *Introduction to Metaphysics*, trans. Gregory Fried and Richard Polt, New Haven & London, Yale University Press, 2000.

— *Kant and the Problems of Metaphysics*, trans. Richard Taft, Bloomington and Indianapolis, Indiana University Press, 1997.

— *Letter on Humanism*, in *Basic Writings*, ed. David Farrell Krell, London and New York, Routledge, 1993.

— *Logik, Die Frage nach der Wahrheit*, in *Gesamtausgabe*, Vol. 21, V. Klostermann, Frankfurt, 1976.

— *Nietzsche* Vol. I and II, trans. David Farrell Krell, San Francisco, Harper & Row, 1979-1987.

— *Nietzsche* Vol. III and IV, ed. David Farrell Krell, San Francisco, Harper & Row, 1979-1987.

— *The Origin of the Work of Art*, in *Basic Writings*, ed. David Farrell Krell, London and New York, Routledge, 1993.

— *The Origin of the Work of Art*, in *Poetry and Language, Thought*, trans. Albert Hofstadter, New York, Harper & Row, 1971.

— *Plato's Doctrine of Truth*, in *Pathmarks*, ed. William McNeill, New York, Cambridge University Press, 1998.

— *Preface* to *Heidegger: Through Phenomenology to Thought*, William J. Richardson S.J., New York, Fordham University Press, 2003.

— *Plato's Sophist*, trans. Richard Rojcewicz and André Schuwer, Bloomington & Indiana University Press, Indiana University Press, 2003.

— *The Principle of Reason*, trans. Reginald Lilly, Bloomington and Indianapolis, Indiana University Press, 1996.

— *On the Question of Being*, in *Pathmarks*, ed. William McNeill, New York, Cambridge University Press, 1998.

— *The Question Concerning Technology*, in *Basic Writings*, ed. David Farrell Krell, London and New York, Routledge, 1993.

— *Zein und Zeit*, Tübingen, Max Niemeyer Verlag, 2001.

— *The Thing*, in *Poetry, Language, and Thought*, trans. Albert Hofstadter, New York, Harper & Row, 1971.

— *Der Ursprung des Kunstwerkes*, ed. H.G. Gadamer, Stuttgart, Philipp Reclam Jun. GmbH & Co., 1960.

— *On The Way To Language*, trans. Peter D. Hertz, San Francisco, Harper & Row, 1982.

— *What Is Metaphysics?*, in *Basic Writings*. ed. David Farrell Krell, London and New York, Routledge, 1993.

Secondary sources

Aquinas, St. Thomas, *The Summa Theologica*, Vol. I, 1.Q3.4, trans. Fathers of the English Dominican Province, London, Encyclopaedia Britannica, 1952.

Aristotle, *Metaphysics Books Z and H*, trans. David Bosteock, Oxford, Oxford University Press, 1994.

Aristotle, *Metaphysics*, trans. Hugh Lawson-Tancred, London, Penguin Books, 1998.

Attridge, Derek, *Introduction* to *Acts of Literature*, Jacques Derrida, ed. Derek Attridge, New York and London, Routledge, 1992.

Audi, Robert ed., *The Cambridge Dictionary of Philosophy*, Cambridge, Cambridge University Press, 1985.

Bannet, Eve Tavor, *Structuralism and the Logic of Dissent*, Hampshire and London, The Macmillan Press LTD., 1989.

Bass, Alan, *Introduction* to *Writing and Difference*, Jacques Derrida, trans. Alan Bass, London and New York, Routledge, 1978.

Behler, Ernst, *Confrontations: Derrida, Heidegger, Nietzsche*, trans. Steven Taubeneck, California, Stanford University Press, 1991.

Beutsch, Eliot, *Culture and Modernity: East-West Philosophic Perspectives*, Delhi, Motilal Banarsidas Publishers Pvt. Ltd., 1994.

Bonevac, Daniel, *Kant's Copernican Revolution*, in *Routledge History of Philosophy*, Vol. VI, ed. Robert C. Solomon and Kathleen M. Higgins, London and New York, Routledge, 1993.

Born, Rainer, *Frege*, in *Routledge History of Philosophy,* Vol. IX, ed. Stuart Shanker, London and New York, Routledge, 1996.

Bullock, Alan and Woodings, R.B. eds., *The Fontana Dictionary of Modern Thinkers*, London, Fontana Press, 1992.

Chakravorty, Spivak Gayatri, *Introduction* to *Of Grammatology*, Jacques Derrida, trans. Gayatri Chakravarti Spivak, Baltimore and London, The John Hopkins University Press, 1974.

Chang, Briankle G., *The Eclipse of Being: Heidegger and Derrida*, in *International Philosophical Quarterly*, Vol. XXV, 1985.

Clark, Timothy, *Derrida, Heidegger, Blanchot*, Cambridge, Cambridge University Press, 1992.

Code, Alan, *Aristotle's Logic and Metaphysics*, in *Routledge History of Philosophy,* Vol. II, ed, David Furley, London and New York, Routledge, 1997.

Collins, Jeff and Mayblin, Bill, *Derrida for Beginners*, ed., Richard Appignanesi, Cambridge, Icon Books Ltd., 1996.

Copleston, Frederick S.J., *A History of Philosophy*, Vol. I, Part 2, New York, Image Books, 1962.

Culler, Jonathan, *On Deconstruction: Theory and Criticism after Structuralism*, London, Melbourne and Henley, Routledge & Kegan Paul, 1983.

Dreyfus, Hubert L., *Heidegger on the Connection between Nihilism, Art, Technology, and Politics*, in *The Cambridge Companion to Heidegger*, ed. Charles B. Guignon, Cambridge, Cambridge University Press, 1993.

Dreyfus, Hubert and Hall, Harrison, *Introduction* to *Heidegger: A Critical Reader*, eds. Hubert Dreyfus and Harrison Hall, Oxford and Cambridge, Blackwell, 1992.

Dreyfus, Hubert, *History of the Being of Equipment*, in *Heidegger: A Critical Reader*, eds. Hubert L. Dreyfus and Harrison Hall, Oxford and Cambridge, Blackwell, 1992.

Fenves, Peter, *Hölderlin, Jahann Christian Friedrich*, in *Encyclopaedia of Aesthetics*, Vol. II, ed. Michael Kelly, Oxford, New York, Oxford University Press, 1998.

Ferry, Luc and Renault, Alain, *French Heideggerianism*, in *Jacques Derrida: Critical Assessments of Leading Philosophers*, Vol. I, eds. Zeynep Direk and Leonard Lawlor, London and New York, Routledge, 2002.

Figal, Günter, *Martin Heidegger—Phänomeology der Freiheit*, Frankfurt am Main, Athenaeum, 1988.

Frede, Dorothea, *The Question of Being: Heidegger's Project*, in *The Cambridge Companion to Heidegger*, ed. Charles B. Guignon, Cambridge, Cambridge University Press, 1993.

Fried, Gregory and Polt, Richard, *Introduction*, to *Introduction to Metaphysics,* Martin Heidegger, New Haven and London, Yale University Press, 2000.

Früchtl, Josef, *Zeit und Erfahrung: Adornos Revision der Revision Heideggers*, in *Martin Heidegger: Innen-und Außenansichten*, eds. Forum für Philosophie Bad Homburg, Suhrkamp, 1989.

Gadamer, Hans-Goerg, *Zur Einführung* to *Der Ursprung des Kunstwerkes*, Martin Heidegger, Stuttgart, Philipp Reclam Jun. GmbH & Co., 1960.

Gadamer, Hans-Georg, *Hermeneutics and Logocentrism*, in *Jacques Derrida: Critical Assessments of Leading Philosophers*, eds. Zeynep Direk and Leonard Lawlor, Vol. I, London and New York, Routledge, 2002.

Gasché, Rodolphe, *Deconstruction as Criticism*, in *Jacques Derrida: Critical Assessments of Leading Philosophers*,

Vol. II, eds. Zeynep Direk and Leonard Lawlor, London and New York, Routledge, 2002.

Gasché, Rodolphe, *Joining the Text: From Heidegger to Derrida*, in *The Yale Critics: Deconstruction in America*, eds. Jonathan Arac, Wlad Godzich, Wallace Martin, Minneapolis, University of Minnesota Press, 1983.

Gasché, Rodolphe, *Like the Rose-without why: Transcendentalism and Practical Philosophy*, in *Diacritics*, Fall-Winter, (19.3-4), 1989.

Gasché, Rodolphe, *The Tain of the Mirror*, Cambridge and London, Harvard University Press, 1986.

Gethmann-Siefert, Annemarie, *Martin Heidegger und die Kunstwissenschaft*, in *Heidegger und die praktische Philosophie*, Hrsg. Annemarie Gethmann-Siefert und Otto Pöggeler, Frankfurt am Main, Suhrkamp, 1988.

Gethmann, Carl Friedrich, *Heideggers Wahrheitskonzeption in seinen Marburger Vorlesungen*, in *Martin Heidegger: Innen-und Außenansichten*, eds. Forum für Philosophie Bad Homburg, Suhrkamp, 1989.

Haugeland, John, *Dasein's Disclosedness*, in *Heidegger: A Critical Reader*, eds. Hubert L. Dreyfus and Harrison Hall, Cambridge and Oxford, Basil Blackwell, 1992.

Heinaman, Robert, *Plato: Metaphysics and Epistemology*, in *Routledge History of Philosophy*, Vol. I, ed. C.C.W. Taylor, London and New York, Routledge, 1997.

Hoeller, Keith, *Introduction* to *Elucidations of Hölderlin's Poetry*, Martin Heidegger, trans. Keith Hoeller, New York, Humanity Books, 2000.

Hussey, Edward, *Pythagoreans and Eleatics*, in *Routledge History of Philosophy*, Vol. I, ed. C.C.W. Taylor, London and New York, Routledge, 1997.

Janicaud, Dominique, *Presence and Appropriation*, in Jacques Derrida: *Critical Assessments of Leading Philosophers*,

Vol. II, eds. Zeynep Direk and Leonard Lawlor, London and New York, Routledge, 2002.

Johnson, Barbara, *Introduction* to *Dissemination*, Jacques Derrida, London and New York, Continuum, 1981.

Kant, Immanuel, *Critique of Pure Reason*, trans. J.M.D. Meiklejohn, Mineola and New York, Dover Publications, INC, 2003.

Kockelmans, Joseph J., *Heidegger on Art and Art Works*, Dordrecht, Martinus Nijhoff, 1985.

Kockelmans, Joseph J., *Language, Meaning and Ek-sistence*, in *On Heidegger and Language*, ed. Joseph J. Kockelmans, Evanston and Illinois, Northwestern University Press, 1972.

Krell, David Farrel, *The Perfect Future: A Note on Heidegger and Derrida*, in *Deconstruction and Philosophy*, ed. John Sallis, Chicago and London, University of Chicago Press, 1987.

Küchler, Tilman, *Postmodern Gaming: Heidegger, Duchamp, Derrida*, New York, Peter Lang Publishing, 1994.

Lafont, Christina, *Heidegger, Language, and World-disclosure*, trans. Graham Harman, Cambridge, Cambridge University Press, 2000.

Laycok, Steven W., *Mind as Mirror and the Mirroring of Mind: Biddhist Reflections on Western Phenomenology*, New York, State University of New York, 1994.

Loesberg, Jonathan, *Aestheticism and Deconstruction*, Princeton and New Jersey, Princeton University Press, 1991.

Lukacher, Ned., *Writing on Ashes: Heidegger Fort Derrida,* in *Diacrities*, (19.3-4), 1989.

Menke, Christoph, *The Sovereignty of Art: Aesthetic Negativity in Adorno and Derrida*, trans. Neil Solomon, Cambridge, Massachusetts and London, The MIT Press, 1999.

Miller, Hillis J., *Derrida's Others*, in *Applying to Derrida*, eds. John Brannigan, Ruth Robbins and Julian Wolfreys, London, Macmillan Press Ltd., 1996.

Nancy, Jean-Luc, *Elliptical Sense*, in *Derrida: A Critical Reader*, ed, David Wood, Oxford Cambridge, Blackwell, 1992.

Nida-Rümelin, Julian und Bretzler, Monika, eds., *Ästhetik und Kunstphilosophie,* Stuttgart, Betzler, 1998.

Norris, Christopher, *Derrida*, Cambridge and Manchester, Hardward University Press, 1987.

Pattison, George, *The later Heidegger*, London and New York, Routledge, 2000.

Plato, *Republic*, trans. Robin Waterfield, Oxford, Oxford University Press, 1993.

Price, A.W., *Plato: Ethics and Politics*, in *Routledge History of Philosophy*, Vol. I, ed. C.C.W. Taylor, London and New York, Routledge, 1997.

Rockmore, Tom *Heidegger and French Philosophy: Humanism, Antihumanism and Being*, New York, Routledge, 1995.

Ricoeur, Paul, *Meta-phor and Meta-physics*, in *Jacques Derrida: Critical Assesments of Leading Philosophers*, Vol. I, eds. Zeynep Direk and Leonard Lawlor, London and New York, Routledge, 2002.

Richardson, J. and William, S.J., *Heidegger Through Phenomenology to Thought*, New York, Fordham University Press, 2003.

Ritter, Joachim and Gründer, Karlfried, eds., *Historisches Wörterbuch der Philosophie*, Vol. 10, Basel, Schwabe & Co. AG, 1998.

Rorty, Richard, *Is Derrida a Transcendental Philosopher?* in *Derrida: A Critical Reader*, ed., David Wood, Oxford and Cambridge, Blackwell, 1992.

Sallis, John, *Doubling*, in *Derrida: A Critical Reader*, ed. John Wood, Oxford and Cambridge, Blackwell, 1992.

Schapiro, Meyer, *The Still Life as a Personal Object—A Note on Heidegger and van Gogh* in *The Reach of Mind: Essays in Memory of Kurt Goldstein*, ed. Simmel M.L., New York, Springer Publishing Company, 1968.

Schürmann, Reiner, *Heidegger on Being and Acting: from Principles to Anarchy*, trans. Christine-Marie Gros, Bloomington, Indiana University Press, 1987.

Silverman, Hugh J., *Textualities*, New York and London, Routledge, 1994.

Steiner, George, *Real Presences*, Chicago, The University of Chicago Press, 1989.

Taylor, Charles, *Heidegger, Language and Ecology*, in *Heidegger: A Critical Reader*, eds. Hubert L. Dreyfus and Harrison Hall, Cambridge and Oxford, Basil Blackwell, 1992.

Teichman, Jenny ed., *An Introduction to Modern European Philosophy*, London, Macmillan Press Ltd., 1995.

Vries, William de, *Hegel's Logic and Philosophy of Mind*, in *Routledge History of Philosophy* Vol. 6, eds. Robert C. Solomon and Kathleen M. Higgins, London, Routledge, 1993.

Whitehead, Alfred North, *Process and Reality: An Essay on Cosmology*, New York, Macmillan, 1929.

Wood, David, *Following Derrida*, in *Deconstruction and Philosophy*, ed. John Sallis, Chicago and London, The University of Chicago Press, 1987.

Wolin, Richard, *The Politics of Being: The Political Thought of Martin Heidegger*, New York, Columbia University Press, 1990.

Zimmerman, Michael E., *Heidegger, Buddhism, and deep ecology*, in *The Cambridge Companion to Heidegger*, ed. Charles B. Guignon, Cambridge, Cambridge University Press, 1993.